Managing Employee Absence for a Competitive Edge

ANDRZEJ A HUCZYNSKI AND
MICHAEL J FITZPATRICK

Pitman

PITMAN PUBLISHING
128 Long Acre, London WC2E 9AN

© Andrzej A Huczynski and Michael J Fitzpatrick 1989

First published in Great Britain 1989

British Library Cataloguing in Publication Data

Huczynski, Andrzej
    Managing employee absence for a competitive
    edge
    1. Great Britain. Personnel. Absenteeism.
    Management aspects
    I. Title   II. Fitzpatrick, Michael J.
    658.3'14

ISBN 0 273 02850 2

Printed and bound in Great Britain

Contents

Introduction vi

Part one   The problem of absence 1

1 **What is employee absence?** 3
Scale of the problem 3
The international and national scenes 5

2 **Reading the research – help or hindrance?** 10
Analysing conflicting survey results 10
Interpreting survey designs and definitions 11
Comparing research conclusions 12
Identifying the limitations of 'quick-fix' solutions 12
Recognizing personal theories 13

3 **Measuring the costs of employee absence** 15
The true cost of absence 15
Importance of measuring cost 19
Controlling absence – problem or productivity improvement
    opportunity? 21
Conclusion 26
Management review questions 26

Part two   The causes of absence 29

4 **Classifying reasons for absence** 31
Introduction 31
Components of attendance behaviour 32
Process model of employee attendance 34

5 **Cause of absence: job situation factors** 38
Job scope, level, design and type 38

Stress 40
Frequency of job moves 44
Shifts/hours of work 47
Leadership style/management quality 47
Work environment 48
Work-group size and cohesion 50

6 **Cause of absence: personal factors** 52
Employee values/job expectations 52
Personal characteristics 55
Satisfaction with the job 62

7 **Cause of absence: attendance factors** 65
Pressure to attend 65
Attendance motivation: summary 76
Ability to attend 77
Other attendance factors 80

8 **Conclusions** 83
Management review questions 85

Part three *Approaches to absence control* 89

9 **Introduction** 91
Problem-solving tips 91
Methods of absence control 93
Management review questions on absence control procedures 96
Deciding on absence control techniques 97

10 **People techniques** 100
Negative (punishment) incentive 100
Positive incentives approach 113
Mixed consequence system 122

11 **Work techniques** 123
Job situation 124
Employee values and job expectations 127
Individual behaviour 128
Influencing attendance 131
Ability to attend 136

12 **Organizational techniques** 139
Diamond Measurements Ltd: a case study 141
High performance, high commitment organizations 147

13 Summary of approaches to absence control 149
Management review questions 150

Part four Developing a strategy to control absence 153

14 ALIEDIM: the seven-step approach to absence control 155
Step 1 Assess the absence problem 157
Step 2 Locate the absence problem 166
Step 3 Identify and prioritize the absence causes 167
Step 4 Evaluate the current absence control methods 175
Step 5 Design the absence control programme 179
Step 6 Implement the absence control programme 184
Step 7 Monitoring the effectiveness of the absence control programme
  191
Conclusion 195

15 Applying the ALIEDIM approach: a case study 196
Introduction 196
Company background 196
Definition, recording and monitoring of absence 198
Arlanda Electronics: Assess the absence problem 209
Arlanda Electronics: Locate the absence problem 214
Arlanda Electronics: Identify and prioritize the absence causes 218
Arlanda Electronics: Evaluate the current absence control methods
  230
Arlanda Electronics: Design the absence control programme 234
Arlanda Electronics: Implement the absence control programme 246
Arlanda Electronics: Monitor the effectiveness of the absence control
  programme 250
Conclusion 255

References 257

Index 273

Introduction

Every year British industry loses millions of pounds as the direct and indirect result of a single personnel problem – employee absence. While much has been written on new initiatives and processes to improve the efficiency and performance of British companies *vis-à-vis* their overseas competitors, the severity of the problem of absence is a topic that has until recently been neglected. To achieve a real competitive edge in industry, innovative managers are realizing the crucial importance of making the most of existing resources – and, taking a lesson from the Americans and the Japanese, they are realizing that their most valuable resource is the workforce.

In some industries, high levels of absence among employees are endangering company profitability, while in others they put the very survival of the enterprise at risk. This book is therefore written primarily to help personnel and line management to understand and control employee absence. A second audience who will find it of value are consultants, both in-company consultants and those who may be called in to help analyse and solve an absence problem. Third, the book is an excellent starting point for those who are interested in studying in greater depth the research work that has been carried out in this area. With the needs of these separate, though related, audiences in mind, the book has been designed to be easily accessible to each. For example, the practising manager looking for practical solutions to an urgent absence problem can refer directly to Part two or Part three of the book, whilst the student or researcher will prefer to read up on the background to the problem of absence in Part one.

We are recommending a 'back to basics' approach by arguing and illustrating that managers can do much to enhance their company's performance, to reduce costs and to improve morale among employees by addressing seriously the problem of absence.

First, we set the absence issue in a national and international context. With so many other pressing problems, is absence one that merits the attention of the busy manager? It is our intention to show that at a national level, absence is the source of unnecessary costs which act to reduce the competitiveness of British industry. We help managers to assess whether or not they have an absence problem. A certain amount of absence is to be expected, but when does it constitute a problem or, as we shall argue, when does control of absence create a productivity improvement opportunity? We go on to review and classify *both* the literature on absence causes *and* that on absence control techniques. We intend to link these two previously separated areas. In so doing, it is our intention to provide the reader with contrasts and comparisons. Certainly we have reviewed the literature, but have done so with the intention of making it accessible, useful and relevant to the busy manager and consultant who, in their different ways, are responsible for dealing with this problem.

What struck us when reviewing the available writing on the subject, was the extreme separation of *understanding* from *control*. The British and American academic literature on absence focused almost exclusively on understanding the causes of absence with no thought being given as to how the problem might be solved. Journals addressed the question of absence from both a theoretical and an empirical basis. Many concepts were defined, survey results summarized, and models presented. One notable exception to this trend was the work of Steers and Rhodes. These writers did attempt to link absence causes with absence controls, and we shall be using their model as the organizing framework in this book. In contrast, the management literature, in the form of newspaper reports, surveys by management consultants and management institutions, accounts by practising managers in management magazines, goes to the other extreme. A few lines were all that was usually devoted to what the author felt might be the cause of the absence problem. The remainder of the contribution consisted of a description of the actions taken by certain companies to control their absence problems, and a set of recommendations was offered as to what the reading manager ought to do. It was as if a literary apartheid existed with a complete and total separation of interest between understanding the causes of absence on the one hand, and doing something about it on the other.

We address the question of the causes of absence. There is no single explanation for absence. The cause may be single and simple, or multiple, complex and interrelated. Not only do causes differ between different groups of employees in the same company, but they also differ for the same employees over a period of time. Third, we consider the solutions, or absence control techniques that have been used to deal with the absence problem. We shall show that these techniques represent three distinct and separate approaches. To supplement the findings of surveys and reports we have ourselves conducted an extensive series of interviews with line and personnel managers on the subject of absence causes and controls. The purpose of this work is not to test any of the summarized absence theories, but rather to use managers' problem descriptions, insights and views, to illustrate and clarify the research findings of other investigators. It is important to stress from the outset that we cannot offer any 'silver bullet', panacea or magic wand which will instantly and completely eliminate absenteeism. The reason for this is quite simple. The causes of absence amongst employees are many and varied. The solutions, or absence control techniques that are available are similarly diverse. A solution that has worked in one company may fail in another and vice versa.

What then is our approach? Not only are the causes of absence in any one company unique, but the manager will also have to design an absence control programme that is acceptable to that organization. In other words, each organization will have to work out its own salvation. Given such diversity, our intention is to offer a step-by-step guide which can help managers to define and isolate their company's absence problem, and lead them to select the solution which is likely to be the most effective, and which will fit in with their organization's culture. The book encourages managers to take their absence problem and fit it into the scheme provided. In the book, we focus upon both *understanding* and *controlling* absence. The two elements are inescapably linked. There is little point in managers merely understanding the causes of absence if they are not going to take steps to control it. Similarly, attempts at absence control that are based on an inadequate understanding of absence causes are likely to fail. Hence, to deal effectively with absence, a manager needs first to understand the problem, and then to design a control strategy based upon that understanding. The structure of the book therefore follows closely the approach a manager might take in addressing an absence problem.

Each of the first three parts of the book concludes with a set of *Management review questions*. These questions seek to relate the material presented by the authors in that part of the book to readers' own experiences of their company's absence situation. The Management review questions therefore act as a bridge between absence research and theory on the one hand, and the practical solution of absence problems on the other. Part four of the book uses the output of those questions to take the reader through the development of a programme of absence control that will be effective for their particular company. We have devised a seven-step approach which we have named ALIEDIM to indicate the processes involved in solving absence problems: Assess; Locate; Identify; Evaluate; Design; Implement; and Monitor.

In the final chapter, we apply the ALIEDIM absence control processes to Arlanda Electronics. This is a real company, whose name has been disguised. Following a background description, the case will demonstrate the application of the ALIEDIM seven-step approach to the solution of an absence problem. Each of the seven steps introduced in the previous chapter is illustrated with actual absence data from Arlanda Electronics. Having completed the book, managers should be able to apply the ALIEDIM approach to the solution of their own organization's absence problems.

It is often said that people think with what they know. We hope to increase managers' knowledge about the causes of absence, and what can be done to reduce it. By increasing their knowledge base, our aim is to increase their chances of diagnosing their absence problem more accurately, and designing an absence control programme which will have the greatest chance of success. Thus, while we do not offer any instant solutions to the problem of absence, we do provide a systematic approach which can be used to help them grasp the productivity improvement opportunity that absence reduction offers. By managing their absence, companies can achieve a real competitive edge.

Acknowledgements

We should like to thank the many managers who gave their time to tell us about their companies' absence problems and the ways in which they were being dealt with.

Our warmest thanks are also due to Amelia Kerr who conscientiously typed the early drafts of the manuscript and to Simon Lake and Howard Bailey at Pitman Publishing who guided the progress of the book.

The following copyright material has been reproduced by permission and grateful acknowledgement is made to the sources quoted.

Tables 1.1, page 7, 6.1, page 57, 6.3, page 59, 14.2, page 160 from the *General Household Survey, 1984*, HMSO. Crown copyright, reproduced by permission of The Controller, Her Majesty's Stationery Office.

Table 4.1, page 34, 'Some factors affecting sickness absence' from Taylor, P. J. (1987) *Absenteeism: Notes for Managers*, The Industrial Society, London.

Figure 7.1, page 76, 'Variables in employee absenteeism', from Steers, R. M. and Rhodes, S. R. 'Major influences on employee attendance: a process model', *Journal of Applied Psychology*, Vol. 63, No. 4, pp. 391–407, copyright 1978 by the American Psychological Association. Adapted by permission.

Table 9.2, pages 94–95, 'Absence control methods ranked by rated effectiveness', from Scott, D. and Markham, S. 'Absenteeism control methods: a survey of practices and results', printed from the June 1982 issue of *Personnel Administration*, copyright 1982, The American Society for Personnel Administration, Alexandria, Va.

Table 10.1, page 118, 'Range of incentives used by companies in possible incentive programmes', from 'Controlling absenteeism, part 2 – discipline or reward?' *Small Business Report*, May 1985, pp. 52–56.

Andrzej A Huczynski
Michael J Fitzpatrick

Glasgow Business School
Glasgow University
May 1988

For Janet, Sophie and Gregory
and Irene, Michael, Neil, Bryan and Simon

Part one

The problem of absence

Chapter 1
What is employee absence?

Scale of the problem

Obtaining agreement as to what is meant by absence is somewhat difficult. Most organizations distinguish between different *types* of absence. Indeed, there are no fewer than six different categories. Incomes Data Services Ltd[1] has produced a useful listing of these:

- **Sickness absence:** subdivided into self-certified (or certificated) and medically certified sickness and industrial accident or injury, with separate records being kept for long-term absentees
- **Statutory time off:** e.g. pregnancy and maternity leave
- **Strikes or other industrial action**
- **Holidays:** including annual leave and statutory holidays
- **Special leave:** e.g. study leave
- **Personal/domestic leave:** e.g. visits to doctor, time off to care for sick relatives

For the purposes of this book however, we shall take *absence* to mean the non-attendance of employees for scheduled work when they are expected to attend. This particular definition distinguishes voluntary absence from the categories above. The definition also seeks to avoid a judgement on the *legitimacy* associated with absence from work.

Interest in absenteeism has often been related to other employee problems identified by management, such as lateness (considered by many as a form of absence), work absenteeism (when the employee fails to fulfil his or her designated tasks while at work), and high rates of staff turnover. Psychologists have treated these as different facets of a single 'withdrawal from work' phenomenon, and have investigated the reasons which underlie all of them.

The process of defining absenteeism and distinguishing different types is, as we shall see in Chapter 2, of limited practical value. Writers have contrasted paid with unpaid absence, organizationally excused with organizationally unexcused absence, genuine with false reasons for absence, voluntary with involuntary absence, and so on. While researchers may find such categories useful, it is difficult and frequently impossible in operational terms for supervisors and managers to confirm their suspicions that employees are, for example, voluntarily absent. Because of this, many companies have adopted a 'no-fault' attendance control procedure, by which a company acknowledges the inevitability of occasional absence, and bases discipline on the *frequency* rather than on the legitimacy of the absence. A no-fault policy relieves supervisors of the task of judging the validity of excuses, and hence the legitimacy of the absence.

A second point is that when companies *do* distinguish between different types of absence, they tend to identify those over which they can exercise some control. We are distinguishing here between different absence *causes*. Thus, a company may not be able to do much about an employee's state of health. However, it can change a sickness benefit scheme through which staff can benefit from staying away from work even once they have recovered.

Third, we can note that organizations may distinguish not between types of absence, but between categories of absentee, for example, between people who take casual, one-day absences; the short-term but persistent absentees who are away every two or three weeks for a few days; and those with a single, severe illness.

Rhodes and Steers[2] argued that the problem of employee absenteeism, while widely recognized by managers, is seldom examined systematically. Instead, absence causes are considered by many to be similar to, or the same as, those of staff turnover. This is not the case. Absence as a category of employee behaviour, differs from staff turnover in at least three ways. First, the negative consequences associated with absenteeism for employees are typically fewer than those associated with turnover. Second, absenteeism is more likely to be spontaneous and a relatively easy decision for the employee, while the decision to leave is more carefully considered over a longer period of time. Finally, absenteeism is often indicative of a wish to leave the organisation, especially when alternative forms of employment are not available. Thus, we argue that the causes of absenteeism should be treated separately from those of staff turnover.

Our starting point for a consideration of the problems resulting from absence is the recognition of the disruption caused to scheduled work processes, resulting in a decrease in production and the under-utilization of productive capacity. The direct and indirect financial costs of absence, regardless of its cause, can be considered as an unnecessary and avoidable expense that makes a company less efficient. Competitiveness and profitability are reduced and, in the long run, the very existence of the company is threatened.

The international and national scenes

International scene

The Confederation of British Industry[3] suggested in its 1987 survey of 'non-attendance' rates, that those of the United Kingdom were four times higher than those of its main competitors. In 1986, it reported, absence from work cost British industry £5 billion. However, managers who examine the international data on how Britain's absence rates compare with those of other countries are likely to come away confused. Comparable absence measures are both difficult to obtain and inherently unreliable. There is no one survey that one can refer to in order to obtain reliable international figures on a comparable basis. Reading through the different surveys, the absence percentages quoted are often gathered on different bases, and it is therefore impossible to compare like with like.

Some of the past surveys have in fact suggested that Britain compares favourably with her European counterparts. Investigating sickness absence in 9 countries, Taylor[4] identified a rising trend during the early 1970s, but stated that Britain's absence trend was rising more slowly than those of Sweden, Holland, Italy and West Germany. In terms of average certified sickness days per annum, he put Britain on a par with West Germany and Poland (15 days), and compared it favourably with Czechoslovakia (16 days), Sweden (18 days) and Holland (21 days).

A report by Incomes Data Services[5] cited a multinational study carried out in 1981 in which Britain was found to have the lowest level of absence amongst seven European countries, being well below Italy, Holland, and Sweden, and a little lower than Germany and France. Contrast this generally positive picture with an analysis conducted by Klein[6] using data from the 1983 Labour Force Sample Survey of the European Communities[7]. This put Britain's absence rate, at 11.8%, well above those of its nearest rivals of France (5.9%), Holland (5.4%), Belgium (3.8%), West Germany (3.0%), Sweden (3.0%), Italy (2.9%) and Japan (2.5%).

Since the United States' *Current Population Survey* (CPS) and the United Kingdom's *General Household Survey* (GHS) calculate the absence rates in broadly the same way, this comparison may be the most meaningful one. In terms of absence, Europe fares very badly when compared with the United States. For example, the Bureau of National Affairs studied 274 employers in 1984 and found an average absence rate of 1.9%[8]. In 1985, the CPS gave a figure of 4.7% for the US (covering absences due to injury, civic duties and personal problems), while the 1984 GHS gave a figure of 7%. Although the US authorities are dissatisfied with their level of absence, it is half the rate of absence typically experienced in Europe. Against this background, the European problem, and in particular the British level, can be put into perspective.

The main point demonstrated by these figures is the unreliability of international comparison tables of non-attendance rates. The most that we can take from them is the observation that Britain's average absence figure is regularly above 6% despite the various calculations.

The UK scene

Our knowledge about absence at work in Britain at this time, comes from five main sources:

- the Central Statistical Office's (CSO) *Annual Abstract of Statistics*[9]

- the *General Household Survey* of 1984[10]

- the 1985 Industrial Society survey of absenteeism[11] (covering 1984 and 1985 with a low 26% response rate from the personnel managers to whom it was circulated)

- a second Industrial Society survey published in 1987[12] (with an even lower 6.9% response rate)

- an absence survey carried out by the Confederation of British Industry[13] also published in 1987.

The CBI study is based upon 431 companies, but the survey response rate is not given.

Problems of survey coverage, response rate and overlap make the findings less than authoritative. Nevertheless, this data is the most recent. These surveys quote a mixture of facts (e.g. numbers of employees absent) and opinions (e.g. the opinions of managers on why they think their employees are absent).

The CSO's abstract contains information on the total number of days lost through certified sickness. It showed that in 1984 about 372 million days were lost during the period July 1981 and June 1982. This figure, however, excludes sickness absence of less than three days, that of married women not paying full Class 1 National Insurance contributions, and attendances not attributed to sickness. The trend is upwards, going from 244 million days (1955), through 328 million days (1971), and on to 372 million days (1982).

The *General Household Survey* provides amongst the most reliable absence data. About 13 000 households were sampled. The data from the 1984 GHS survey was published in late 1986. It therefore represents the most comprehensive albeit somewhat dated information about absence. The overall absence rate figure was 7% for both men and women. This was down from 9% in 1979. Most of this absence was the result of sickness. The sickness rate in 1984 was 4.0% for men and 4.6% for women. This figure, however, includes strikes, short-time working and layoffs. The 1984 *General Household Survey* clearly showed the absence rates amongst different classes of employees (Table 1.1).

Table 1.1 Percentages of employees absent from work in the previous week for different reasons (illness, injury, strike, short time, lay-off, personal reasons) by socioeconomic group

Socioeconomic group	Total absent from work % (all reasons)	Base 100% All employees
Managers in large establishments	5	685
Managers in small establishments	3	461
Professional workers – employees	5	362
Intermediate non-manual workers	7	1279
Junior non-manual workers	7	1954
Personal service workers	7	618
Foremen and supervisors	9	435
Skilled manual workers	10	1506
Semi-skilled manual workers	9	1049
Unskilled manual workers	6	530
Agricultural workers	8	122
Total	7	9001

General Household Survey, 1984.

These figures accord with the Industrial Society data of 1984–5 which showed that manual workers took an average of 12 days off. Full-time, manual employees were the highest absence group in the 1987 CBI survey with a 4.7% rate and took 11 days off a year. Part-time employees had the next highest rate with 4.3%. In contrast, full-time, non-manual employees had the lowest rate of non-attendance at 2.6%. These figures lead to the rule of thumb, often quoted by personnel and line managers, that manual workers are absent almost twice as often as non-manual staff, who themselves are absent almost twice as often as management. An article in *The Director* magazine[14] claimed that 200 million days were lost to British industry each year through absenteeism, as compared to 3.2 million days lost due to strikes. The cost of absence from work to British business was £5 billion[15]. Reduced to individual terms, on average, each employee will miss work anywhere from 7 to 12 times a year. On any given day, 3–7% of a company's workforce will be absent. For every £1 the employee loses due to absenteeism, the company loses £2.

The National Economic Development Council[16] stated that:

'Hours of work have been reduced, medical services and working conditions have been improved, and we are living longer. We should therefore be healthier and absenteeism should be less, yet statistics indicate that this is not so.'

The *General Household Survey*[17] showed that, from 1974–84, total absence from work for all reasons varied between 6% and 9%, with an average of

7.5%. In the 1980–82 period, a constant level of 8% was reached. These somewhat dry statistics have been translated into more meaningful statements describing Britain's absence problem:

'There are forty times more days lost through certified absence than through strikes.'
Taylor[18]

'There are over one million people absent from work every day.'
Arbitration and Conciliation Advisory Service[19]

'On average, each member of the working population is taking some 15–17 days sickness absence each year.'
Matthewman[20]

'Employers should realize that an 8.35% absence rate is equivalent to a four week strike.'
Barlow[21]

Those writers who have studied the subject of absenteeism generally criticize British management's failure both to recognize the absence problem and systematically to resolve it. Matthewman's[22] views on this matter are fairly representative. He argued that most companies did not cost out the effect of absenteeism, failed to keep adequate records, and generally had no idea whether their particular level of absenteeism was worse than, better than or similar to those of other companies in their area, industry, or the country as a whole. As a result, he said, ignorance abounded. Many companies claimed that their absence levels were 'reasonably acceptable'.

While it is possible to argue about the detailed statistics, the point that comes over loudly and clearly is that absence from work is costing British industry a great deal of money. It can be seen as an extra tax on the goods that British manufacturers send to their customers. Its effect is to blunt the competitive edge of companies. Viewed in this way, control of absence represents an area of potential productivity gain, and hence a challenge to British management. Progress can be made provided that we take heed of Monty Finniston's warning,

'We have become accustomed to deplore ... such interruptions as strikes, embargoes, work-to-rules, and go-slows, while ignoring the continuous background of disruption – absence from work.'
Finniston[23]

Amongst the key legislative changes, introduced during the 1980s, that have affected absence have been the introduction of Statutory Sick Pay in April 1983, and the introduction of self-certification in June 1982. The former required organizations to keep detailed absence records, while the latter required employees to complete self-certification forms for absences of seven days or less. This legislation has had a number of effects on absence.

In particular it has led companies to reassess their attitudes to absence. Most organizations expected the introduction of self-certification to increase levels of absence. In fact, a number of surveys have found that it has made no measurable difference. Indeed, because many companies began to assume a greater responsibility for controlling absenteeism, the situation actually improved in many cases.

As far as personnel executives or line managers at plant level are concerned, theinternational comparative statistics on absence rates are of little direct interest. Such data are likely to be of more relevance to government in planning national industrial and manpower policy. However, even here, the different data collection methods make an accurate comparison of the absence rates of different countries difficult. National absence figures, especially those which compare average absence rates in different industrial sectors, are also of limited value. Their function seems to be primarily a defensive one: managements are able to claim from the data that, 'our figures aren't as bad as the average'.

In our opinion the most useful comparative absence statistics for companies seeking to achieve a competitive edge through absence reduction, are those supplied as part of a *benchmarking* approach. This strategy will be discussed in greater detail later. Essentially it involves a company obtaining key statistical information on the productivity performance of a recognized 'excellent' performing company in a comparable industrial sector. Amongst the statistical data, is information about absence rates. The key point is that this absence figure is one that *has actually been achieved*. It therefore acts as the goal or target for the organization engaged on a performance improvement drive.

Chapter 2
Reading the research – help or hindrance?

The manager who sets out to read up on the effects of absence on business performance faces a number of difficulties, each of which we will examine in detail. Though the body of research in surveys, professional and academic journals and the press is growing, the very diversity of reports and findings presents problems. There are difficulties in:

- analysing conflicting survey findings;
- interpreting survey design and category definitions;
- comparing research conclusions;
- identifying the limitations of 'quick-fix' solutions;
- recognizing 'personal theories'.

Analysing conflicting survey results

A common complaint from managers is that the results presented by the surveys conducted on absence tend in general, to obscure rather than to clarify. Frequently, the results quoted contradict one another. A good example of this occurred in 1987 when two surveys on absence were produced within months of each other. One was prepared by the CBI[1], and the other by The Industrial Society[2]. The CBI survey covered 450 companies, 'employing 1.25 million people across the business spectrum'. It found the non-attendance rate to be 4.7% for full-time, manual workers, and 2.6% for non-manual staff. This contrasts sharply with The Industrial Society's figures of 5.05% as 'the mean sickness absence rate' in a group of 275 companies. The discrepancy in findings is larger than the figures suggest because the CBI defined absence more broadly than the Industrial Society to cover all kinds of non-attendance except for short-time working and strikes. The Industrial Society figures, in contrast, are limited to 'medically certified absence, self-certified absence, and uncertified/unauthorized absence'. The

CBI also collected figures for sickness alone, and produced a figure of 4% for full-time, manual workers, and 2.2% for full-time, non-manual employees. The Industrial Society asked its respondents: 'Has your absence rate gone down over the last five years?' Of those replying, 59% said 'No', and 41% said 'Yes'. The Industrial Society authors concluded that: 'This agrees with our results which show a slightly higher rate now than in 1985.' In contrast, the CBI's figures for 1983-6 which, although a slight increase on 1984, suggest that 'absence had returned to 1983 levels by 1986'.

Interpreting survey designs and definitions

First, one can say that much of the variation in statistics identified above can be attributed to the design of the survey, the method of its conduct, the wording of the questionnaires used, and the techniques of analysis used. The way that absence is defined, the base of measurement, and the way in which the companies are grouped by number of employees all tend to differ between surveys. The surveys necessarily take a 'snapshot' of the absence picture at a point in time by looking at one or two weeks' absence. Depending on how that week is chosen, the absence rate may be much higher or lower in the preceding and succeeding weeks.

Second, the representativeness of the responding companies is rarely discussed, and the response rates are low. Frequently they drop to 25%, when most statisticians do not make generalizations at anything below 65-70%. The 1987 Industrial Society findings are based on a response rate of only 6.9%. The effect of all this is that the manager is unable to make a reliable comparison either between the different surveys, or between his or her own company and the survey results quoted for companies in the same industrial group or geographical region. Some reports speak of various types of absence, while others consider sickness absence only. Still others, such as the General Household Survey, distinguish between absence caused by own injury or illness, by strike, short-time working and lay-offs, and absence for personal and other reasons. When comparing absence figures, readers should ensure that they are comparing like with like.

Third, the survey results, although strictly numerical, often imply the causes of absence problems. Thus, the higher absence rate for women which most surveys reveal, is often attributed, without any substantiation, to female psychology, mental attitudes, and the social attributes which sex imposes. The fact that women generally have the more boring, repetitive work in companies, is not taken into account. Related to this is the tendency for the surveys to treat managers' opinions about the causes of absence, as if they were irrefutable. Management associations such as the CBI, BIM, and the Industrial Society, rely on managers for their answers. Since managers can not always know the real causes of employee absence, they can only offer opinions, and it is these opinions that are revealed in the surveys. The reader of the survey is therefore generally none the wiser as to what the real causes of absence in the organizations are.

Fourth, the same can be said for the solutions. Managers are invited to offer their opinions on factors which, in their view, *might* have curbed absence in their companies. Once again, opinions, unsupported by any evidence are offered. The conclusion that one can draw is that these absence surveys have been singularly useless in terms of their ability to point serious managers in the right direction towards solving their absence problems.

Comparing research conclusions

The articles that managers can read about absence are neatly divided into two groups. The first group consists of the academic articles published in British and American learned journals, most frequently, in psychological and economic journals. They consist of the reports of well-executed investigations, impeccably planned experiments and well-organized field trials. The theoretical issues are discussed, the data is evaluated and the weaknesses of each study are commented upon. Cumulatively, these investigations have added to our true stock of knowledge about the causes of absence. These studies have shown that variables which affect or cause absence include the degree of personal involvement of the employee in his or her work, distance to be travelled to work, the existence of a company sick-pay scheme, differences in age, and many others. However, this literature has two major deficiencies. First, most of it is impenetrable for the average manager. It is written in a lumbering, academic style. Second, it concerns itself solely with the task of explaining absence behaviour, to the complete exclusion of advice on what should be done about it.

In contrast, the articles in the professional, management practitioner journals go in completely the opposite direction. They report accounts of various absence control programmes, all of which, to varying degrees and for varying reasons, are claimed to have had an effect on reducing absence. Generally, little or no attention is paid to the causes of the original absence behaviour. These are either taken for granted, or judged not to be worthy of consideration. This lack of consistency inevitably leads to a listing of a diverse (and frequently contradictory) set of recommendations on what to do about absence. Managers have been recommended to exert firm management control, to give employees more discretion in how they do their jobs, to manipulate group attitudes, to institute a system of warnings and punishments and to pay bonuses for good attendance.

Identifying the limitations of 'quick-fix' solutions

Quick-fix solutions abound. The articles rarely if ever pay any attention to the underlying mechanisms and concepts of the different approaches to absence control. Techniques are offered as instant solutions, and the results of absence interventions are reported with little consideration of the underlying issues. Yet these factors are important. Which techniques are appropriate in what circumstances? Why should this be? Are there any distinguishable patterns or groupings of techniques – families or groupings, based on similar assumptions? One writer[3] warned that: 'One company's answer could be another's disaster'. If this is so, then one needs to move away from the universally applied 'quick-fix' solution to a more customized approach.

Recognizing 'personal' theories

In the absence of a proper understanding of the true causes of absence, the responding managers in the CBI survey are inevitably thrown back on their personal theories of absence. As Raymond Miles[4] observed, the typical manager has a set of views and concepts which influence his or her behaviour and affect his decisions. Related to absence, these are detectable within the company as folksy axioms. For example:

'If supervision is poor, employees will abuse the system'.

'When jobs are repetitive and boring, absence is bound to be higher.

'Salaried staff have a different code of behaviour from shopfloor workers'.

We found examples of such personal theories amongst the managers that we interviewed in our own study. We were told that: 'Women are more complex physically than men, so you'd expect them to be off more', and that: 'It's a terribly boring job, no wonder they go off absent'. At a recent absence control seminar that one of the writers attended, the question *why* people were absent was neither addressed by the speaker, nor raised by the audience. The seminar participants must have all shared a common personal theory about the causes of absence, which made any discussion of absence causes both superfluous and unnecessary.

Although it may seem somewhat grand to elevate these statements to the status of management theories, Miles argued that such axioms did in fact contain the basic components of a theory. This was because:

'A theory usually begins with a set of assumptions, then describes or prescribes a set of actions possible under the assumed conditions, and finally predicts and explains the causal linkages determining the set of results'[5].

For example, the statement that employees will abuse the system when the supervision is poor implies a set of beliefs about employees' attitudes towards work and their predispositions towards company goals. Given these assumptions, the personal theory will indicate what will happen (employees will take excessive time off) if management does not behave in a given manner (exercises control and supervises closely). The assumptions of the seminar participants mentioned earlier, led them all to concentrate on an individually focused, punishment-centred approach to absence control. This stressed the importance of the contract of employment, and the taking of prompt disciplinary action within the prescribed legal framework. In consequence, the participants' personal theories led them to ignore the potential contribution of individually focused, reward-centred approaches (e.g. attendance bonus schemes), or work-focused strategies (e.g. job enrichment).

The real significance of these sets of beliefs lies in their influence on management actions and decisions. Clearly, the absence reduction programmes that management designs will depend upon these beliefs. For example, if management believes workers are absent because they are lazy, then it will design programmes which punish absence. The situation becomes more complicated as inconsistencies arise between the theories of different managers and supervisors. It is hardly surprising, therefore, that in such a situation the company has difficulty in establishing a cohesive view of the absence problem, and agreeing on a suitable approach to its control and reduction. In this climate there is a strong temptation to reach out for the quick-fix solution mentioned earlier. There is no shortage of such prepackaged advice on offer from the retailers of management consultancy. Shephard cautioned managers:

'... not [to] kid themselves or be kidded by plausible peddlers that problems in the management of human resources ... are capable of simple solutions'[6].

Chapter 3

Measuring the costs of employee absence

The true cost of absence

Even those companies which do monitor their absence levels may be unaware of the true magnitude of the absence costs incurred. Taylor[1] has identified not only the direct costs of employee absence (those that come immediately to mind), but also the indirect ones (those which are often not as apparent, but which are nevertheless as real). Taylor listed the following costs:

Direct costs

- sick pay and the continued payment of fringe benefits to the absent (e.g. insurance, pension, holiday),

- overtime payments for those who fill in,

- costs incurred in overstaffing to cope with the problems posed by absence.

Indirect costs

- disruptions or shutdowns of sections,

- reduced productivity as work is done by people who are less experienced and/or tired,

- lower product quality if replacement staff are not sufficiently competent,

- loss of customers due to failure to meet deadlines or through an inferior service,

- management/supervisory time used in revising work schedules, counselling, disciplining, and checking the work quality of substitutes,

- extra administration required to maintain and administer the absence control programme.

- cost of recruitment, selection and training of replacements,
- dissatisfaction – adverse effects on other employees when they see unwarranted absence and resent doing the absentee's work.

In one of the companies we studied, some of its products were affected to such an extent that an 'absence allowance' formed 9% of the labour content of the product cost. Employees who are absent can cost the company more than just salaries. Benefits continue to be provided to absent workers. Insurance, holidays and pensions all have to be paid for. Our own interviews with managers confirmed that the costs involved were substantial. Sick pay is a figure which is immediately identifiable as a direct, and highly visible cost to the company. All the managers with whom we talked were either able to quote the costs of absence immediately, or else were able to calculate it on the back of an envelope. What was most striking, in many cases, was the magnitude of the amount, and what that meant in day-to-day company terms.

'In the year 1985–6, the group of companies of which we are a part, paid out one million pounds in company sickness alone. That was 36% up on the previous year. One case of whisky earns us one pound, so we have to sell a million cases of whisky just to cover our sick pay.' (*Whisky producer*)

The use of *overtime* as a means of overcoming the problems caused by absence was also regarded as a visible and a high cost. Excessive overtime that is related to absenteeism can lead to other problems. Employees who have worked a great deal of overtime may decide to reward themselves with a 'sick day'. This can snowball as other employees are forced to work overtime to cover those absences. They then award themselves sickness holidays as well.

'To catch up the hours, you've got to lay on overtime. That's a cost the company should not have to stand. It pushes the price of your product up. It doesn't help in the market-place'.

*   *   *

'Here it's cheaper to employ temporary labour than to use overtime. We have a historical agreement which gives people time and a half for working overtime plus a four-hour 'follow-on' payment. We have to pay sixteen hours to cover eight.' (*Glass manufacturer*)

There are also the indirect or consequential costs of absence. These are the ones which are often more intangible and difficult to measure. In the long term, these may turn out to be the critical ones. They will determine the profitability of the company and its long-term performance. Thus, *over-*

staffing or overmanning is a commonly used technique to deal with an absence problem.

'We have a rate of absence of 7–8% among shopfloor staff. We've never really costed it because you're talking about a loss of profit perhaps, loss of production, loss of productivity, and that is difficult to cost. We do employ additional operatives to cover for absence. We carry an extra eight employees at a cost to the company of about £10,000 a head. Add to that the cost of sick pay, and the final cost to us is about £100,000.'

* * *

'We used to have extra people on the payroll to cover for absence. They were called "spares", but it didn't work. The person who was absent was always the person for whom you didn't have a spare, or else the spare was absent at the same time. We gradually moved away from the idea of "spares".' (*Electrical components manufacturer*)

In some cases, the figures involved can be even more substantial. A manager from a shipbuilding company explained how, in order to ensure that 75 cleaners were always available, 100 had to be employed. With an overall payroll of about 3000 shopfloor employees, he estimated that about 10% of them would not be needed if absence was reduced. Calculating that out, he estimated that the annual cost to the company of the present level of absence was £3.3 million. He added: 'That can be the difference between winning and losing an order.'

Supervisory and managerial time had often to be used both to ascertain whether employees were coming in or not, and to reschedule jobs and workers. Our respondents talked about the extra administrative work that absence caused.

'If a foreman has so many men to produce a job, he's got the problem of juggling people about. You can lose between two and three hours work in the morning trying to get people to do that particular job, so that creates a problem. It causes delays'. (*Shipbuilders*)

Low product quality was an inevitable consequence of absenteeism. A personnel manager explained:

> 'Because you put people on one job, it means you're taking them off another. So the job suffers. It creates inefficiencies that you shouldn't have, and they're difficult to manage.'

Sometimes, absenteeism by individuals from key employee groups can have a disproportionate effect on the production process. Thus, for example, in a heavy engineering plant, if the cranes cannot be manned because of absence, then nothing can move on the shopfloor.

There is always the danger of a loss of customers due to a *failure to meet deadlines or to inferior service* caused by absence. In the case of production, absenteeism can mean missed deadlines or deliveries. Costs can be even higher when they are not planned for, or when they exceed forecasts.

An industrial relations manager from a shipbuilding company explained: 'Last year, our paintwork went behind primarily because the painters and the red leaders went sick. We had a delay of about three months because of high absenteeism. It wasn't a disaster because the customer asked for a change (to the original specification given), and that allowed us to catch up, but in terms of the first date that we got for delivery of the ship, it did cause a problem.' (*Shipbuilders*)

The *cost of recruitment, selection and training replacement* are also relevant issues. The additional administrative costs related to absenteeism include those of hiring, training, and orienting new employees. In addition, maintaining and administering an absence control programme, whether effective or not, costs the company money. Absenteeism forces supervisors to spend time revising work schedules, counselling and reprimanding workers, and monitoring the process of replacement.

As one might expect, absenteeism had *adverse effects on those employees who were good attenders*. First, there was the natural resentment that they were being inconvenienced through the actions of others. Employees resented doing work for absentees, especially when they knew that there was no valid reason for their being away. This could cause a decrease in morale which, in turn, could lead to higher rates of staff turnover, more grievances and increased latecoming. Morale suffered when work was done by those who were less experienced or fatigued.

'Occasionally there is resentment when, in order to get everything out of the plant, someone, somewhere has got to make the extra effort. The absent person can be the cause of grievance amongst the others. We have established manning levels for various jobs, and if we decide that we have to run the job with fewer men because of the absences, perhaps we reorganize it, then occasionally we get a kick-back'. (*Plastics factory*)

* * *

'When absence is high, then it has an effect on morale. When it gets to 14–15% average, then the employees who are conscientious, and who are giving their full commitment, find it soul-destroying. On the shopfloor, if there is high absence, then the people who do come to work really have the pressure put on them. They have to do that bit extra – be more flexible, do more coverage, pull out all the stops. We did find that when we did really have high absence rates, we got a lot of complaints.' (*Canning factory*)

Dissatisfaction may also be caused when, in order to achieve coverage for those absent, natural groups or teams of workers are shuffled around. Such disruption can reduce morale, and in itself can lead to the absence of those who were previously good attenders. The problem can thus become self-generating. When workers fail to report for work, resources are wasted. Expensive machinery and equipment stand unused. Additionally, the spoilage of unused materials increases costs, and the absence of key workers, may mean that the remaining materials are inefficiently used. Even when an employee is finally dismissed for excessive absenteeism, the company has to hire and train a replacement. During that training, the company will suffer reduced output and profitability due to employee errors and delays.

Against this background, absence clearly represents not only a major problem for many companies, but also a great challenge. The Institute of Directors' Information and Advisory Service, and the Industrial Society, both receive frequent enquiries from members on the subject of absence.

Importance of measuring cost

The measurement of absence represents a topic in itself and it is not our intention to deal with the minutiae of the procedure. Instead, we wish only to make a number of general, although in our view crucial, points about the measurement of absence. First, we believe that the *keeping of accurate records* is the cornerstone of any effective absence control strategy. Company sources of information on attendance come from time clocks, attendance sheets, medical records, personal files, and 'return to work' interviews. Record analysis tells the company whether an absence problem exists and where it is located. Such records are also necessary in case disciplinary action is taken against employees. The act of measurement has itself been used as an absence control tool. Companies have reduced their absence by management making an effort to measure it and, as importantly, showing *employees* that it is measuring it.

In recent years, companies have improved their systems for recording and monitoring absence levels. In many cases, records have been computerized. Computerized databases can be built up by the company, to monitor the overall absence levels, hold attendance records on all employees and produce detailed analyses when required. We talked to an industrial relations manager who had a section of his department which spent a substantial part of its time collecting and monitoring employee absence statistics. Time clocks were linked to the computer, and printouts were readily available on an individual, group, trade and departmental basis. As late as 1976, a study conducted by the Ontario Ministry of Labour in Canada revealed that only 17% of the organizations surveyed compiled formal statistics on absenteeism.

A second point that we wish to stress is the one made by Taylor[2]. This is that absence is a repetitive event. He wrote that, while births and deaths were singular and could be expressed by a single measure of rate, absence had to be measured both in terms of the amount of time taken off (expressed in days or as a percentage) and in terms of individual episodes of absence (its frequency). To do otherwise would be misleading in his view. He commented that most organizations produced a time off rate, but rarely a frequency one. While the former was helpful to accountants (allowing them to cost time easily), it was the latter which was much more valuable to those responsible for absence control. Indeed, as we shall see later, the frequency rate forms the basis of the 'no-fault' absence control approach.

Thus, one has the

- absence rate,
- absence percentage rate and
- absence frequency rate.

The first refers to the total number of days that a person is absent each year. The second expresses that number of days as a percentage of the total time that he or she is expected to be at work. The third measure refers to the number of spells or instances of absence. It is expressed as a number. Thus an employee may be absent for 10 days during a year – 10 days is thus his or her annual absence rate. Assuming that person was required to attend 225 days in the year, his or her absence percentage rate would be 4.4%. If those days were taken off in the following sequence: 1 day, 1 day, 2 days, 4 days, 2 days, he or she would have a frequency of 5 spells of absence. Despite the range of sophisticated types of statistical analyses available, these three basic measures are the most straightforward and most useful in terms of identifying an absence problem, and of doing something about it.

Third, we would emphasize the importance of standardizing the *basis of calculating absence*. Inter-company comparisons, and to an even greater extent, international comparisons of absence, often flounder because everybody calculates their absence rate differently. For example, some companies include holidays in their calculations while others do not. The most common measure of absence is the 'time lost rate'. It is this which is most often used by companies to determine the overall severity of their absence problem. The rate shows the percentage of time lost through absence in relation to the total time available for work, viz:

$$\text{Total time lost} = \frac{\text{days lost to absenteeism for a year}}{\text{average number of employees} \times \text{total days in year}} \times 100\%$$

Studies have found that the total-days-in-year varied greatly between companies. This variation produces differences in the final overall percentage. The higher the working year figure, the lower the absence percentage will be. While a variation of two or three days will have little effect, a difference of 30 days will greatly modify the picture, and make comparison either difficult or impossible. A survey carried out by The Industrial Society[3] showed a 138-day variation in the base for calculating the absence figure. Amongst the companies surveyed, the base figure varied between 227 and 365 days. The majority of responding companies used a figure in the 227–33 days range. The Industrial Society itself recommended a base figure of 230 days in its most recent absence survey[4].

Finally, we would stress the importance not only of collecting absence data, but also of analysing it on a regular basis. The purpose of regular analysis is to identify absence trends in particular areas of the company. An overall company absence figure of 5% may hide the fact that in certain departments there is no absence at all, while in others it may be running at 10%. The 1987 Industrial Society study[5] revealed that there was no general pattern of how absence data was relayed back to managers, and hence how often it was analysed. They did find, however, that the largest organizations tended to provide weekly or monthly feedback, while the majority of the smaller ones only did so in response to absence problems. The figures were as follows:

Frequency of feedback	%
Weekly	15
Monthly	35
Quarterly	10
Six-monthly	4
Annually	5
Only when there is a problem	30
Never	1

In this section, we have sought to stress the importance of managers having a clear picture of what is happening in their organizations in terms of absence. We now have to consider whether absence should be seen as a problem to be solved, or an opportunity to be grasped.

Controlling absence: problem or productivity improvement opportunity?

While a company may be able to state what its level of absence is, it is rarely able to say definitively whether this figure is satisfactory or unsatisfactory. It does not know the relative size of its problem. Managers may be aware of some tell-tale signs. There may be unnecessarily high manning levels for the tasks involved, high overtime expenditure, lost or delayed production, lost orders, a reduced range or standard of service, regular disruption of the workflow, low morale amongst employees, a higher than average level of safety incidents, and so on. The companies in our study had current rates of absence which ranged from 3% to 14%. Each company tended to assess this rate in historical, comparative terms. Thus, one firm which has had an absence rate of 20% in the past now considered its 12% absence as a major improvement. Other managers, after stating their absence rate, added that this figure was either good or bad *for their industry*. The 1987 Industrial Society survey[6] discovered that of its 289 responding companies, only 30% had a target rate for absence. These rates are shown in Table 3.1

In most regions, the survey indicated that the greatest number of responding companies had a target rate of between 3% and 4%, while in London and the South-east, where the absence rate was already lower, the target absence figure was between 0% and 2%. We should remember that it is not immediately possible to say whether a certain level of absence represents a problem. In some organizations such as casinos, a 3% absence rate amongst croupiers does severely impede overall company performance. In another organization, a 3% rate may have a negligible effect on performance. Rather than argue whether a certain absence figure is good or bad, it is perhaps more useful to ask whether it represents a *productivity improvement opportunity*.

More and more managers are becoming aware of the need to improve productivity in order to remain competitive in the international business environment. The first half of the 1980s was marked by rates of improvement far in excess of anything previously achieved in the post-war period. Productivity is a much used, and abused, term often meaning different things to different people. Richard Thorpe[7] has offered a helpful and simple definition. Productivity in his view refers to: 'An increase in the relative output for a given input.'

However, even this straightforward definition raises the question of which inputs and outputs are being referred to. Ray Wild[8] wrote about three dimensions of productivity – machines, materials and labour. He suggested that in each case, the achievement of high productivity could be considered in terms of maximizing the use of the available resources, or of minimizing loss or wastage. When labour productivity is considered in these terms, it becomes clear that absence levels represent a key factor in determining the level of a company's productivity. As has been pointed out elsewhere, the traditional view of productivity measurement, as typified by work study approaches, may be incomplete. It tends to focus only on the performance of labour while it is working, but ignores other crucial aspects such as downtime and absence[9].

When management considers the company's relative absence performance, it needs to avoid focusing purely on a narrow, internal, subjective assessment – for example, by comparing a factory's current absence rate with what it has been in the past. Where management strives for, and accepts, only annual marginal improvements, it may be ignoring the true opportunity available to the organization by failing to recognize objectively what could actually be achieved.

Table 3.1 Company target absence rates: 1987
Industrial Society survey

Target absence rate (%)	0-2	3-4	5-6	7-9
Percentage of respondents having this target (%)	22	47	26	5

Benchmarking

Benchmarking is a new and powerful method now being used by organizations which are seeking to achieve major improvements in their productivity. It involves establishing what can actually be achieved (the benchmark), against either a wide range of business metrics obtained through the systematic study of the practices of recognized 'excellent' companies, or through a comparison of one factory with others within the same group. We shall refer to the former as *external benchmarking* and the latter as *internal benchmarking*.

For the purposes of external benchmarking, the companies chosen for comparison need not be in competition or even in the same business as the organization carrying out the review. For example, a manufacturing company engaged in the high volume assembly of hi-fi equipment recently developed a set of benchmarks by studying successful companies engaged in computer, photocopier, and car manufacture. An extract of the results of this study is shown in Table 3.2.

The realization that such levels of performance are actually being achieved by companies doing the right things can have a dramatic effect on

Table 3.2 Example of an external benchmark table

Metric	Calculation	Feasible benchmark	Current hi-fi company performance
Inventory turns	Output versus average inventory	16 turns	7 turns
Equipment changes	Average time to retool for alternative production	2 hours	2 days
Production scrap	Scrap value as a percentage of good output	0.3%	2.5%
Materials quality	Rejected incoming materials as a percentage of total receipts	1.0%	5.0%
Indirect manning	Ratio of direct workers to indirect staff	2:1	1.4:1
Absence	Total absence as a percentage of time available	3.0%	7.4%

management's thinking. It can lead to previously acceptable performance being critically reappraised, and breakthrough productivity goals being developed over short-, medium- and long-term timescales. These goals are accompanied by supporting programmes and the appropriate cost-benefit analyses.

A company whose management team engages consultants to supply it with benchmark data on a comparable, top-performing organization, is signalling its own commitment to improving productivity. Its overall performance will be enhanced if it is able to secure improvements in the 6 areas detailed in Table 3.2. The comparative statistical information indicates to management where significant gains can be made. In the case of absence it shows that the company rate is more than that of the comparative company. The benchmark table sets the agenda for change. Managers will need to agree in which order to address the issues and decide which areas can be changed relatively quickly and with ease, and which will require more time and effort. The relative effect on bottom line results can be a decision criterion here. In the case of absence, for example, Chapter 14 presents a checklist for calculating the likely cost savings which can accrue from reduced absenteeism. These can be compared with the financial benefits to be gained from increasing inventory turns, or reducing the time on equipment changes.

Turning now to the topic of internal comparison, we can see that many companies already employ a system of *internal benchmarking*. In one Australian insurance company which has 18 branches, each branch manager receives a printout comparing his or her branch's performance with that of the other 17. The performance indicators used are financial, productivity, costs and staff-related. The latter includes figures on staff turnover and absenteeism. The figures that the branch manager receives first compare the branch to the company as a whole. Next, the branch is ranked on each indicator against the others. While the branch manager does not receive the detailed figures on the costs or productivity of the other branches, he or she does know where the branch stands in relation to them. An international garment manufacturer with branches in Europe, including some in Scotland, produces similar cost data every quarter for the managers of its European manufacturing plants.

The underlying rationale for this approach is contained in work done by Edward Lawler[10], and called the *valency theory of motivation*. What this theory states is that individuals can be motivated to improve their performance if the company sets goals which are challenging but achievable, and if it sets up a system which allows employees to achieve those goals. Specifically in the area of absence, we would suggest that this benchmarking technique, whether external or internal, can help managers to assess the productivity opportunity that exists within their own organization. Our studies show that a benchmark of 3% absence or less should be used by organizations seeking excellence in line with the best current practice. The guide, shown in Table 3.3, can put an organization's absence opportunity into perspective.

Table 3.3 Absence levels and productivity opportunities

Organization's absence level	Productivity opportunity
Under 3%	This level matches an aggressive benchmark which has been achieved in 'excellent' organizations. Attention should predominantly focus on individual problem areas or pockets of absence.
3%–4%	This level may be viewed within the organization as a good absence performance but it still represents a moderate productivity opportunity, particularly if sectional analysis is conducted.
5%–8%	This level is tolerated by many organizations but clearly represents a major productivity opportunity when viewed against the benchmark of excellent organizations.
9%–10%	This level indicates that a serious absence problem exists. It represents an outstanding productivity opportunity.
Over 10%	This level of absence is totally unacceptable, and if sustained could undermine the future viability of the company. Urgent improvement is both essential and achievable.

The measurement of absence is a necessary first step to its elimination. Andrew Sargent, author of a management training video on absenteeism[11], argued that, while the keeping of proper records was a vital factor in overcoming an absence problem, it was extraordinary how many companies did not bother to keep such records. Even those which had serious financial problems. Whether such criticism is wholly justified is uncertain. The reality of the absence problem is more complex. Certainly there is a considerable scope for improvement in the many administrative aspects of absence control. However, this should not be taken as a confirmation of complacency amongst management about the problem. Both personal experience and published information suggests that managers do take a very serious view of the matter. The managers we interviewed expressed deep concern about the topic, proudly described their successful attempts to reduce absence, and expressed disappointment when these strategies had failed. Their comments, contained in this book, express their views.

In our view, the main obstacle to addressing the absence problem is not complacency. The real difficulty seems to be that managers do not fully understand the nature of the absence problem. Consequently they are unable to develop an effective strategy to resolve it. This is in spite of the fact that a great deal has been written on virtually every aspect of the subject. Absence is a problem with a great appeal to behavioural scientists[12]. Many studies have sought to measure absence and to correlate it with other variables such as age, sex and so on. On the prescriptive side, a large number of solutions have been marketed. Despite all of this information and advice, there is little doubt that the goal of systematic absence control is as elusive as ever. A survey of management practices used by 22 Scottish companies revealed that the attempts to control absence varied widely[13]. To put it simply, many managers experience a sense of futility when trying to determine how to get from 'where they are' to 'where they want to be' in terms of their absence rates.

Conclusion

Despite the problems of surveys, confusing literature, offers of quick-fix solutions, and the prevalence of personal theories, absence remains an important issue. It is a key ingredient in the search for increased productivity and the competitive advantage. Traditional productivity measures have in the past ignored this element.

By understanding the nature of their company's absence problem, and by developing and implementing an appropriate absence control programme, managers can achieve significant productivity improvements rapidly. Absenteeism therefore, is an issue that is of real importance to the employee on the shopfloor, to management and to the country as a whole. Moreover, it is one of the few human relations puzzles for which we have all the pieces. The problem is deciding how they should be assembled to meet the needs of each particular organization.

Many organizations have grappled with their own absence problem and have achieved outstanding success using a variety of approaches. The example of the Tees and Hartlepool Port Authority is a case in point. In 1968, unauthorized absence amongst registered dockers employed by this organization was 18%. In 1987, the overall rate for what is now known as Teesport is just 2.8%. This shows that major improvements can be achieved, and that there are many different roads to salvation. Each firm has to find its own.

Management review questions

Below are listed a number of management review questions, based upon the topics of the first three chapters. Managers intending to address their company's own absence problem should assign a staff member to write a report answering the following eight questions:

1 Does our company maintain accurate records of employee absence?

2 What is the overall absence level in our organization?

3 Does our company produce statistical analyses of absence records?

4 Are there any work areas or employee groups which represent a particularly large absence problem?

5 Can any unfavourable absence trends be identified?

6 What are the hidden costs to our organization of absence?

7 What arrangements, if any, are built into our company's plans to mitigate the effects of absence?

8 Where in our organizational structure does 'ownership' for resolving the absence problem reside?

Part two
The causes of absence

Chapter 4
Classifying reasons for absence

Introduction

The popular management literature on employee absence suggests a range of causes. An article in *The Director* magazine argued that:

> 'The majority (of employees) ... will opt out of work depending on how important the company makes them feel'.

All managers have their own personal views about the causes of absence in their organizations. Newspapers frequently ignore the question *why* employees fail to turn up to work, and report the topic by calling them lazy or 'skivers'[1]. The 1987 CBI survey on work absence concluded that absence was:

> ... often symptomatic of a general failure to abide by agreed rules and procedures, and of a low level of commitment, morale and responsibility within the workforce'[2].

Some companies have engaged management consultants to carry out detailed studies of the causes of absence, and what should be done about it. A manager may make an educated guess as to the causes of absence as a prelude to implementing some absence reduction strategy but without detailed research, long-term solutions are impossible to achieve.

Although this chapter will deal in detail with what have been found to be the main causes of absence, it is well to remember that absence in all organizations is a problem related to a *minority* of employees, even though it may have major implications for the company. Knowing that 20% of the workforce is responsible for 80% of absenteeism, brings the problem into better focus. Moreover, the realization that certain groups in the workforce, for example, young people, and in some cases, women, are major contributors to the adverse absenteeism rates, often assists in finding a solution. Absenteeism often relates to individuals in certain identifiable groups. However, the important word is 'individual', and addressing absenteeism with a particular individual's situation in mind is very often the key to solving the problem.

Our argument is that much of what is done by managers to combat absence in their organizations is taken in total ignorance of the causes of absence. Most managers neither understand, nor have investigated the causes of their absence problem. Instead, personal hunches, prejudices and rules of thumb represent the basis on which corrective action is decided. The failure of managers to deal effectively with their absence problem derives, to a large extent, from a lack of proper understanding. Personalized theories, rather than educated thought, dictate the actions of many managers and supervisors with respect to absence. At this juncture it is appropriate to broaden our consideration to review the main research findings into causal factors, and those that have been associated with absence.

Components of attendance behaviour

Absence can be viewed as a very personal decision based on both the *ability* to attend, and the *motivation* to attend. One definition of non-attendance sees it as:

> 'The manifestation of a decision by an employee not to present himself at his place of work at a time when it is planned by management that he should be in attendance, and when he has been notified of such an expectation'[3].

The individual decision to come to work will be influenced by many factors. At one extreme, there will be those conditions which make attendance virtually impossible, a serious illness or an accident. At the other extreme, there are those circumstances where management would say that there is no justification whatsoever for non-attendance.

In practice, the reasons stated for absence are not always the real ones. Some writers have concluded that it is virtually impossible to determine the true cause of absence[4]. This difficulty is complicated by the fact that identical conditions will give rise to different employee responses. For example, research carried out into sickness absence indicated that most of the factors which were significantly associated with sickness absence could be considered to be *behavioural* rather than *medical*[5]. The same study revealed that when employees in the 'never sick' category were examined, over a quarter were found to have had some organic disease.

These findings, and the examples given, highlight the very *personal* nature of the absence decision for each employee. Moreover, absence may not be due to a single factor or cause, but to an interdependency of influences. Management must therefore guard against seeing absence as an exclusively organizational phenomenon, or as a one-cause problem[6]. If it does not, then it will fail to take adequate account of what absence and attendance may mean to different individual employees.

If managers are to stop relying on personal axioms and prejudices, from where are they to seek better information about the causes of absence? The answer has to be in the research literature. A review of psychological, sociological and managerial studies has identified a great number of influencing factors. It has been found that:

- Lower levels of absence among shift workers (as opposed to day workers) have been attributed to their 'degree of personal involvement in their work and the social structure of the working group'[7].

- Workers who had high certified and uncertified absence rates spent more time travelling to work each day[8].

- The lack of a sick-pay scheme for workers during the first six months of service contributed to particularly low absence rates amongst this group[9].

- Significant differences in absence behaviour could be directly related to age[10].

- It was doubtful whether job dissatisfaction was a major cause of absence[11].

- Job strain was positively related to absence[12].

These extracts represent a very small sample of the diverse research findings that we examined. The remainder of Part two will seek to distil the essence of a wide range of academic and non-academic research studies. Taken in isolation, such research presents a complicated and potentially confusing picture of the main causes of absence. In an effort to bring some order to the task of understanding these multiple influences, it is helpful to categorize the main influencing factors. The Industrial Society[13] recommended a three-way grouping of geographical, organizational and personal factors (Table 4.1).

Such a classification can help to organize the many variables, assist managers to get an overall picture, allow them to review absence causes, and highlight those factors over which they can exert personal control. The weakness of the framework is that in trying to understand absence it tends to be *content*-focused rather than *process*-oriented. This means that it suggests what might influence an employee to be absent from work (the content), but it fails to pay adequate attention to explaining the way in which one variable, such as supervisory quality, relates to another one, for example, job satisfaction. This is referred to as the *process*.

One can imagine that many of the different variables appearing on the list are very closely related to each other. Research has discovered other relationships between, for example, personality and medical condition, and between job satisfaction and the nature of the organization. In situations where a number of influences may be involved, the preceding classification

Table 4.1 Some factors affecting sickness absence (*Industrial Society*)

Geographical	Organizational	Personal
Climate	Nature	Age
Region	Size	Sex
Ethnic origin	Industrial relations	Occupation
Social insurance	Personnel policy	Personality
Health services	Sick pay	Life crises
Epidemics	Supervisory quality	Job satisfaction
Unemployment	Working conditions	Medical condition
Social	Environmental	Family
attitudes	hazards	responsibilities
Pension age	Occupational health	Alcohol
	service	Journey to work
	Labour turnover	Social activities

offers little assistance in understanding either the interdependencies between the various factors, or in pinpointing the key ones.

Interestingly, none of the personnel managers interviewed, who lived with the absence problem on a day-to-day basis, were confident in making a definite statement as to the causes of absence in their companies. In the absence of hard data about absence causes, but under company pressure to take action, they were inevitably forced to rely on their own hunches and theories about the causes of the absence problem.

Process model of employee attendance

Both the single-cause suggestion, and the category listing are examples of content-focused approaches to absence-cause identification. Because of the weaknesses of this approach, we intend to offer a process model. This not only classifies the various causes of absence, but also recognizes the interdependent processes involved. The model itself was developed by two American writers, Richard Steers and Susan Rhodes[14]. Their process model of employee attendance is based upon a review of over a hundred research studies on absenteeism.

As the name of their model suggests, the focus is on *attendance behaviour*, rather than upon absenteeism. After all, absence is not strictly a behaviour. It is more an absence of a behaviour. Steers and Rhodes argued that more attention should be paid to the process associated with attendance. They felt that the research into employee absence had two main shortcomings. First, it largely assumed that job dissatisfaction was the primary (and often sole) cause of absenteeism. That is, people did not turn up to work because they did not like it. This view continues to be held, even though research evidence to support it is weak. Second, they found that there was an implicit assumption that employees were generally free to choose whether or not to attend. Clearly, there were frequently situational constraints which influenced the attitude-behaviour relationship.

To deal with these problems, Steers and Rhodes devised a process model to explain the causes of absence. Their model not only includes job attitudes (and other influences on attendance motivation), but also *situational constraints* which may inhibit the motivation-behaviour relationship. The model is shown in Figure 4.1.

This model will be used as the main organizing framework within which to consider the complex issue of absence causes. The variables which have been shown to affect attendance behaviour are listed in Figure 4.1. We have extended the Steers and Rhodes model slightly, and have grouped absence causes under three main headings, each of which will constitute a chapter of its own.

The first set of variables focus on the *job situation*. Steers and Rhodes saw attendance motivation as being composed partly by the individual's job situation (1), mediated by his or her values and expectations (2). Chapter 5 will consider the empirical evidence concerning the effect of the job situation on attendance behaviour.

Personal characteristics (3) represent the second main set of variables affecting attendance behaviour. These affect employee values and job expectations (2) and, together with the job situation (1), determine employees' satisfaction with their job situation (4). For ease of explanation, boxes 2, 3 and 4 in the Steers and Rhodes model will be considered together in Chapter 6.

Pressure to attend was the third major force determining employee attendance. It was affected by the personal characteristics of the employee (3), and these combined with factors such as illness, family responsibilities and transportation issues to establish whether the worker was able to attend. Factors which impeded a person's ability to attend, as well as other absence causes revealed in the literature, will be examined in Chapter 7.

A glance at Figure 4.1 will reveal that Steers and Rhodes present their model as a process, one in which feedback from attendance behaviour can subsequently influence both the job situation and the pressure to attend.

We have conducted an extensive literature review of absence causes and variables. As each item was identified, it was allocated to one of the main categories in the Steers and Rhodes model. We sought to focus particularly on those variables which revealed themselves most consistently, and which therefore can be considered to be of greatest interest to the manager. These included job design, age, sex, incentive systems, illness and so on. In addition, we have also discussed attendance factors which have received relatively less attention, but which, nevertheless, can provide us with significant insights into the absence problem. Their inclusion, we believe, can enhance our overall understanding of the absence problem. Such

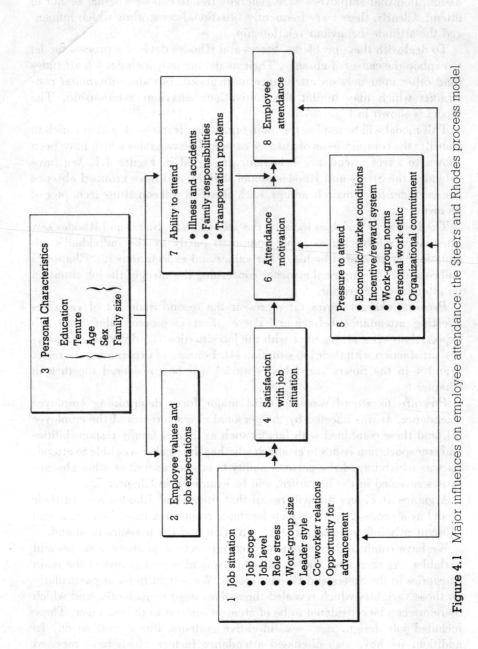

Figure 4.1   Major influences on employee attendance: the Steers and Rhodes process model

Table 4.2 Factors affecting absence from work

---

1   Job situation
    1a   job scope, level, design, type
    1b   stress
    1c   frequency of job moves
    1d   shifts/hours of work
    1e   leadership style/management quality
    1f   work environment
    1g   work-group size

2   Employee values/job expectations

3   Personal characteristics
    3a   tenure/length of service
    3b   age
    3c   sex
    3d   personality

4   Satisfaction with job situation

5   Pressure to attend
    5a   economic/market conditions
    5b   incentive/reward system
    5c   sick pay/NHI benefits
    5d   work-group norms
    5e   personal work ethic

6   Attendance motivation

7   Ability to attend
    7a   illness/accidents
    7b   transportation/distance
    7c   family responsibilities

8   Other
    8a   day of week/time of year
    8b   past absence patterns
    8c   self-certification

---

variables include frequent job moves, personality and past absence trends. Where possible, we have tried to illustrate the points being made with comments from the line or personnel managers whom we interviewed in our study.

Chapter 8 ends Part two of the book. The management review questions contained in it are based on the Steers and Rhodes model. The questions are organised into a checklist to allow managers to analyse the likely causes of absence in their organizations or parts of their organizations. The output from this audit represents one of the steps in the ALIEDIM approach to absence control which will be the subject of Chapter 14.

Chapter 5

Cause of absence: job situation factors

Job situation

(a) Job scope, level, design, type
(b) Stress
(c) Frequency of job moves
(d) Shifts/hours of work
(e) Leadership style/management quality
(f) Work environment
(g) Work-group size

Job situation refers to all those aspects which determine the nature of the job, and the overall work environment. Put simply, the argument is that if employees enjoy the work situation, and the tasks associated with that job, then they will be more likely to want to come to work. Under these circumstances, the work experience would be a pleasurable one for employees.

According to the process model, the nature of the job situation represents a major influence on job satisfaction. This in turn contributes directly to attendance motivation. The research literature provides information on seven aspects of the job situation. Amongst those which are most likely to lead to increased job satisfaction are increases in the job scope or challenge, an increase in the job level, or the position that one holds in the organizational hierarchy, low amounts of stress, few or no job moves, a considerate and democratic leadership style, a pleasant working environment and positive relations with fellow group workers related to the size of the work group.

(a) Job scope, level, design and type

Generally speaking, there seems to be a consensus, supported by research, of a very *modest* inverse relationship between the scope and nature of the job and absence. That is to say, the more that employees identify with the task the greater will be their degree of both autonomy and participation in decision-making. The higher the level of their responsibility the greater will be their feeling of achievement and the less likely they are to be absent. Because this explanation has such a commensense ring to it, it should be treated with the utmost caution. After an extensive review of the literature, one group of researchers[1] concluded that:

'At best it seems that job satisfaction and absence from work are tenuously related'.

In a medical study at an oil refinery, those employees who were classed as being frequently sick regularly reported an active desire for more responsibility in their job, while the never sick group did not[2]. In another study, this time in a government department, the researchers were able to establish an inverse correlation between job involvement and absenteeism. As job involvement went up, so absenteeism came down[3].

Identification with the task has much to do with its quality and the challenge that the task offers. A great deal of research associates high levels of task repetitiveness with low job satisfaction[4,5,6]. This in turn has been positively correlated with absenteeism[7,8]. Many of the managers that we interviewed acknowledged, with regret, that the people in the groups which constituted the absence problem in their organization, had jobs which were intrinsically boring. More specifically, the jobs offered little to employees in the way of task identification possibilities, or gave them any autonomy, responsibility, or the chance to make decisions.

'This is an industry where there isn't a great deal of technological development or new products, new designs or new machinery. The people are really machine minders, packers and fork-lift truck drivers. The work is highly automated and highly repetitive.'

* * *

'The high absence groups do not have a job that's particularly interesting. Not a job that you or I would be satisfied with.' (*Whisky bottling plant*)

Our managers often pointed to some of the worst jobs that were performed by the employees.

'One job is called *sighting*. This is an inspection function. On the so-called automatic machines, you sit, and the bottles come along and are inverted in the machines with opaque white lighting behind. The bottles run across this. Because it's a high-speed operation, all you can do if you see a fault is to put a sticker on the bottle. Once it is back on the line again, another girl lifts the faulty bottle off. Now, that's a mindless, soul-destroying job that.'

* * *

'Of those who are affected by the job, they just find the job boring. They wake up ten minutes late and say they won't bother today, because there's nothing in the job, other than coming in and rolling the casks. I think it's the repetitiveness of the job and that it's not interesting.' (*Whisky bottling plant*)

It is easy to be carried away with the belief that jobs with limited job scope are the main or only cause of absenteeism. Other factors, including the employee's personality, are likely to play a part in the attendance decision. As a manager commented: 'I don't think the type of work helped. Repetitive type work. What effect it had I don't know. You get two apparently similar people, doing the same jobs. One is never off, and the other's never at his work.'

Not all people, however, want the same thing from a job. Nevertheless, many do want more than they are currently getting. The dilemma for management is that attempts to make any significant changes in the type of job and its scope have, at least in the past, been seen as being limited by the existing technology. It is not so much that managers are unaware of this cause of absence, it is more that they, at their level in the organization, feel that there is little they can do to change the jobs of these workers.

One effect of this dilemma is that some managers, because they would hate to do many of the worst jobs themselves, feel a certain sympathy for the job-holder who may be absent frequently. Perhaps they see absence as a form of psychological defence against an intolerable situation, which indeed it often can be. The more recent research studies of job satisfaction's effect on absence, which were carried out in the late 1970s and early 1980s, suggest that it is not as good a predictor of absence as other factors[9,10,11,12,13,14].

(b) Stress

Recent research in Britain suggests that 40 million working days are lost each year due to stress at work. The 1987 CBI[15] survey of absence reported that 33% of responding managers thought that work-related stress was a cause of absence amongst non-manual workers. Other data suggests that stress is a problem lower down in the organizational hierarchy as well. The US government's National Institute of Occupational Safety and Health has recently identified psychological disorders at work as one of the top ten occupational diseases in that country. The National Council of Compensation Insurance reported that stress at work represented 11% of all occupational disease claims. Dr Andrew Mason of the Gresham Centre in Suffolk, which runs stress management courses, has been quoted as saying that 1 in 4 male managers will die before they collect their pensions.

Stress has been defined as, 'an adaptive response, mediated by individual characteristics and/or psychological processes, that is a consequence of any external action, situation or event that places special physical and/or psychological demands upon a person'[16]. This definition focuses our attention on the three major components of stress:

- the situational demands that force one to adapt, i.e. the stressors,

- one's perceptions of those demands and one's ability to cope with them,

- the biochemical stress response.

Dr Hans Selye[17], a pioneer of stress research, argued that the usual response to stressful events followed a fairly consistent pattern which he called the *General Adaption Syndrome* (GAS). The GAS consists of three stages labelled alarm, resistance and exhaustion. In the alarm stage, the body is mobilized to meet the challenge posed by the stressor. If the stressor continues, the resistance phase is entered in which fighting or fleeing from the stressor was evident. The individual becomes tense, anxious or fatigued. Since the activation of the GAS puts extraordinary demands on the body, the more frequently it is activated and the longer it remains in operation, the more wear and tear it causes to the person. Prolonged continuous exposure to stress can use up the available adaptive energy, and this leads to the exhaustive stage. When the adaptive energies of the organism are depleted, collapse can take place. This occurs in the form of severe depression, mental breakdown or total exhaustion. Any or all of these can cause absence from work. Equally, people may escape from the work situation so as to avoid contact with the stressors which cause this reaction.

In much of the popular literature, job stress is held to be synonymous with management stress. The stereotype of the highly stressed employee is the hard-working, heavy-drinking top manager who puts in 100 hours a week. Making difficult decisions under pressure, the manager is exposed to acute conditions which lead to illness and absence from work. While many senior managers may drive themselves hard, and are absent from work as a result, researchers have found stress-induced absenteeism in jobs all the way down the organizational ladder, right down to the shopfloor. In a review of the literature, Cary Cooper[18] identified a number of major sources of occupational stress. Five of these are particularly relevant to the subject of absenteeism:

1 Factors intrinsic to the job
2 Role in the organization
3 Career development
4 Relationships at work
5 Organizational structure and climate

As one would expect, there were a number of factors intrinsic to the job which could cause stress for employees, and thus indirectly cause them to be absent. Five job factors appeared to be particularly relevant. The first of these were *poor working conditions* and physical danger of the job. This was true of both manufacturing and office environments. A study of casting in a steel plant revealed that heat and danger were major stressors which led to below standard employee performance and absence[19]. Another of Cooper's job-focused stress factors was *physical danger*. Although some occupations such as those of firemen, soldiers, policemen and miners involve high risks of physical danger, the potential stress can be reduced if the employees feel they are adequately trained and equipped to deal with emergency situations[20,21]. Our own discussons with managers in the shipbuilding industry emphasized the effects of outdoor working, noise levels and the wearing of safety equipment. In office environments, distractions may be a problem. Work areas may need to be changed using modern environmental and ergonomic designs.

A second job stressor identified by Cooper was *shift work*. He quoted numerous occupational studies which showed that shift working impaired mental efficiency and work motivation. Air traffic controllers were particularly susceptible. While other stress factors in the job played a part, shift working was singled out as being of particular importance[22]. Exactly how shift working contributes to absence is not yet clear from the research.

Third, the volume of work required to be done could cause stress. *Work overload* seemed to cause stress and absenteeism[23,24]. One could have too much work to do (quantitative overload) or the work might be too difficult (qualitative overload). Overload manifested itself in cigarette smoking (leading to coronary heart disease), low self-esteem, work motivation and escapist drinking[25]. All of these have consequences for absence. *Job underload* was also identified as a stressor. It involved having to do repetitive, routine, boring and unstimulating work. Machine-paced assembly lines have been associated with ill health[26]. Our own studies show that many jobs, such as working in bottling plants, warehousing, and light-bulb manufacture represent similarly non-stimulating environments. There are jobs which are characterized by long periods of boredom, but which require the employee to maintain sufficient vigilance to be able to respond quickly to a potential emergency. One would list here jobs such as those of a fireman and the nurse[27]. Interestingly, it has been found that policemen are not stressed by horrific road accidents or by violent people but by the mountains of paperwork that they have to do, and by having to appear in court.

The second broad category of stressor that Cooper identified (after factors intrinsic to the job), was the person's *role in the organization*. The stress here came from having an unclear or ambiguous role, or when a person's different roles came into conflict. This was particularly characteristic of managerial, clerical and professional positions. Being responsible for people was also stress-inducing[28]. *Role ambiguity* is a situation where the role expectations for the employee are unclear. It has been shown to be linked to stress and to absenteeism[29,30,31]. Finally, *role conflict* refers to a situation where the expectations placed on an employee are clear, but are in conflict with each other. In seeking to meet one set of expectations, for example, being a hard-working and diligent employee, the individual necessarily fails to meet another set of expectations, such as being a good spouse and parent. It has been shown that role conflict too, can cause stress and absence[32]. Brooke[33] argued that these different types of role problem (overload, ambiguity and conflict) have an indirect effect on absenteeism by producing lower satisfaction, poorer employee health, and increasing drinking problems. The evidence indicates a relationship between role ambiguity and conflict and stress-related illnesses such as coronary heart disease[34,35].

The roles that people play in organizations, define the demands that are placed upon them, and the authority and responsibility that they receive. It is this which can make stress a feature of jobs at all levels in the organization. In order to determine what makes jobs stressful, Richard Karasek[36] proposed a job strain model. It contains two dimensions:

1 job decision latitude   how much decision-making authority the occupant of the job has

2 job demands: the extent to which the job occupant can control the demands placed on him/her in the job

Using these two dimensions, Karasek produced four job groupings. These he labelled passive, active, low strain and high strain (Figure 5.1).

The critical point that Karasek made was that stress was caused by a coincidence of factors. Specifically, a combination of high job demands that could not be controlled or reduced by the job occupants, and the extent of their decision latitudes. Such a combination of circumstances can occur anywhere in the organizational hierarchy. It depends upon how the company is structured, and how responsibility, authority and accountability are divided up. However, it tends to be most commonly found at the bottom, rather than at the top of organizations.

Jobs which make great demands on individuals, over which they have control will not, on their own, necessarily cause stress. Similarly, jobs which offer their occupants only limited freedom to make decisions on their own (limited decision latitude), need not cause stress. The high-strain jobs, argued Karasek, typically made high job demands on employees while *at the same time* giving them low decision latitudes. It was this combination which produced an unresolved strain in the person involved.

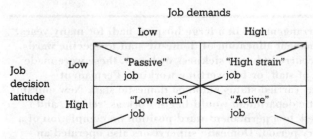

Figure 5.1 Karasek's job strain model

Thus, the high-strain jobs included those of assembly workers, waiters, cashiers, materials handlers, cooks and telephone operators. Our stereotype of a top manager making many decisions, was more an example of an Active Job. He/she was exposed to job demands, but this was accompanied by a great deal of freedom to make decisions about what should be done.

Career development was the third of Cooper's work environment stressors. It referred to the effects of either overpromotion, underpromotion, status incongruence, lack of job security or thwarted ambition. Thwarted career ambition was a particularly important stressor for women[37,38].

Fourth on the list of stressors were *relationships at work*. The quality of these and the social support available from other members of the organization were found to be related to the level of stress[39]. Interpersonal relations might be strained by role ambiguity[40] which produced strains that showed themselves in the form of low job satisfaction, and hence possible absence. In contrast, strong support from colleagues could relieve job strain[41].

The fifth and final source of potential stress identified by Cooper was *organizational climate and structure*. Under this heading he put factors such as office politics, inadequate consultation, little or no participation in decision-making, and restrictions on behaviour. Indeed greater participation was found to increase performance and productivity, and to reduce staff turnover and illness[42,43]. Again, having acknowledged that the combination of certain job characteristics can produce stress, it is not always clear how stress relates to absence. In some people it causes mental and physical illness, which may lead to their being absent from work. Overall, it should be noted that there is evidence to show that absence is greater in jobs characterized by high levels of stress[44].

(c) Frequency of job moves

Although this factor has not received a great deal of attention in the literature, those studies which have examined the effect of frequent job transfers, do suggest a relationship to absence. An account by a hospital administrator provides an excellent illustration of how permanent attachment to a group increases group cohesion and how regular moves can destroy it[45].

The domestic service arrangements in a large hospital had, for many years, been based on the permanent allocation of domestic staff to specific wards. When staff shortages occurred (due to sickness or leave), these were made up from a reserve pool of staff, or by overtime working. Permanent allocation to a ward thus carried status amongst domestic staff. New entrants to the hospital's domestic department would begin work as 'reliefs', and would then be 'promoted' to a permanent ward position on completion of a satisfactory probationary period. Domestic supervisors also operated an unofficial sanction system whereby staff off sick frequently, or for long periods of time were penalized for their absences by being 'demoted' to the reserve pool. They only returned to a permanent ward position, when their record of attendance once again proved to be satisfactory.

An Organization and Methods (O & M) team was brought in to review the work practices of these domestic staff and recommended that efficiency could be increased, and overtime reduced, by changing work patterns and the type of equipment used. The new equipment was purchased. These two changes meant the replacement of the old labour-intensive system which, in order to work, had to be based on staff co-operation and co-ordination. Changes in work patterns resulted in the dissolution of the reserve pool and the allocation of staff to ward areas on a rotational basis. This was intended to increase flexibility in the transfer of staff on an *ad hoc* basis to any areas of shortage.

Much to the surprise of management, problems arose as soon as the revised system began to operate. Levels of sickness and absenteeism rose, productivity and efficiency fell, and problems of liaison at ward level between domestic and nursing staff were reported which suggested a deterioration in working relationships. Management hurriedly re-established the original working practices.

An analysis revealed what the O & M team had overlooked. Under the original method of working, domestic staff had a permanent placement within a particular ward. Over time, the domestic staff working on the same ward began to perceive themselves as an informal group with a measure of collective identity. By going to tea and lunch breaks together, by identifying with the particular type of patient on their ward, and by building up working relationships with regular nursing personnel assigned to their ward, they gradually evolved into cohesive, informal groups.

The organizational goal of getting the work done was achieved by a group approach, encompassing group norms and goals. These included warning other group members of the impending approach of a supervisor, supporting other group members in the event of 'harassment' by management, and defending or bragging about their own ward's happenings.

The formation of such groups served several purposes. It provided members with an opportunity for social interaction. It gave them a sense of belonging in an otherwise large, anonymous organization, and it provided them with a measure of protection against the power of the bureaucracy. Simply stated, being permanently attached to a group fulfilled the individuals' needs for friendship, identity and security. By providing opportunities and outlets for needs not allowed for in the system, the groups completed and supplemented the formal organizational structure and goals.

The effect of the revised working patterns was twofold. First, it forced the disintegration of the groups. Second, it destroyed the co-operative nature of the work, and thus undermined the interdependence of individuals within the groups. The domestic staff could no longer associate themselves with particular areas of the hospital, as they moved so frequently from one location to another. Practical working relationships with other ward personnel could neither be forged nor maintained for the same reason. The

former integration of domestic staff into the multidisciplinary ward teams dissolved, leaving domestic staff as outsiders alienated from ward activity. This sense of alienation was reflected in increased absenteeism and reduced productivity. (*Administrator—hospital*)

This account illustrates how easily management action can destroy group loyalties and ties, and group cohesion, by requiring individuals to change work colleagues and work areas. An important consequence of constant job moves is the serverance of employees' ties with their small work group. It encourages them to think and act as individuals. One of the managers from a bottling plant made the following observation:

'The shopfloor operates as a workforce of 150. They are all flexible and interchangeable. So if you're one of the 150, and you have a day's absence, then you feel that someone else will cover for it. They don't think they're leaving someone in the lurch if they're off'.

The same manager was also surprised by the attitude of the drivers in the warehouses who worked outside in the yard all day. During the bleak Scottish winter they were exposed continually to the elements each day. The warehouses were often freezing and the rain sheeted down. He observed however that:

'If you tried to move the men away from that job and rotate them into a job indoors, they didn't want to know. They've become a unit in themselves. They tend to be reasonably highly motivated people'.

In the manufacturing environment, the requirement for labour flexibility which results in frequent job moves, has been found to be a dominant factor in the total absence equation[46]. As in the case of the hospital domestics, the effect has been attributed to the uncertainty, insecurity and lack of work-group identification created by this type of labour policy. At the shopfloor level, high levels of absence have resulted in the attending workers being reallocated to fill in for their absent colleagues. Such rejigging has itself led to absence amongst those who have been moved around.

One should never forget the preference of some people to continue doing the same job, however boring it may appear to an outside observer. One manager described the work of his warehouse staff. The task involved feeding a conveyor to bring the casks into the whisky filling department, filling the casks themselves, putting the bungs in, and then removing the casks. He felt this job and some similar ones, would be prime candidates for job rotation. In fact, the warehousemen resisted this proposal and insisted on remaining in the department in which they worked. The manager himself continues to be amazed that he should have a group of reasonably well-motivated people in the warehouse, doing well a repetitive and boring job. There is a warning here to those considering instituting job enrichment or job rotation schemes, or those who are seeking to implement productivity programmes which rely on flexible manning.

(d) Shifts/hours of work

It is difficult to give an unequivocal answer to the question whether shift working causes, or is associated with, absence. This is because the nature of the job is as important as the mode of working. Assembly line workers and hospital doctors are both shift workers. Earlier, Cooper was quoted as saying that shift working does produce stress, which can lead to absence. However, other evidence suggests that absence is lower amongst shift workers than amongst day workers. This is particularly apparent in studies involving rotating shift working[47]. However, research which has compared permanent day workers with permanent night workers has shown less conclusive results[48]. The lower absence rate amongst rotating shift workers has been attributed to three factors: the availability of premiums for shift working, the ability to cope with social/domestic working, and group norms and improved work-group involvement on shifts. The diversity of these conclusions, again emphasizes the problem of interpreting results.

'An awful lot of the shopfloor is on shiftwork. Again, it is understandable. If you get up at 4.30 a.m. to be here at 6.00 a.m., and you're not feeling too well, it's less likely that you'll drag yourself up on a cold winter's morning, and give it a go. The shifts rotate morning – afternoon. We have some people on permanent nights, who turn out to be good attenders. I don't know why.'

* * *

'Any continental shift working system of seven days a week will cause absence. In that system, you get rota days off. As such, occasionally, there will be a request from employees for holidays, etc. Depending on the level of sickness or absence in the specific group or crew, it may not be possible to grant them a holiday. You then get the person who just takes the time off. The absence causes are thus related to the existence of the continental shift system which we work.' (*Domestic lighting products manufacturer*)

(e) Leadership style/management quality

There are conflicting views on the effect that leadership style and the quality of management have on the absence level. The popular view is that management in general, and first line management in particular, has a vital influence on absence behaviour[49,50]. This influence is held to be particularly strong on brief spells of absence[51]. A study carried out in the Detroit Edison Company by Floyd Mann and John Sparling of the University of Michigan considered the effect of the supervisor–employee relationship on absence. They found that men in the 'low frequency-of-absence' groups felt free to discuss their job problems with their supervisors. Their supervisors had time to talk over personal problems with them. They often held meetings with the whole work group on common problems.

Another study, this time by the US Bureau of Business Practice, embraced nearly a quarter of a million employees in 39 companies. It asked them about a range of issues connected with absence. These were pay, their view of the company, how they rated their immediate supervisor, working conditions and the amount of work that was expected of them. The study was able to make only two significant connections or correlations. One of these was between the employee's attendance record and how he/she felt about his/her supervisor. This survey identified the quality of first line supervision as a major factor contributing to the amount of absence.

One of the key elements in supervisory style would appear to be the degree of recognition that is given to employees by their supervisors, for work well done[52]. Although supervisory behaviour was an important variable in influencing job satisfaction, its direct relationship with absenteeism was found to be more tenuous. This finding is consistent with the process model of employee attendance which proposes that leadership style does not have a direct influence on absence levels, but interacts with other factors such as job satisfaction.

Considering management more broadly, some writers have talked about *organizational permissiveness*. The underlying idea here is that of frequent absences without consequence[53]. Thus, an organization or department in which employees were able to take unscheduled days off easily, or in which numerous casual absences resulted in little or no apparent adverse consequences for the individual concerned, would be considered as being highly permissive of absenteeism[54,55]. The notion of organizational permissiveness is implied by leadership style, and that is why it is being considered here. However, it also has implications for the incentive and reward systems, and for work group norms. Evidence exists for a direct causal relationship between permissiveness and absence[56,57,58,59]. One example of a non-permissive environment was studied by Winkler[60]. Once teachers were required to demonstrate proof of illness, and were required to report their absences directly to the school principal, a large reduction in their short-term absence was noted.

(f) Work environment

This refers to the physical conditions at work. Many of the managers interviewed, especially those in factories where the working conditions were poor, gave this as a reason for absence.

'We've done a tremendous amount of work in terms of improving the environment that people work in. We're conscious now that the noise and the heat affects them. We've put murals on the walls, and spaced the machines out better.'

* * *

'Give people a better environment, better surroundings, then they don't get as bored with their work, and don't feel as if people are ignoring them.' (*Electrical components manufacturer*)

* * *

'In the shipbuilding industry, there are a number of hazards. High levels of noise, working in fumes, as well as out in all types of weather. Many employees are therefore absent for medical reasons.' (*Shipbuilders*)

In the Bureau of Business Practice survey mentioned in the previous section, the second significant connection found with absence were the working conditions. In that study, those employees who rated their working conditions as good or very good, were the same ones who showed a lower level of absence. More narrowly, Odiorne examined the relationship between poor equipment and machinery maintenance and employee morale. This was found to suffer when a person's machine was not in proper working order, or if that person felt that he or she did not have the tools to do a proper job. Odiorne found that the absence rate amongst workers on poorly maintained machines was 22% as compared to only 3% on well-maintained ones.

Taylor[61] confirmed this point. He wrote that, while it is generally accepted that good housekeeping and well-maintained machinery were necessary for good safety, it was not widely known that these factors also had an effect on absence rates. He described the case of an engineering factory where the output of ten well-maintained machines was compared with that of ten poorly-maintained machines. The results showed that the output was much higher from the well-maintained machines. Moreover, the absence rates, grievances and shopfloor arguments amongst the operators on the well-maintained were also significantly lower than those on the less well-maintained machines.

Another survey, this time a British one concerned with office work, was carried out by Reed Employment[62]. It questioned 500 secretaries and other office staff, all of whom were under 35 years of age. One half said that they liked nothing about their office environment. The biggest complaint was that their workplace was drab, dull and boring, or tatty, scruffy and dirty. They concluded that if the office did not damage their health, then it could easily bore them to death. A previous survey on the same subject by the same company revealed that staff faced 'physical battering from badly designed furniture, central heating, strip lighting stress and new technology'. Nearly half of the office workers questioned said that they suffered from backache, and two out of three blamed this on office chairs. Others claimed that sore throats and colds were caused by heating systems. Secretaries and their colleagues claimed that they were 'browned off' by offices with drab colour schemes. Brown, cream or beige were the common office colours. They wanted lighter colours such as green or blue.

It is difficult to interpret the significance of the comments and statistics about employees' views on their working conditions. At a basic level, inadequate working conditions, whether in the factory or the office can increase accidents through illness. People working in the open are affected by the weather. Bad working conditions can cause accidents which require time off. In the office, certain types of work layout can cause stress, while air conditioning systems have been shown to encourage the breeding of germs and the spread of viruses.

Beyond this, however, the complaints about working conditions may represent concerns about other, more fundamental, issues. People often go to their local doctor with some minor physical ailment which they use as a 'ticket' to get into the surgery to discuss a deeper, perhaps psychological, problem. Thus, the discovery of the relationship between machine maintenance and absenteeism may signal a failure of the company to give the employee a significant and meaningful job to do. The complaints of the secretaries about the colour schemes may identify unreasonable demands being made by their bosses, role conflict, or boring, unfulfilling work. In his now famous theory of motivation, Frederick Herzberg[63] listed working conditions as a *hygiene* factor, rather than as a *motivator*. That is, employees only complained about them when they were bad, but improving them beyond a level of adequacy did not motivate staff to achieve improved performance.

(g) Work group size and cohesion

One of the stable statistics in the absence literature is that which shows that the bigger the employing organization is, the higher its absence rate is. In the 1985 Industrial Society[64] study, companies in the 1–250 person range had an annual absence rate of 2.8%, while those in the 5000–10,000 plus range, had a rate of 4.7%. Two years later, the 1987 Industrial Society study[65] produced broadly the same figures. Sites with 1–99 staff had an average of 2.4% absence, while those with over 1000 employees had 5.1%. These figures are virtually identical with the 1987 study by the Confederation of British Industry[66], whose company size banding was a little different. Nevertheless, in this survey, the absence rate for companies with 1–100 employees was 2.4%, for those with 101–500 was 3.9%, and for those with 501 plus was 4.6%. This size–absence trend was first identified in the United States in the 1950s and 1960s for blue-collar employees.

The relationship seems to operate in the following way. Increases in work-group size come about as a result of increases in organizational activity. As the work-group size increases, so organizational factors act on the group members to reduce their motivation to attend. First, group cohesiveness tends to decrease as the group gets larger. Second, the tasks to be performed by the group members get more specialized and less interesting. Finally, effective interpersonal communications tend to deteriorate. Thus, it appears that increased work-group size results in reduced job challenge, and in a reduced ability of group members to satisfy their social needs at work. In consequence, job attendance becomes less appealing. Bendell's[67] observation of sickness and turnover rates amongst nurses in training clearly showed that where nurses, like the domestics described earlier, were moved frequently from one ward to another, their sickness and wastage rates rose dramatically.

This is a good example of a feature that will be common in our attempts to identify the causes of absence, namely that the different causes of absence interact with each other. Thus, here we have an example of one variable (work-group size) interacting with another variable (more specialized and less interesting work) to produce the consequence of lower job attendance. This is a regular feature of the studies, and it is this which prevents one from easily and unambiguously identifying the causes of absence.

Chapter 6
Cause of absence: personal factors

Employee values/job expectations

Not all employees want or expect the same things from a job. For some, having an interesting task is an important job outcome, while for others, satisfactory supervisory or co-worker relations are more desirable. Consequently, a major influence on the extent to which employees experience satisfaction from the work situation are the values and expectations that employees have concerning their jobs. These values and expectations are, to a large degree, shaped by their personal characteristics and backgrounds. For example, their age, sex, education, family, and length of employment with the firm. Thus for example, more highly educated people can be said to be more concerned with having a job that provides them with challenge and achievement opportunities than are less well-educated people. Moreover, peoples' values and expectations are not fixed. They can change over their working careers. Of particular importance is the initial employment period. It is at this initial selection and induction stage that the organization can ensure that there is a close match between individual and organizational expectations.

From research carried out amongst assembly line workers in the motor car industry[1], we know that people who already have an instrumental attitude to work (that is, who regard work as merely a means to an end and not as a source of satisfaction in itself) are attracted to those jobs where they can earn most. It is not expected that they will necessarily express a liking for the work or identify with the firm, but they will value good pay and security. Thus, although they may dislike the work and the company, they will not necessarily be absent often. The origins of the attitudes to work from this perspective are likely to be outside rather than inside the organization. They will be rooted in the individual's personal history, family circumstances and social class position rather than in the structure and patterning of the work within the company.

A manager in our study, whose factory was located in one of the poorest and most deprived areas of Glasgow, gave his view of the relationship between employee attitudes and environment:

'The attitude of some people here is that the employer is exploiting them, coming as they do from a poor background. We have a poor environment here. The catchment area from which we take people means that we pick up both people who have radical views of industry and exploitation, and also people who just don't care. They wouldn't care if the place closed, or whether they came to work or not. It's an attitude that has become built into them through school and their home environment.' (*Whisky bottling plant*)

Clearly, it is not possible to confirm or refute this manager's view about the motivation of the shopfloor operators. What his comments voice is not so much a vindictive attitude as one of powerlessness. On the one hand he sees people devoid of any internal drive, while on the other the mechanized technology used in the factory does not offer him any scope for changing their attitudes. His particular solution to this impasse was to suggest 'boredom breaks', so that employees could withdraw temporarily from the processes of production which reinforced their basic attitudes.

In some cases the aspiration level of employees may be very low. They may seek only enough money to get by. The level of required income may in fact be lower than that paid to them in their job. If the resulting excess of money has no great value, then some employees may prefer to take the time off.

A personnel manager had a personal theory about the different motivations of managerial and shopfloor employees.

'We always strive for a bit more. But the lower paid people have reached a level that they're quite happy at. They're happy with their lot in life. They don't seem to be motivated all that much. I'm not saying that they're all bad guys, not by any stretch of the imagination. But they don't have a lot of ambition left. They're probably in a job that's a dead end job anyway, so they don't have a lot of interest in the job.' (*Whisky bottling plant*)

This 'just getting by' idea that was voiced by several managers had a particular variant with regard to women. One respondent believed that some of the female staff came to work in order to be able to afford specific items for their home and family. Once this basic goal had been achieved there was less motivation for them to seek more money. However, since employment was full-time, five days a week, they had to have a five-day job even though the money from three days' work would have been sufficient for their needs. The effect of this was that once the required purchases had been made, the women took random days off until the next purchase need came into focus.

'The attitude of some of the women is; "I want a week's work, but I don't need a week's pay". These people, mainly but not exclusively women, may want to save for their holidays or a carpet. A certain logic says: "I've got

enough money, I don't need any more". The same thing applies to some of
the men, particularly the younger ones.' (*Whisky bottling plant*)

There is some research to suggest that the ability to miss work repeatedly
while keeping one's job was a characteristic considered desirable by many
workers, regardless of whether the time used was for recovering from a short
illness, or enjoying a three-day weekend[2]. This has been referred to as the
basic underlying motivation to, 'be away from work'. Doing less work for
the same financial reward improved the deal made by the worker with his
employer ('the effort–reward bargain'). Taking time off, even unpaid time,
may, in the eyes of some of the employees, represent part of the reward
structure to the deal – a 'compensation mix' of time and money. Many
workers find companies which tolerate absenteeism attractive because it
gives them flexibility to schedule activities outside their work.

Most jobs are characterized by uniform work schedules in terms of both
the days and hours worked. These are not adjusted to fit in with the
preferences of workers. As a result, employees create their own flexibility by
taking the time off when they need it. Absences permit an employee to
increase his leisure time or reallocate his leisure. He can work a varying
number of hours across time periods without having to renegotiate his work
contract or having to look for another job. Recovering from an illness or
accident, or relief from boredom at work, are activities for which the
demand for scheduled time flexibility tends to be greatest amongst
employees.

What then are the motivating consequences of being absent? The
following positive outcomes of absence were found to be particularly
important to employees: break from routine, leisure time, dealing with
personal business, and having a break from co-workers[3]. Because these are
positive consequences for the individual, they are likely to encourage further
absence in the future. Therefore, the company has a choice. It can adopt
either a negative (punishment) strategy, or a positive (rewarding) one. The
negative strategy involves management countering such absences by creating
undesirable outcomes or consequences for the individuals concerned. In
effect, it punishes workers for their absenteeism. However, studies have
shown that those employees who were frequently absent, considered the
motivating consequences of absence to be the realization of justified desires.
Given this value position, companies might choose to adopt a positive
strategy instead. They can operate an absence control plan which provides
employees, not with negative consequences such as punishments, but with
positive and valued outcomes. They could arrange to give employees the free
time that they desire, without at the same time, disrupting production
schedules. Strategies such as time off in lieu, four day–forty hour (4–40)
weeks, flexitime, and the annual hours approach are some examples of
approaches currently being used in companies.

Personal characteristics

(a) Tenure/length of service
(b) Age
(c) Personality
(d) Sex

Personal characteristics may have an influence on employee values. These in turn affect job satisfaction and the ability to attend. Both are directly related to employee attendance.

(a) Tenure/length of service

The relationship between length of service and absenteeism is unclear. The data provides inconsistent conclusions. Some studies have found little variation in absence rates relative to age[4], while others have reported a rise in absence as service increases[5]. Yet another study has identified an opposite trend with the level of absence, particularly of short spells, reducing with increased service[6].

Each group of writers who offer these different points of view, gives its own explanation. There are those who argue that the decreasing frequency of absence is associated with increasing work identification. The longer people are at work, the more they identify with, and become attached to, their jobs. Hence, the less likely they are to become absent. One might then expect the opposite to be true: that increased frequency of absence can be associated with decreasing work identification. One can say that the length of service studies provide no direct evidence of a link between absence and the duration of employment. Many of these inconclusive findings have been attributed to the limitations of the research methods used[7].

After conducting some long-term studies of his own, Pocock[8] concluded that an employee's length of service *per se*, probably had very little impact on absence, except as an indicator of other factors, such as sick-pay provision, job satisfaction and age. The question that remains concerns the degree to which absence behaviour reflects a new recruit's learning of company rules and informal (group) norms[9].

Length of the time in a job may also inculcate certain past traditions. The following speculation from a whisky bottling plant personnel officer illustrates the point.

'We had a lot of people with long, long service. There was a tradition prior to the 1970s where, instead of taking on temporary staff to meet peaks, the company laid off people to meet troughs. So some of the old-stagers who had been here a long while will tell you how management would come up to you on a Friday night and tell you 'Right, it's your turn, don't you lot come in next week." Another lot of people who had been off that week, would report in the following week. That was the way the thing worked. So perhaps it was a hangover from those days that you took a few weeks off in addition to your holidays.' (*Whisky bottling plant*)

(b) Age

There is a general, although not unanimous, consensus in the research literature that younger employees have more frequent absence spells than their older colleagues[10]. However, these absence episodes are usually very brief. Older employees' absences tend to be longer, and there is a particularly marked increase in the duration of absence after the age of fifty. This may be explained by the fact that while job satisfaction and work identification increases with age[11], so too do health problems. As generalizations, these are true, but the reasons for these absence patterns are less clear. Amongst the explanations offered are the lower level of responsibility amongst young people, differences in their status, and the higher incidence of serious illness amongst older employees.

'The worst problems were with the young girls, the middle-aged women, and those who had recently married. These women always seemed to be taking plenty of time off. They were the really bad ones. Single women, once they got to a mature age, were never a great problem. The older married women were OK. That's why I probably think that children were a factor that you never heard about.' (*Assembly plant*)

Horgan[12] reported the findings of a study on the work attitudes of American adolescents. His conclusions are relevant in the British context. The majority of youngsters he discovered had not yet developed the motivational patterns associated with success at work. Those that did have them, had satisfying and meaningful after-school and week-end jobs. They were given meaningful responsibilities at work, and were supervised by adults who both encouraged and controlled them. The individuals in that age group, argued Horgan, are on the bridge between childhood and maturity, and need both freedom *and* control. They are painfully surrendering a carefree life-style for the satisfactions that come with responsibility.

These beliefs are reflected, to some degree, in the comments of our respondents in the study. The age factor cannot be completely separated from job satisfaction. Absenteeism is usually higher on the more undesirable shifts, either late in the evening or early in the morning. These shifts may be worked by the newer and younger employees. The same people may be requested or required to do overtime. Younger workers may have more income and fewer financial responsibilities, and their attitude towards work discipline is not to let it interfere with their preferred life-style.

'The younger generation, they don't take a lot of time off. We call the ones who do, the "rascals". This group doesn't want to work anyway, and wants an easy life. They come from the lower paid groups. They're the ones who get a holiday outside of the normal holiday period. I think it's because they can get holidays abroad cheaper at certain times of the year. They suddenly go ill at that time. You can almost set the trend every year. You know when that guy's going to be off. You can never prove it.' (*Shipbuilders*)

The implication for management action in terms of the appropriate control method will be discussed later in the book. However, given that young workers are especially sensitive to free time, they will appreciate any steps taken by management to accommodate this priority. Typically they resent overtime, and will resist a rigid absence policy. In contrast, they are more likely to respond well to flexitime systems and to absence control programmes which reward good attendance with time off.

Some managers believe that younger employees often have higher rates of absence because they are unmarried, and hence do not have any family responsibilities. This in turn means that they lack an in-depth sense of commitment to the job. Because of this, they may be absent for any number of complicated reasons, many of which are not related to on-the-job conditions.

To what extent do the statistics confirm this view? The data from the Government's own General Household Survey of 1984[13] supports the view that absenteeism is more prevalent amongst the younger age groups (Table 6.1).

Table 6.1 Percentages of workers absent from work in the previous week for different reasons (illness, injury, strike, short time, lay-offs, personal reasons) by age and sex

Employee age and sex	Male (absence %)	Female (absence %)	All (absence %)
16–17	12	13	12
18–24	8	7	7
25–34	8	9	8
35–44	7	6	6
45–54	7	7	7
55–64	7	9	8
65 and over	5	0	4
All employees	7	7	7
Self-employed	10	12	10
Total	8	8	8

Source: General Household Survey, 1984

The US Bureau of Labor Statistics confirmed this finding, and showed that the absence rate of employees decreased consistently as the age of the employees increased. Workers under 20 years of age had the highest absence rates of about 15.5%, while those who were 45 years old had an absence rate of only 3.4%. Given the differences in the way that the statistics are collected, more emphasis should be placed on the general trends rather than on the specific numbers.

(c) Sex

Nearly every published study which has compared female with male sickness absence has generally shown a higher rate for the former group as compared with the latter. Historical data confirms this point. Table 6.2 shows that since 1979, women workers' sickness levels have always been higher than those of men. Meanwhile, the figure for men in 1984 was lower than at any other time over the previous ten years[14].

The 1984 General Household Survey data shown in Table 6.3 indicates that full-time working women had more sickness absence than men, 5% as opposed to 6%. The difference is particularly marked in the 55–59 age group, where it was 9%, compared to the 5% for men. Numerous organizational studies have confirmed this trend[15]. However, as far as absence patterns over working life are concerned, these are similar for both men and women. The absence levels for both full-time men and women are relatively stable during the first 20 years of their working lives. The figures are about 5% for men, and 6 per cent for women. The absence rates for both sexes then dip slightly during middle age. Finally, once full-time workers approach retirement, the absence levels for both sexes rise sharply.

Table 6.2 Percentage of workers absent from work in the previous week because of own illness/injury by sex, 1974-84[14]

Year	Men (absence %)	Women (absence %)
1974	5.4	5.3
1975	5.0	5.7
1976	5.2	5.1
1977	4.4	4.4
1978	5.0	4.9
1979	5.0	5.4
1980	4.3	5.3
1981	4.1	4.7
1982	4.2	5.4
1983	3.5	4.8
1984	4.0	4.6

Table 6.3 Percentages of full-time and part-time employees absent from work because of their own illness/injury by age and sex

Age	Males		Females		
	Working full-time	Total +	Working full-time	Working part-time	Total
	Percentages absent because of own illness/injury				
16-24	5	5	6	3	6
25-34	5	5	6	3	5
35-44	4	4	5	2	3
45-54	3	3	4	5	5
55-59	5	5	9	6	8
60-64	7	7	[1]	5	4
65 and over	nil	2	nil	nil	nil
Total	4	4	5	4	5
Base = 100%					
16-24	919	984	740	93	836
25-34	1220	1243	497	367	868
35-44	1143	1165	423	585	1009
45-54	943	960	371	407	780
55-59	359	369	149	171	320
60-64	268	280	34	81	117
65 and over	28	93	9	39	50
Total	4880	5093	2223	1743	3980

Source: General Household Survey, 1984

In the United States where proportionately more women work, their work loss from unscheduled absences is substantially higher than for male workers. In 1978, the female figure was 4.3% compared to 3.1% for men. US absence incidence rates are also higher for women, 8.6% of female workers experience a spell of absence during a typical working week, compared to 5.4% for men. The majority of unscheduled work absences are classed as being due to illness or injury. In 1979, the average US female worker lost 5.4 days from work for health reasons compared to 4.7 days for her male counterpart.

In Britain, the 1985 Industrial Society survey on absence indicated that women were more prone to sickness absence than their male counterparts. The figure for women was 9.5 days sickness absence in a year, and 7.4 days for men − a difference of 22%. Two years later, the 1987 Industrial Society absence survey[15], once again confirmed that male employees had less medically certified absence than females. This difference existed amongst both full-time and part-time female workers. In global terms over the years, women are typically found to have up to 50% more absences than men. However, it should be noted that there is considerable controversy about the causes of the consistently higher figures relating to women's absence.

The reasons for this difference are likely to be sociological since there is no clinical or pathological evidence to suggest that women are more susceptible than men to disease. Thus, the higher levels of absence amongst women are generally not accounted for by a difference in the incidence of illness. Instead, popular commentators attribute it to the types of job typically held by women, and to the traditional role of women in relation to their family responsibilities. It has been argued that, where women do a worthwhile job, there appear to be no absence problems. Banks and airlines which employ considerably more women than men, do not report any major absence problems[16]. However, where absenteeism among females is high, observers point to the fact that the jobs are routine, boring, and mundane. Writers have noted that both women and youngsters are treated unsympathetically by management, and are often given the worst jobs. Hedges[17] wrote that:

'It is quite common for people to develop very real illnesses arising from frustration or the stress of boredom'.

However, in our own study of an international garment manufacturing company which employed only women doing a highly repetitive, and intrinsically boring job, the absence rate was only 3%. This further supports the proposition that sex alone is not the determining factor in the absence equation.

So far as the traditional role of women in society is concerned, it has been found that female absence reduces as the age of dependent children increases[18]. However, Paringer[19] reported that, an increase in women's family responsibilities appeared to reduce the amount of time they missed from work. She stated that married women with family responsibilities exhibited a stronger attachment to work than unmarried women. These different reports further support the proposition that factors other than sex, may be as important, if not more so, in understanding absence behaviour. As examples we may cite such issues as the age of the woman (young or old), her marital status (single, married, divorced, widowed), her family responsibilities (does she have children, what are their ages?), and her economic status (is she a single parent, is she the main or sole family breadwinner?).

In this context, a study in the United States on sex differences in absenteeism, concluded that these had been overstated[20]. It was found that in blue-collar occupations, the absence rates of both men and women decreased as their wages rose. Both groups were more likely to increase their absences if they were employed in hazardous jobs. Finally, poor health increased absenteeism for both sexes. However, a number of fundamental differences were discovered. Women apparently assumed more responsibility for children, and reported more absences as the number of young children in the household increased. Women reported more minor health complaints such as insomnia, and were more likely than men to be absent as a result. Women were also more likely than men to miss work if they were employed in a large organization. Men, on the other hand, were more likely to report absent if they had experienced a recent work-related injury.

All the managers that we interviewed in our study were men. It was significant that in most cases they took a sympathetic attitude to female absence and appeared to expect women to be off more frequently than men. Gibson[21] referred to the common expectation that women will be absent more. This could create a situation where, because they are *expected* to be off more by men, they *will* be off more. That is, women may come to consider higher absence as part of the consensual contract, created by the climate of organizational permissiveness operated by a predominantly male management.

Male interviewee:

'Women are a problem. Their family responsibilities come first. Who can blame them? If there is a family problem, they do tend to take time off. Women are more susceptible to absence being more complicated physically than men. Our female absence figure is higher than male. Women, when they are off, will take fairly long spells, and that's even women who are away quite a lot. They will take a week or two off, even three, and they'll go to their doctor.' (*Bakery*)

(d) Personality

Most attendance–absence decisions are ultimately attitudinal. A number of studies have been carried out to discover whether people with certain types of personality are more absence-prone than others. These studies have shown that absence (and sickness absence in particular) is distributed unevenly amongst any group of staff. A small number of people, usually between 5% and 10%, account for about half of the total absence, while a few are never absent at all. The latter are by no means the most healthy, while the former are not necessarily suffering from chronic ill health. In one study of a telephone company, it was found that 10% of employees were responsible for 45% of the recorded absences, while the top third of absentees, accounted for three-quarters of all the recorded absences.

Such a distribution was first discovered in the 1920s in the studies of injuries at work. It was this which gave rise to the idea of *absence proneness*. Studies suggest that there is evidence which relates rates of absenteeism to certain personality traits. The term *absence-proneness*, therefore echoes the notion of *accident-proneness*. However, the identification of a small group of regular absentees does not mean that these people necessarily have a personality feature which makes them go absent. Some writers have argued that while absence-proneness is not necessarily an inherent or unalterable personal characteristic of these individuals, if they are left in an uncontrolled situation, their absence pattern, once established, will persist throughout their lives.

Managers want to know, for example, if extroverts are absent more often than introverts. Such studies have involved the use of personality tests. Fairly consistent findings have been reported on this topic. The personality profile of the absentee is the person who is '... characterized by manifest anxiety'[22], and who, '... is more tense, and less emotionally stable'[23]. These observations are further supported by the results of an Eysenck Personality Inventory Test. A study using this instrument concluded that those who were in the 'never sick' category, were characterized by 'introversion and stability'[24]. These findings support the distinction between *illness behaviour* and *illness as such*, the emotional and personality factors being particularly relevant to illness reporting[25,26]. It is well known that there is a progressive strengthening of personality traits such as stability, rigidity and perseverance with age[27,28,29]. The impact of this on attendance motivation is probably the major determinant of the well-established inverse age–absence relationship. This relationship shows that as people get older, they tend to be absent less[30].

Satisfaction with the job

Job satisfaction is the degree to which individuals like their jobs[31]. All the major reviews of absenteeism literature have examined the relationship between job satisfaction and absenteeism. Some writers have treated absence as a pain-reducing response on the part of the worker to an unsatisfying job. Others say that this is an overstatement, and that job satisfaction plays an important but indirect role with respect to the attendance decision[32]. The effects of job satisfaction are shown by job involvement, organizational commitment, health status and alcohol involvement. Low job satisfaction is often a precursor to reduced physical and mental health. Satisfaction with the job situation therefore, may perhaps be best said to constitute an important influence on attendance motivation generally, rather than specifically. Job satisfaction is an important although imprecise concept. It depends upon several specific attitudes which are related to the job, the working environment, supervision, and to work-group relations.

There is a widespread view, disseminated in the 'popular' management literature, that absence is somehow a natural consequence of a lack of job satisfaction. Indeed, in the past, employee absence rates have been used as an indicator of the level of work dissatisfaction amongst the workforce. All the managers in our study made this connection, either implicitly or explicitly.

'Given the industry, the technology and the workers, the absence rate is an unfortunate fact of life' (*Confectionery manufacturer*)

* * *

'The technology is old, but the process is complex, and intrinsically
difficult, but the product is simple. Since it is fairly old technology, there
are inherent problems in actually operating it, and making thousands of
electrical units, all to the same standard. A lot of work on the shopfloor is
mundane stuff. (*Electrical components manufacturer*)

* * *

'Traditionally, absence has been higher on the shopfloor. Lots of reasons
have been put forward. It's just in the nature of the job they have to do. If
you're feeling a bit off colour, you're maybe less likely to be prepared to
turn up to work under these conditions, than say, if you work in an office
environment.' (*Meat products factory*)

* * *

'Given the work environment and processes, I believe that you're always
likely to get a slightly higher absence level on the shopfloor. I wouldn't like
to ride on a fork-lift truck in the cold, whereas, I'd be prepared to work in
an office with a cold. There will always be that kind of gap.' (*Engineering
components manufacturer*)

* * *

'You've got to look at the conditions people work under. It wouldn't be
quite as acceptable for a clerk in a nice office to say he would be away for
four days with a chill, as it would be for a fork-lift truck driver.' (*Food
processing*)

* * *

'Production is a noisy, dirty area. If it's running reasonably well, it's a
reasonable job. If they hit problems, they are under pressure, and have to
build that performance back up.' (*Glass manufacturer*)

Our interviews revealed two interesting phenomena. First, when talking
about absence and work satisfaction amongst the workforce, our managers
used their *own criteria* against which to judge how much or how little
satisfaction the shopfloor workers might be getting from their jobs. In fact,
many employees do not expect to receive any satisfaction from their jobs
whatsoever. Second, having made the judgement based on their own
criteria, and having thereby acknowledged how much more satisfying their
own jobs were, these managers appeared to express a view which, while not
condoning absence behaviour, nevertheless expressed an understanding of
it. The effect of this might be to move the boundary point at which they
might be prepared to take action on absence in order to curb it. Given that a
public demonstration of management concern about the problem is a major
absence control strategy, as will be shown later, this point is important.

A number of studies have provided supporting evidence to demonstrate a
link between job satisfaction and absence, but an equal number have

questioned it[33]. A review of these studies concluded that it was doubtful whether job satisfaction was a major cause of absence, even though this was a popularly held belief amongst managers. From the available evidence, it is perhaps most appropriate to treat job dissatisfaction as a contributory rather than as a primary cause of absence.

Chapter 7

Cause of absence: attendance factors

Pressure to attend

According to the Steers and Rhodes model, *pressure to attend* represents the second major influence on attendance motivation.

(a) Economic/market conditions
(b) Incentive and reward systems (including overtime)
(c) Sick pay/National Insurance payments
(d) Work-group norms
(e) Personal work ethic

(a) Economic/market conditions

A number of authors have argued that absenteeism is affected by internal and external forces acting upon individuals[1]. This perspective assumes that workers are aware of, and respond to, the environmental forces that they perceive to be affecting them. The argument goes that, during periods of economic downturn, one of the worker's greatest fears will be job loss. To prevent this, a worker makes extra efforts not to jeopardize his or her employment. Furthermore, a downturn in the economy often requires management to reduce costs. As a result, supervisors will be more active in controlling absence. Additionally, if there is a need to make employees redundant, selection may now be made less on the basis of 'last-in, first-out', and more on the worker's past performance record, including the absence rate. Conversely, it is argued, when unemployment is low and the economy booming, job opportunities are more readily available and employees can usually obtain work elsewhere. Moreover, at these times, managers are less concerned about the occasional absence, because their attention is turned to meeting increasing customer demands.

Generally speaking, the little research that has been done on the connection between unemployment and absence, was conducted in the 1950s and, at the time, confirmed this fact[2,3]. This research established an inverse relationship between changes in regional unemployment levels and subsequent changes in the corresponding absence rate. As unemployment went up, so absenteeism went down. While this general relationship was supported by the evidence at the time, it had to be qualified by such factors as an individual's ability to change jobs, and the improvements that have taken place in unemployment benefits during the last thirty or so years, as well as changes in internal company disciplinary procedures and payment policies in relation to absenteeism.

If this theory was widely applicable in the 1980s, then one should expect to find the lowest absence rates in companies situated in the areas of highest unemployment. Although inadequate in themselves, the available statistics do not support this view. The 1985 Industrial Society survey[4] in fact produced exactly contrary evidence. London and the South-east with the lowest unemployment had the lowest absence rate (3.5% and 3.8% respectively). In contrast, the absence rates for firms in the following unemployment blackspots were as follows: North-west (5.0%), North-east (5.0%) and Scotland (4.3%). Northern Ireland (albeit on a very small sample), had both the highest unemployment and the highest absence rate (8.5%).

It is possible to compare the 1985 Industrial Society's absence survey figures with those produced in its 1987 study[5]. The changes and movements are shown in Table 7.1. The authors of the 1987 survey commented that there was something of a north–south divide in absence rates. However, the South-east did have an absence rate higher than the mean, and the North-west one that was below the mean. Additionally, the Midlands, North-east, Scotland and the South-east were above the mean, while the North-west, Eastern, Wales and London were below it.

Considered another way, one can rank the regions in a league table in terms of the magnitude of their absence rate for each of the two survey years. These rankings are shown in Table 7.2. However, given the low response

Table 7.1 Comparison of results of the Industrial Society's 1985 and 1987 absence survey results (by region)

Region	1985 Absence (%)	Change	1987 Absence (%)
London	3.5	down	3.3
South-east	3.9	up	5.4
Midlands	4.6	up	6.4
North-east	5.0	up	5.8
North-west	5.0	down	4.6
South-west	3.7	down	2.4
Eastern	4.1	down	3.9
Scotland	4.3	up	5.4
Wales	4.1	down	3.9
Northern Ireland	8.5		not included

Table 7.2 Regions ranked by the magnitude of their absence rate (the Industrial Society absence surveys 1985 and 1987)

	1985			1987	
	Region	Absence (%)		Region	Absence (%)
1	Northern Ireland	8.5	1	Midlands	6.4
2	North-west	5.0	2	North-east	5.8
2	North-east	5.0	3	Scotland	5.4
			3	South-east	5.4
4	Midlands	4.6			
5	Scotland	4.3	5	North-west	4.6
6	Eastern	4.1	6	Eastern	3.9
6	Wales	4.1	6	Wales	3.9
8	South-east	3.9	8	London	3.3
9	London	3.5	9	South-west	2.9

rate achieved by both Industrial Society absence surveys, these figures should be treated with the greatest caution.

The 1987 Confederation of British Industry survey[6] broadly supported these findings. Considering full-time manual employees, the highest absence figures were found to be in the North-west (5.9%) and Wales (5.4%). Absence in the southern part of Britain had, however, risen. The figures were London 5.3%, South 5.2% and the South-east 4.8%. While the differences in sample size and survey methods may account for differences in the detailed results, the broad indication is that absence, at the present time, does not appear to be greatly affected by the prevailing economic conditions. Nevertheless, the managers we interviewed did feel that the unemployment rates of recent years had had an effect.

'We have had redundancies. The economy is in recession. There are not a lot of jobs that you can walk into. We pay £XXX a week to a shopfloor operative, but it's still good for that type of work. There are still redundancies in this industry, and still recession and uncertainty, and people are still afraid. This is partly a contrived policy by the company. We have said that if there are redundancies, we won't select on the basis of last in first out, but on the basis of attendance at work. That is a deterrent, I've no doubt about it. This creates a feeling of insecurity which acts to encourage attendance. It's not a very good solution, but it has nevertheless had an effect' (*Whisky bottling plant*)

*   *   *

'The high local unemployment gives the employees the almost certain knowledge that if they lose their jobs, they won't get other ones. This has played a tremendous part. There's fear in the system in that everybody knows how competitive the market is. Now, there is a greater willingness to protect their own skins.' (*Electrical components manufacturer*)

There is an argument that sickness rates tend to be higher in depressed areas. In addition, some writers feel that social security and company sick-pay schemes have altered the attitude from that which prevailed in the pre-war and immediate post-war period when absence levels and unemployment did show an inverse relationship.

(b)   Incentive and reward systems (including overtime)

Could res. uk in Presat.
eism

The type of incentive or reward system used by an organization is another factor that exerts pressure on an individual to attend. Two aspects are particularly important. The level of wages, and the availability of overtime at premium pay rates.

Let us first consider the actual wage rates paid (as opposed to people's satisfaction with their pay). Research shows that as wages increase attendance improves. Hence, one can expect a salary or wage increase to represent a pressure to attend, even in circumstances where the employee does not like the tasks involved in the job. A wage rise causes two conflicting changes in incentives. On the one hand, the worker achieves a higher level of income and can therefore afford not to work as much. On the other hand, working less becomes costly because of the increase in the wages forgone. However, if employees receive increases in fringe benefits, they can better afford free time without its being expensive for them. This is an argument against rewarding good performance by increasing fringe benefits and for raising basic pay instead.

Let us now consider overtime pay at premium rates. For many employees this represents a large element of their income. Studies have revealed that employees who worked a great deal of overtime, had a greater tendency to be absent than other workers. This was particularly the case in industries which had characteristically low wage rates[7]. It may be that substituting premium pay work for regular work was a means used by the employee to achieve either wage equity or time flexibility. Wage equity is the notion that, if you as an employee feel that you are being underpaid by your employer, you adjust your work hours to bring your effort into line with your view of a fair (or equitable) reward. Doing this might involve staying off work, receiving sickness benefits, working overtime at a premium rate, coming in late, leaving early, and so on. Time flexibility means taking time off during the week to attend to personal matters, and picking up the lost time and money, by working overtime at unsocial hours. One can argue that the availability and operation of the overtime system with its premium pay can lead to a situation which encourages and rewards absenteeism rather than attendance.

It is widely felt that certain aspects of a company's incentive/reward system can have a direct effect on attendance motivation. In studying this topic, researchers have tried to account for the influence of the effect of related variables such as age and length of job tenure[8]. In our opinion, the apparent relationship between absence and pay may owe more to the nature of the jobs studied than to the actual pay system in operation.

'The coopers are on a PBR system (payment by results). Although no overtime is worked on the site, the earning potential of coopers is £XXX, which is high. But they have a big incentive to come along. They aren't problem attenders. They're not an unhappy group. The job is a lot more interesting. It's repetitive, but skill is required.' (*Whisky blending plant*)

Some reward systems may encourage non-attendance. This can be either as a result of their poor design, or their inefficient administration. For example, the practice of allowing employees a set number of *sick days* which they receive without any effect on their earnings, is one example. It can create a situation where the company-funded insurance policy comes to be seen as both an individual right and as an additional holiday entitlement.

'Although it died out with self-certification we used to have five days in the year which, if people did not take them more than two at a time, they did not have to submit evidence of illness. A supervisor was heard to say to an employee, "Remember, you've still got your five sick days to take." People regarded it as a right to take all five days off. There were some who abused it.' (*Food and drink company*)

The poorly managed allocation of overtime to employees who have been absent can allow some people to play the system. They can thus take time off while increasing their overall earnings through the overtime premiums. It should be noted, however, that general research has not established any strong or consistent link between overtime and absence. One manager said that those employees who worked overtime to increase their basic earnings were the least likely to take unauthorized absence[9]. In contrast, he said, other groups of employees, perhaps unconsciously, achieved a target level of wages by working the highest paying hours.

He explained that, if an employee was requested to work two shifts during a week, he achieved a high level of wages. It was a great deal of money. He might have worked two shifts and, if the week-end came along and if the weather was nice, he would take time off. Thus the wage level achieved by overtime working gave him the opportunity to 'fall by the wayside', as this manager put it. Usually this occurred on a Friday or on a Saturday backshift or nightshift. That, historically, had been a problem throughout that company.

'At one time we averaged 17-18% absence amongst our industrial personnel. To get output out, we had to work two nights a week overtime. We also had to work virtually every second Sunday. In 1977 we worked 32 Sundays. The problem became self-generating. What we were doing was that, if someone was off one week, they gained through the sickness benefit scheme. We didn't allow them to work a Sunday if they'd missed a day the previous week. The chances were that if they put in a full week the following week, they'd end up working Sunday. So, they'd end up with Sunday, and two nights' overtime. So it became a self-perpetuating thing. What happened was that people started avoiding overtime, and it became difficult to plan things.' (*Whisky blending plant*)

The answers provided by the managers whom we interviewed suggest that many of the employees give a different meaning to, and have different purposes for, working certain types of overtime. From a managerial perspective, the primary purpose of overtime is to level out the peaks and troughs for the demand for labour over the year. Because it is capable of being easily turned on and off, it can be selectively applied. Because it can be applied quickly when needed, overtime working by existing staff is preferred by management to recruiting additional labour.

The use of overtime is based on the idea that workers will want to put in extra hours at an increased hourly rate in order to secure higher weekly wages. To a large extent this is true. Although the working week has been reduced over the years, most shopfloor employees work as many hours as they did before (and in many cases more than before). The difference is that more of these hours are paid at overtime rates. Indeed, it has been estimated that, if companies eliminated overtime and hired people from the dole queues to do the extra work, unemployment could be reduced substantially. Large sections of the workforce rely on overtime, some of it guaranteed, to maintain their standard of living.

Provided that employees see overtime as a way to maximize their income, as something that they must have, and indeed they are dependent upon, then absenteeism is unlikely to be affected. However, if, in contrast, the employee is interested in merely achieving a regular weekly sum in the easiest way, then the availability of overtime can encourage absence. Managers, accustomed to increasing and maximizing their own incomes, may find it difficult to understand this alternative income management strategy of their employees. Nevertheless, by working a full Sunday at the double-time rate, a shopfloor operator can have a day off during the week and still maintain or better his weekly earnings. This is a problem when overtime is available on a regular basis. To some extent companies seek to counter it by treating overtime as a perk and not offering it to bad attenders.

'People who work a weekend, you can guarantee, they'll have a day off during the week because they've lost nothing. Anything they could lose would have been made up by working a Sunday. One gets that with groups when there's regular overtime.' (*Storage/distribution company*)

When overtime is used occasionally to ensure that a valuable order is completed, it is money well spent. However, in some circumstances it has to be used to get the ordinary week's production out which high absenteeism has prevented. In such circumstances, overtime represents a cost of absence.

When it is available regularly, workers may see being off not as inconveniencing their colleagues but as positively helping them. The absentees, far from feeling guilty about letting their mates down, see their own absence as a sort of blank cheque for the person who will cover for them. They feel that they will recoup it when they come to cover for that other person in the future. This provides a positive incentive to be absent.

Individual preferences are clearly important here. Employees' personal values and financial commitments will determine whether the overtime payment will be translated into additional income, or used to finance additional leisure time. Once again, one can suggest that companies design wage payment systems on the basis of managerial values and commitments. This might be the difference between 'working to live' and 'living to work'. One manager put it this way: 'We have had a sort of four-day week mentality among the workforce. Because they were being paid for five, there seemed to be no great incentive to turn out if you didn't feel like it.'

The distinction is perhaps best summarized in the now famous reply given by a coal miner to Lord Robens when he was Chairman of the then National Coal Board. Asked why so many of the men seemed to be working only four days a week, a miner replied that they were unable to live on only three.

(c) Sick pay/National Health Insurance benefits

Sickness pay schemes can themselves cause absence. Taylor[10] quoted the best-documented cases from West Germany which showed that shortly after each increase in benefit (which usually followed an election), the sickness absence rate went up. For many firms in Britain, however, the company sick-pay scheme is more important than the changes in the rates of nationally paid State benefits. However, the two are related.

'It used to be that if someone was absent they got sickness benefit from the State at fixed amounts and a proportion of sick pay from the company. They actually got more money when they were sick than when they were at work. The State benefit was based on gross pay rather than take-home pay. SSP now is taken from net pay (take-home-pay). So now, you can never earn more when you're absent than if you're at work.' (*Food and drink company*)

* * *

'Our policy is that when someone is ill they shouldn't gain by it, but they shouldn't be out of pocket. That was, historically, one of the problems that we had with absence. We used to work a system whereby when people went off sick, they claimed from the DHSS, and we took back, at most, a single man's allowance. So if he had 3–4 children, it was extremely profitable for him to be off work because he was making a packet.' (*Whisky blending plant*)

The provision of company sick-pay benefits does encourage absence. This phenomenon has been neatly summarized in Parkinson's Law of Sick Leave Abuse. This says that days lost due to sickness expand to equal the number of paid sick days allowed. Data from the United States suggests that companies that offer sickness benefit to employees experience almost twice as much absenteeism as those that do not. Paid sick leave is often perceived by employees as another fringe benefit which is rightly owed to them. They may, therefore, have no compunction about collecting it. Moreover, when management allows such leave to be abused, often this can cause a snowball effect amongst the other workers who resent having to do the work of their absent co-workers.

Many employee-benefit packages include paid sick leave of up to 12, 15 or 18 days per year. Depending on how the individual scheme works, employees can often accrue unused sick-pay leave to a maximum of 30, 40 or more days. In a small number of cases, there is no maximum of sick days leave that an employee can accrue. According to most policies, certainly in the United States, sick leave is only to be used for the illness of the employee or to care for a member of the immediate family who is ill. In reality, sick leave is often viewed by many employees as additional holiday time. The attitude of these workers is that sick days are 'coming to them'. If pressed, the employee may justify taking sick leave because of a hostile supervisor, boring job, disagreeable co-workers, or simply because the practice represents a long-standing part of the organization's culture.

Violations of the sick-leave policy are very difficult to control. Rarely will the supervisor challenge the authenticity of the statement: 'I can't come in today. I'm sick.' Some firms require a doctor's slip upon return to work, but most managers will admit that such certificates are easily obtained, and self-certification has largely negated this practice anyway.

Improved sick-pay provision both at government and company levels, has been associated with rising trends in absenteeism. The doubling of the relative National Insurance benefits in the last 20 years has been accompanied by a one-third increase in the average number of 'certified days' of sickness[11]. This trend may be used to provide evidence of 'social security scrounging', although some observers have argued that workers can now afford to take adequate time off work for medical treatment and recuperation. In this context, the effect of the introduction of self-certification in 1982 has led to a shift in numbers away from 'unaccounted absence' (absence without a medical certificate) to 'sickness'.

At the company level numerous studies have shown that those employees not covered by company sick-pay schemes, for example, new starters and temporary workers have considerably less absence than those who do have such cover[12]. While most studies support this view, Taylor[13] has challenged it. Our own research revealed a high level of agreement amongst managers that the abuse of company sick-pay schemes by employees did contribute to absence.

'The cause was people being cosseted by our sick-pay scheme. There was no incentive for them to turn up to work.' (*Whisky bottling plant*)

* * *

'Most managers were convinced that the absence was due to the sickness scheme. The scheme gave them, and still gives them, 13 weeks of pay within any period of 12 months. The sum is 90% of earnings less SSP. The scheme has been exploited.' (*Whisky bottling plant*)

* * *

'They get the company sick-pay scheme which will pay 50%, 80% or even 100% of their wages. But even though they have received sick pay during their period of absence, if they've had an accident, they will still claim against the company for the pain, suffering and any loss of overtime earnings. That figure for two days may be £60–100, but they also get the sick pay, albeit ten days late. As far as they look at it, it's money in the bank with their insurance claim. Most large companies have two insurance schemes, so employees have two bites.' (*Glass manufacturer*)

* * *

'In some work areas, the absence levels have been high. The reason for this is that the company pays manual workers sick pay of £40 per week on top of the SSP which, because of our rate, is £47. Thus, in lower paid areas, they're as well off being sick. It is in these areas that we get the major problems. We have had an absence rate of 20–25% which is just intolerable' (*Shipbuilders*)

(d) Work group norms

Considerable pressure for or against attendance can be exerted by one's co-workers. Where work-group norms emphasize the importance of good attendance for the benefit of the group, one would expect increased attendance. This relationship will be particularly strong in highly cohesive work groups. In such groups, employees see coming to work to help their co-workers as highly desirable. Hence, job attendance is seen as more attractive than absenteeism. However, group norms can also exert a negative effect. They may reinforce the notion that it is acceptable to report sick periodically, although one is well, in order to claim the sick leave entitlement.

A number of writers have discussed this sort of 'normative' absence[14]. Absence behaviour is seen as a habitual response to the norms of the work group with respect to absence. It does not show itself in random days off, but can be deduced from definite patterns, from which management should be able to predict not only absence frequency but also when it is likely to happen. One study investigated the effect of organizational size on absenteeism. The literature review suggests that increasing size makes the individual's absence less 'visible'. Large group size, it is argued, fails to activate the control of absence by group norms. The argument is that increases in company size lead to greater bureaucracy, which involves reductions in the informal controls associated with higher levels of inter-personal rewards and greater attachment to the job. The expressive (or emotional) needs of workers will involve a strong moral commitment to their fellow workers, and this may prevent various group behaviours of a negative type taking place. Hence, absence behaviour will be high or low in a group, depending on the group norms. Being committed to their workmates, their absence would be relatively independent of economic considerations. Even the most individualistic action will reflect the accepted norms of group behaviour[15].

Since the Hawthorne experiments were conducted in the 1930s, work-group norms have been recognized as exerting an important influence on individual behaviour. This aspect has been specifically researched in relation to attendance decisions. The results generally confirm the importance of the power of group norms in this area[16]. This is especially the case where individual member attendance is important to the well-being of the group as a whole[17].

Group size and cohesion have been found to be of considerable signific-ance in this respect, especially amongst blue-collar workers where absence rates have been found to increase in line with the creation of larger work groups[18]. Where increased size has been associated with a division of labour, it has often led to an increase in the privacy of work performance. Such privacy increases the area of discretionary performance, and permits the employee a greater latitude of absence from work. Increased size results in a decrease of communication and a reduction in group cohesion and job satisfaction. These factors are of particular importance today, as companies experiment with new forms of work organization. These seek to increase productivity in its broadest sense. New working arrangements such as autonomous work groups have generally been associated with reduced absenteeism[19].

In our own investigations, managers commented on the lack of group norms and group cohesion, and the effect that they felt that this had on absence. One respondent felt that individual working was one of the reasons for their absence problem. Sometimes it was a case of management allowing the wrong norms to become established.

'We used to put people who weren't as fit together. That created a problem. We put too many people of the same age group into one work area. That was wrong. You create an older age group which creates problems. You wouldn't get it with younger persons. We're trying to change that pattern now by mixing older with younger.' (Construction company)

(e) Personal work ethic

Another influence on attendance motivation is the personal value system that individuals have. There seems to be a considerable variation amongst employees in the extent to which they feel morally obliged to work. In particular, several investigators have noted a direct relationship between the existence of a strong work ethic, and the propensity to come to work. A major pressure to attend seems to be the belief by individuals that work activity is itself an important aspect of life almost irrespective of the nature of the job.

Many absence decisions are essentially attitudinal. An important consideration here is the system of values to which a person adheres. This may impose a moral obligation to attend, except in extreme situations such as serious illness. We all know people who are motivated by such principles and who are virtually never off work. The intuitive validity of this assertion has been confirmed by a number of research studies.

It has been found that employees who adhered to the *Protestant ethic* (doing a job well, getting on in life, strong sense of family responsibility) had particularly low rates of absence.

Such values are an integral part of an individual's personality and as such may, over time, be influenced to some extent by the culture and environment that they encounter at home and at work[20].

'There's been an attitude of change amongst the workforce as well. As jobs become more precious, then they are less willing, as individuals, to accept a malingerer. There used to be an attitude, "good for you, you got away with it, you pulled the wool over their eyes". But now there is such a fear of losing your job that, there's a recognition that anyone doing that will actually be jeopardizing the prospects of all the workers, and not just of themselves. It's much less acceptable on the shopfloor now to be a malingerer. It's been quite a noticeable change.' (*Food processing plant*)

Related to the personal work ethic is the notion of organizational commitment. Organizational commitment is defined as loyalty to the organization[21,22,23]. As an attitude of loyalty, commitment includes the notion of a strong belief in, and acceptance of, organizational goals and values, a willingness to exert considerable effort on behalf of the organization and a strong desire to maintain membership of it[24].

On the part of the employee, commitment means agreement with the goals and objectives of the organization and a willingness to work towards these goals. In short, if an employee firmly believes in what the organization is attempting to achieve, he or she should be more motivated to attend and to contribute towards its objectives. This motivation exists even if the employee does not enjoy the actual tasks required of the job. For example, the job of a secretary may be boring but, when performed in the intensive care unit for children, takes on a greater significance and creates a high degree of commitment in the job holder.

One's commitment to the organization is influenced by a variety of factors including personal, job and organizational characteristics. In a situation where an employee's primary commitment lies elsewhere, there will be less internal pressure on him or her to attend. This may occur in the case of a worker with very small children, who will feel a greater commitment to her family than to her company. From the research evidence we have, organization commitment appears to be causally determined by job satisfaction and job involvement. Studies have shown a direct linkage between the organizational commitment of employees and absenteeism[25,26,27,28].

Attendance motivation: summary   *Use this - Rewards*

The *motivation to attend* is one of the two main influences on absence in the Steers and Rhodes model. Its role is made clearer, if the model is slightly redrawn, as in Figure 7.1. It represents a cognitive belief which describes the degree to which a person psychologically identifies with his or her current job[29]. From the model, motivation to attend is a consequence of the forces that determine a person's job involvement. Individuals who possess high levels of job involvement believe that their current job has the ability to fulfil

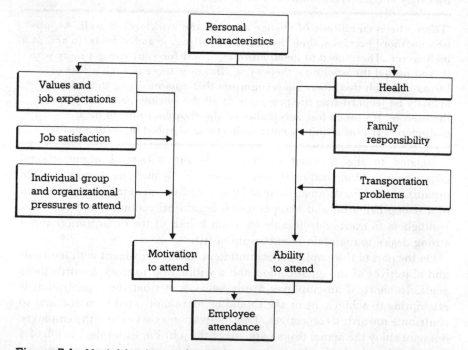

Figure 7.1 Variables in employee absenteeism (Steers and Rhodes)

important needs, whatever these may be[30,31,32,33]. Job involvement is a major determinant of commitment and may be a major determinant of employee absenteeism[34,35].

Let us now consider the second major influence on employee attendance described in the Steers and Rhodes model – the *ability to attend*. As we shall see, the personal characteristics of employees, affect *both* their motivation to attend and their ability to attend. Absenteeism can occur when the employee either does not want to attend work (because the job is too boring or stressful), or because he or she cannot work (having problems with transport or illness). These two variables can interact. Although tired, but physically able to work, an employee may decide, because the job is boring, the supervisor unfriendly, and the sick-pay scheme generous, not to bother going into work. The example illustrates the point that each individual has different personal characteristics and a unique work situation. Thus no two employees will ever be absent for exactly the same reason.

Ability to attend

(a) Illness/accidents
(b) Transportation/distance
(c) Family responsibilities

The preceding sections have suggested that attendance motivation will be influenced by both satisfaction with the job situation and by the pressure to attend. However, according to the Steers and Rhodes model that we are using, the *ability to attend* may place situational constraints on this attendance motivation. Ultimately it will be the interaction of these two factors which will determine employee attendance.

(a) Illness/accidents

Poor health and injury clearly represent primary causes of absence. Absenteeism due to illness is often associated with increased age, while younger employees are more likely to have work-related accidents. Included in this category of health-related absences are the problems of alcoholism and drug abuse since they inhibit attendance. Alcoholics have been found to have higher sickness absence rates than people without a drink problem.

The direct effects of health status on absenteeism have tended to be ignored by researchers, even though illness is widely recognized as a most important cause of absenteeism[36,37]. It has been estimated that it accounts for between a half and two-thirds of all absence[38]. Within the broad category of illness, the primary causes of absenteeism appear to be social psychological ones which include personal maladjustments, emotional disorders and alcoholism. The section on stress in this book is therefore also relevant in this context.

Many non-attendance decisions may follow from the interaction of a person's physical state of health, their self-concept, and their health attitude. The meaning of health is now expanded to include stress and neurosis. The national medical records show a threefold increase in, 'nerves, debility and headaches' over the last thirty years. Such considerations, however, should not cause us to overlook the fact that, irrespective of an employee's motivation, poor health or injury represents a primary cause of absenteeism. It is not intended here to analyse the medical factors related to absenteeism[39]. It is worth noting, however, that the state of health of employees can have different effects on their *working capacity*. This will depend on the nature of their work. The importance of such considerations is often overlooked when comparisons are made of the attendance rates of manual workers with their colleagues in office jobs.

'Particularly in poor areas of Scotland, the incidence of ill-health is higher, and the pressures on people living on supplementary benefits, making ends meet, causes problems. They don't have the diet, and this leads to physical and psychological difficulties that cause them to be absent.' (*Confectionery manufacturer*)

* * *

'The time of year, January to March, is a low period. There are medical theories that it's coming to the end of winter and people are getting weary.' (*Construction company*)

As already mentioned, it is appropriate to treat the issue of alcoholism under the illness heading. A study by Alcohol Concern[40] published in 1987, estimated that alcohol loses industry between 8 and 14 million working days through absenteeism. Employees in certain industries, particularly the brewing and hotel trade, are particularly prone to alcohol-related absence. However, managers from the heavy engineering sector also identify this problem amongst the shopfloor workers.

'You can tell by the high absenteeism that people have been overindulging at the weekend. We've reduced it. The habits are changing for the good. There's nothing worse than seeing a person who has got a drink problem. It's quite depressing actually when you see him. The big difficulty is getting people to identify that problem themselves. Once they've recognized it, there's certainly a lot we can do to help.' (*Shipbuilders*)

While there is overwhelming empirical evidence to suggest that higher amounts of drinking are causally related to higher levels of absenteeism[41,42,43], both in the US and in Britain, absence does not appear to be the result of accidents at work.

The studies of work performance and problem drinking[44,45] revealed that, although problem drinkers had above average absence rates, they did not have above average accident rates. This intuitively surprising finding has been attributed to, amongst other things, the way in which heavy drinkers are protected from accidents by other workers. Since these people are especially vulnerable to accidents, they tend to be assigned to less hazardous work by their supervisors. American researchers claim that the notion of an accident-prone problem drinker is a myth which does not recognize the various opportunities in the workplace for accident avoidance that are not available in non-work settings.

(b) Transportation/distance

It appears that difficulty in getting to work can sometimes influence actual attendance. Travel distance, the amount of time required, and the weather conditions, can all interfere with travelling. Such transportation problems can inhibit attendance, even when the individuals are motivated to attend.

Aspects of the problem, such as the mode of transportation, distance from work and travelling time, have received considerable attention from researchers. A number of themes have been revealed. The relative convenience of the mode of transport can affect individual attendance[46]. Higher absence is associated with employees travelling into major towns as compared to individuals working in rural areas[47]. Taylor[48] wrote that the time required to travel to work only affected sickness absence rates if the journey time was more than one hour.

The number of transportation changes made during the journey was found to affect absence. A study of London office workers showed that more sickness absence (both in terms of frequency and duration) was found amongst those people whose journey was complicated by several interchanges. One-day sickness was more common amongst those who used a car for all or part of their journey[49]. A study of teachers indicated that the longer the distance between a teacher's home and the school, the more likely it was that the person would have days off. Economically, assuming that travel time is a disutility to the teacher, the opportunity cost of a day of absenteeism is smaller for the teacher who has far to travel than for one who lives nearer his or her place of work[50].

It therefore appears that absence rates are positively related to the nature of travel to work, and to the duration of travelling time. With staff commuting ever greater distances, especially in the South-east and London areas, this is likely to be a factor of increasing significance. Our own managers, who recruited shopfloor workers locally, were also aware of the effect of transport problems on absence. One explained his company's recruitment policy for shopfloor jobs: 'We draw our labour locally because most of the people we're looking for will be doing shopfloor operator jobs. They tend not to be very affluent, and don't have a car, so the further away you take them the greater the transport difficulties they have.'

(c) Family responsibilities

Family responsibilities represent the second constraint on attendance. As this limitation, like health, relates to attendance, it is largely determined by the personal characteristics of the individuals concerned (their age, sex, family size). In general, women are absent more frequently than men. This finding seems to be linked, at least partly, to the traditional responsibilities assigned to women. That is, it is mother who cares for sick children. Hence, as family size increases, so does female absenteeism. However, the research evidence indicates that the absenteeism rate for women declines throughout their work career. This may be due to the fact that family responsibilities associated with young children become reduced. For males, on the other hand, unavoidable (sickness) absenteeism apparently increases with age, while avoidable absenteeism does not.

The 1987 CBI[51] study sought to obtain managers' opinions on what they thought lay behind persistent non-attendance. Forty-five per cent of managers said that, in their view, the hidden absence problem amongst manual workers was caused by family responsibilities. This was the second highest rating achieved, coming slightly behind 'poor motivation' (46%). These same managers felt that family responsibilities were the number one reason for absence amongst their non-manual employees (39%). Evaluated over a broad spectrum, the research data does suggest that higher levels of family responsibilities will lead to higher levels of absence[52,53,54].

Other attendance factors

(a) Day of week/time of year
(b) Past absence patterns
(c) Self-certification

(a) Day of week/time of year

Since research was first carried out on work absence in the 1920s, studies have consistently shown that absence patterns have a definite relationship to the days of the week. Single day absences tend to be highest on Mondays[55,56]. Sometimes, these are three times higher than those of Thursday (if Thursday is a pay-day). Patterns, however, depend on company pay practices, self-certification arrangements and other factors. It is worth while studying these aspects, both at the group and the individual level, to see if any trends can be identified. The managers we asked all had their own personal theories as to how the days of the week were related to absence.

'We've seen patterns of absence alter now. It is quite interesting. In the production areas, people used to be off for full weeks 5, 10, 15, and 20 days.

The only area that was different was the skilled men area. They used to be off for either 4 or 9 days. That was their pattern. This was because the weekend overtime roster went up on Thursday. You had to be really ill to miss Thursday because it cost you £60-70 in your pay packet. So if somebody was absent on Thursday, you really knew they were ill. Having missed that D-Day, there was no incentive to come back until the following Thursday. The skilled men were the only category of people who came back midweek apart from the office staff. The shopfloor was always fit on Monday. This was a trend which suggested that there was a bit of malingering going on.' (*Electrical components manufacturer*)

* * *

'Absence rates tend to be highest on the shopfloor and follow a seasonal pattern. We have fixed holidays, and other long spells which people are supposed to fill with personal holidays. If you did the absence graph, the peaks were the same year in, year out - Easter and the September weekend - and it fell away as they came towards the Fairs Holiday. That was people taking absence leave rather than holiday leave in order to cover for a period when children were off school, and maybe husbands were off too.' (*Glass manufacturer*)

* * *

'Analysing the trends, we found that 2 to 3 weeks before the Glasgow Fair, and 2 to 3 weeks before Christmas, the absence rates went down. Once the holidays had passed, absence began to climb again, until the next major holidays, before which it came down again.' (*Shipbuilders*)

* * *

'There's a fair percentage who feel like having a lazy weekend, and stay off on Friday or a Monday. That small percentage may represent the difference between whether your business survives or it doesn't.' (*Transport company*)

* * *

'The average absence amongst the industrial staff is two to three days, and then it's usually muscle strain or sore throat. You do pay attention to the days of the week when the absences occur. We're always looking for people off on Mondays and Fridays.' (*Telecommunications products manufacturer*)

The 1987 Industrial Society's absence survey[57] asked participants to indicate absence levels for each specific day of the week. Amongst those firms which had a high percentage of manual workers (more than 75%), Monday was found to be the highest absence day. The study also showed absence at weekends to be particularly low.

(b) Past absence patterns

Long-term studies have been conducted into absence behaviour to establish whether employees' past patterns of absence can be used to predict their future absence behaviour[38]. In one such study, the attendance of new recruits was monitored over several years to determine the relationship between early absence and longer-term absence trends for the individual employees[59]. It was found that absence sickness rates in the first six months of service were less than half the rates found during the next four and a half years. This was attributed to the lack of a sick-pay scheme for new starters. However, it was also concluded that early sickness absence experience did serve as an indicator of future *absence liability*, especially in the prediction of the frequently sick group.

Ivancevich[60] investigated how prior absenteeism in one job was related to subsequent absenteeism in a new job within the *same* company. Such a situation could occur when, for example, following the introduction of new technology, some of the present employees might have to be selected for the newly engineered or structured jobs. The question this researcher was trying to answer was which employees were least likely to be absent in the future. He found that past absenteeism was a better predictor of future absenteeism than was work attitude. Moreover, the *frequency of absence* measure (the total number of periods or spells that an employee was absent without regard to the length of each period) was found to be a more stable indicator of that worker's future absenteeism rate than was the *total days absent* measure. These findings have been confirmed by other studies[61,62]. Past absenteeism is a better predictor of future absence than either work satisfaction, job involvement, or satisfaction with supervision.

(c) Self-certification

Managers questioned in the 1985 Industrial Society survey[63] were unsure whether the rises in absenteeism that they reported were caused by the introduction, in 1982, of self-certification for illness of up to seven days. The respondents were equally divided with 40% believing that it had, and 43% saying that the change had not made any difference. Two years later in 1987, the CBI survey[64] again specifically asked managers whether, in their opinion, self-certification had had any effect on sickness absence. Most of the managers reported that the introduction had had no effect on the overall levels of sickness absence, but the results of the survey did suggest that it may have led to a shift towards periods of absence lasting between four and seven days, particularly amongst manual workers. This is the period for which, under SSP scheme rules, employees must now provide self-certification statements. Breaking down the CBI's survey figures, no recognizable effects on manual workers were reported by 37% of respondents, while the figure for non-manual workers was 57%. Of those companies which did report some effect, more reported an increase in absenteeism, than a decrease.

Chapter 8
Conclusions

Part two has sought to review and summarize the vast amount of research into absence causes and associations. It has illustrated some of these with examples drawn from managers' own experiences of dealing with absence problems. It is clear that the possible influences on absence behaviour will be many and varied in any given situation. However, it is useful to group them under the two broad headings of *motivation to attend* and *ability to attend*. The Steers and Rhodes model which was presented at the start of this chapter, provides a useful organizing framework for thinking about absence causes.

Moreover, the absence model being presented here is a process one in the sense that the act of attendance or absenteeism often influences the subsequent job situation and the subsequent pressures to attend in a cyclical fashion. For example, a superior attendance record is often used in companies as one criterion of noteworthy job performance and readiness for promotion. On the other hand, a high rate of absenteeism may adversely affect an employee's relationship with his or her supervisor and workmates, resulting in changes in leadership style and co-worker relations. Changes in a firm's reward or incentive system may occur due to high rates of absenteeism. Many other outcomes could be mentioned. The important point is that the model is a dynamic one. In it, employee attendance or absenteeism often leads to changes in the job situation which in turn influences subsequent attendance motivation.

It is one thing to know the range of possible causes of absence, but quite another to be able to pin-point those which relate to one's own organization. Yet accurate absence cause identification is a crucial element in designing an effective, absence control programme, which seeks to meet the specific needs of a particular organization. Many companies do not pay any attention whatsoever to identifying the causes of their absence problem. Being 'solution-led', they implement the current, most popular idea which they hope will reduce absence. This can be an attendance bonus scheme, Quality Circles, or something similar. In other organizations, managers have a hunch about the cause of absence (what we have called a personal theory). They base their actions on that hunch without investigating it further. In order to discover the real causes of absence, it may be necessary to conduct an attitude survey amongst the employees.

Such a survey is best conducted by an independent, outside body such as a consultancy firm or a business school. Nevertheless, a company's management needs to be closely involved at all stages. A number of guidelines have been developed about how such a survey can best be organized[1]:

- The members of the organization, including the senior management, should be involved in the preliminary planning process. They explain their needs to the outside consultant, as they relate to the identification of the causes of absence.

- The survey questionnaire is administered to all the employees of the organization. Although sampling may be used, for motivational and practical reasons, everybody in the company can usefully be questioned. Instead of, or in addition to the questionnaire, in-depth interviews can be carried out with employees. All the information is anonymous in that no names are identified with any of the responses.

- To emphasize confidentiality, the external consultant analyses the survey data, and tabulates the results. Responses are organized by department, by full-time and part-time employees, by direct and indirect operatives, or by any other classification which is significant for the firm. The consultant can also suggest approaches to diagnosing the causes of the absence problem.

- The consultant then feeds back the data to top management, and highlights what the findings indicate about the absence problem.

The questionnaire used in the survey can either be tailor-made for each company, or a standardized version used. What is important to note is that employees should neither be asked directly why they go absent, nor what they think the causes of absence in the organization are. Instead, the questions should seek to obtain answers which will allow management to assess employees' motivation and ability to attend. Questions will be related to topics, such as organizational climate, leadership and job satisfaction. Examples of the areas that can usefully be probed with the opinion survey questions are shown below:

Organizational climate:

- communication within the company
- motivation of respondent
- decision-making
- control within company
- co-ordination between departments

Leadership:

- managerial support
- managerial goal emphasis
- managerial work facilitation
- peer support
- peer work facilitation
- peer interaction

Satisfaction:

- with company
- with supervisor
- with job
- with pay
- with work group

Employees may be questioned on other topics that are considered relevant, and that can provide a clue to the causes of absence in the different parts of the company. Through analysis, the survey should reveal the true causes of employee absence, and allow management to answer the review questions that follow.

Management review questions

1 Identify any sections, departments or division of your organization, where absence is high.

2 Enter the name of the first of these at the top of the questionnaire on the following page.

3 Listed on the questionnaire are the 24 common causes of employee absence. Using your own experience, your company's absence data, and the information contained in this chapter, tick those causes which you believe are most likely to be the ones responsible for the absence in that section, department or division.

4 For each cause ticked write down, in the space provided, the *evidence* on which you base your judgement.

5 On the basis of the resulting evidence, determine whether there appear to be any interrelationships between the causes

identified, e.g. women and boring jobs; high-absence employees are frequently moved around.

6   Following this analysis, *rank* the identified causes (or inter-related sets of causes) in order of importance relative to their likely impact on the actual absence area.

7   Repeat this process for any other section, department or division in your organization which has a high level of absence.

Although this questionnaire can be used for individual analysis by the manager, it is often more valuable to get a group of managers, and/or supervisors together around a table. In this way, more information about the absence problem can be obtained. The requirement to produce evidence to support suggestions places an onus on management to collect and regularly analyse absence statistics. It also is a guard against the introduction of personalized theories and the prejudices of individuals.

Section/department/division: ....
Absence cause   (✓) Evidence

In this section/work group:		
1 The job is boring and lacks challenge.		
2 The job causes the individual stress.		
3 Frequent job moves disrupt employee work patterns.		
4 The organization of shifts and the hours of work contribute to absence.		
5 The quality of supervision contributes to the level of absence.		
6 The physical work environment demotivates employees.		
7 The work-group size is too big to allow individuals to identify with the group.		
8 Dissatisfaction with the job situation seems to affect absence levels.		
9 The work-group norms either do not operate, or else they discourage regular attendance.		
10 Genuine illness and accidents at work are a regular cause of absence.		
11 Employees have incompatible values and job expectations.		
12 The length of time employees have been with us seems to influence their absence rate.		
13 The age of the employee seems to determine likelihood of absence.		
14 People with certain types of personality seem to be off more frequently.		
15 The sex of the employee affects the chance of being off.		
16 People are absent when the financial pressures on them are lower.		
17 Our incentive/reward system contributes to the absence problem.		

Section/department/division: ....
Absence cause   (✔) Evidence

18	The sick pay/NHI benefits that employees get do not encourage them to come to work.	
19	The personal work ethic of the employees does not demand that they give of their best.	
20	Many employees come from far away, and local transport problems put many off from coming in sometimes.	
21	The family responsibilities of employees often take precedence over work attendance.	
22	Certain days of the week have exceptionally high absence levels.	
23	Certain employees have a history of poor attendance.	
24	Self-certification has resulted in employees taking extra days off.	
25	Other causes (*please insert*)	

Part three

Approaches to absence control

Chapter 9
Introduction

The previous chapters have shown that while managers are aware that the problem of casual absence exists in their organization, few of them either know the extent of the problem or its cost. The calculation of the costs of absence includes not only the direct and immediately visible financial costs, but also the undermining of employee morale, and the general reduction in productivity and efficiency. If the Industrial Society's figure of 200 million working days lost each year is broadly accurate, then the reduction of absence represents a primary target for management attention and action. It is to this action aspect that this chapter addresses itself.

Presented with an absence problem, it is easy to reach for an instant, all-purpose solution, based on a superficial determination of absence causes. One 'popular' management journal may tell you that the cause is, 'management's failure to inspire employees'; another says that, 'management does not communicate with the workforce enough', while yet another criticizes management for not laying down, 'sufficiently strict procedures'.

A review of the research literature on the causes of absence, and the comments of the managers interviewed, which were presented in the previous chapter, all suggest that there is no one cause of absence. The corollary of this point, is that there can never be a single all-purpose, sure-fire solution to the absence problem. Although a number of employees may be absent at the same time, they can all be absent for different reasons. In the same way, over a period of years, the same people will be absent for different reasons. All of this leads us to conclude that, if there are a range of causes for casual absence, then one would expect there to be a range of absence control techniques. The effectiveness of each one will be determined by the manager's ability to analyse the unique features of his particular absence problem, and to select the most appropriate technique to deal with it.

Problem-solving tips

Books, reports and articles on absence contain an endless supply of useful hints for managers to help them solve their absence problems.

'There is no substitute for firm managerial control techniques'
Glasgow Chamber of Commerce[1]

'There have been a multitude of studies showing that monetary bonuses contingent upon coming to work, increase attendance'
Latham and Napier[2]

'In order to bring down the level of absence in an organization, some system of warnings and potential penalties is needed'
McCurdy and Bowey[3]

'Changing the climate of a plant or office as regards concern for absence involves primarily the manipulation of group attitudes'
Taylor[4]

'The key to successful absence control is efficient record keeping and monitoring of all absences from work'
Matthewman[5]

'An overall approach to absence is essential, and companies may find that significant organizational or procedural changes are called for'
ACAS[6]

We suggested earlier that many managers developed personal hunches or theories about the causes of absence when they lacked a thorough grasp of the issues involved. They also had hunches about why absence had gone down. The 1987 Industrial Society study[7], for example, asked the 41% of respondents who had said that their company's absence rate had gone down in the last five years, to give their explanation for this. Their answers are shown in Table 9.1.

One of our respondents admitted that he found 'it awfully difficult to firm in, and establish why people just take time off'. Asked about the causes of

Table 9.1 Managers' opinions about the reasons for the decline in their companies' absence rate (*Industrial Society Survey, 1987*)

Reason	Number of managers
Close monitoring	27
Warning/discipline	26
Interviewing/counselling	16
Reduction in headcount	11
Economic climate/environmental factors	5
Attendance bonus	5
Pre-employment medicals	1
Transferring responsibility to departments	1
Agreement with unions on absence policy	1
'We ask all poor attenders not to come back'	1

absence in their companies, many line and personnel managers that we interviewed laughed. They admitted that their explanations ranged from, 'workers being bloody lazy', through to, 'bad working conditions'.

More authoritative research findings, and informed opinion, should act to increase management's understanding of the absence problem. Such information can help to form the basis of an effective absence control strategy. The preceding quotations are, however, reminiscent of the axioms concerned with the problem definitions referred to at the start of the chapter. Some of their writers do attempt to support their recommendations with evidence, analysis or deduction. Many, however, do not.

Methods of absence control

When asked to explain how they controlled absence in their companies, most managers referred to their organization's absence control policy or pro-gramme and the methods that it contained. In our view, while this is a useful starting point from which to consider absence control technique selection, it needs to be developed further.

Scott and Markham[8] in a unique piece of research, conducted a study of the practices used by US firms to deal with absenteeism. In addition, they asked each company to judge the effectiveness of their absence control techniques. A total of 987 respondents identified the methods used in their companies, and graded each one on a scale of one to four:

1 – not effective at all;
2 – marginally ineffective, the benefits just below costs;
3 – marginally effective, the benefits barely worth the costs;
4 – definitely effective, successful.

The results of their research are shown in Table 9.2.

In this table, the absence control methods are listed in descending order of perceived effectiveness. They range from those rated most effective (item 1) to those rated to be least effective (item 34). For each method, its average rated effectiveness is shown. The next column shows the percentage of respondents who used the absence control technique indicated. A wide variation of utilization is indicated here. The third and fourth columns contain the averaged absence rates of, first the companies who indicated that they used this particular control method, and then those who did not. The choices are not mutually exclusive, since a company may use more than one method. For this reason, the total does not add up to 100%.

Commenting on this data, Scott and Markham raised a number of interesting questions. These can be presented as management review questions for readers to ask about with respect to their own organizations.

Table 9.2 34 Absence control methods ranked by rated effectiveness (Scott and Markham)

	Control method	Average rated effectiveness	% in use	Absence rate: non-users	Absence rate: users
1	A consistently applied attendance policy	3.47	79%	4.8%	4.2%
2	Termination based on excessive absenteeism	3.47	96%	4.4%	4.3%
3	Progressive discipline for excessive absenteeism	3.43	91%	4.8%	4.3%
4	Identification and discipline of employees abusing attendance policies	3.39	88%	4.8%	4.3%
5	At least monthly analysis of daily attendance information	3.38	57%	4.7%	4.1%
6	Daily attendance records maintained by personnel department	3.36	48%	4.6%	4.1%
7	Employee call-in to give notice of absence	3.35	99%	7.3%	4.3%
8	A clearly-written attendance policy	3.33	76%	4.2%	4.4%
9	Daily attendance records maintained by supervisors	3.31	68%	3.8%	4.6%
10	Allow employees to build a paid 'absence bank' to be cashed in at a percentage at a later date, or added to next year's vacation time	3.28	10%	4.3%	4.2%
11	Employee interviewed after an absence	3.26	35%	4.4%	4.2%
12	Flexible work schedules	3.25	21%	4.3%	4.5%
13	Inclusion of absenteeism rate on employee job performance appraisal	3.19	66%	4.5%	4.2%
14	Perfect/good attendance banquet and award ceremony	3.19	9%	4.4%	3.8%
15	Formal work safety training program	3.17	42%	4.2%	4.4%
16	Screen recruits' past attendance records before making a selection decision	3.16	67%	4.7%	4.2%
17	Supervisory training in attendance control	3.15	39%	4.4%	4.2%
18	Inclusion of work unit absenteeism on supervisor's performance appraisal	3.15	18%	4.4%	4.2%

Table 9.2 (*Continued*)

	Control method	Average rated effectiveness	% in use	Absence rate: non-users	Absence rate: users
19	Wiping clean a problem employee's record by subsequent good attendance	3.14	47%	4.3%	4.3%
20	Improvements of safety on the job	3.13	57%	4.2%	4.4%
21	Public recognition of employee good attendance (i.e. in-house bulletin boards or news letters, etc.)	3.10	25%	4.6%	3.6%
22	Job enrichment/enlargement/ or rotation implemented to reduce absenteeism	3.09	12%	4.3%	4.2%
23	A component on attendance in a formal orientation program for new hires	3.07	71%	4.5%	4.3%
24	Require written doctor's excuse for illness/accidents	3.05	77%	4.0%	4.4%
25	Spot visitation (or phone call) to check-up at employee residence by doctor/nurse/ detective/other employee	3.00	21%	4.3%	4.3%
26	Operation of day care for employee's department	3.00	< 1%	4.3%	3.6%
27	Substance abuse program (drugs, alcohol, etc.)	2.99	28%	4.4%	4.2%
28	The absenteeism control policy has been negotiated in the union contract	2.98	32%	4.3%	4.9%
29	Employee bonus (monetary) for perfect attendance	2.96	15%	4.4%	4.1%
30	Education programs in health diet/home safety	2.81	13%	4.4%	3.9%
31	Attendance lottery or poker system (random reward)	2.77	< 1%	4.3%	4.8%
32	Peer pressure encouraged by requiring peers to fill in for absent employee	2.62	43%	4.3%	4.4%
33	Chart biorhythms for accident prone day	2.50	< 1%	4.3%	5.3%
34	Letter to spouse indicating lost earnings of employee due to absenteeism	2.50	< 1%	4.4%	1.8%

Management review questions on absence control procedures

1 *Is the appropriate person/department maintaining the absence data so that action can be taken upon it?* The study found that 48% of attendance records were maintained by the personnel department (item 6), and 68% by supervisors (item 9).

2 *Does your company have a clearly written attendance policy?* Of the companies surveyed, 24% did not (item 8).

3 *Are employees interviewed on their return to work after their absence?* Only 35% of companies had the conduct of such interviews as a formal requirement (item 11).

4 *Should some of your absence control procedures be replaced?* While a doctor's certificate was required by 77% of companies to verify the legitimating absence, it ranked 24 out of 34 as an effective absence control tool. Seventy-one per cent of organizations discussed the importance of attendance with their employees during their induction programme, but the judged effectiveness of this technique was ranked only slightly higher than the doctor's certificate at 23. It appears that companies have a number of old absence control procedures which are neither well maintained nor effective but which, nevertheless, continue to be used as part of an absence control policy.

5 *Does your company unconsciously exclude potentially effective control programmes?* Whatever the arguments for and against rewarding good attendance, the survey revealed an unexpectedly infrequent use of such techniques. Rewards for perfect and good attendance in the form of banquets and award ceremonies were conducted by only 9% of the companies studied (item 14); public recognition for good attendance (item 21) was reportedly used by only 25% of the firms. The point here is not that these techniques should be used, but whether or not there is an unconscious reaction against them amongst managers, and hence a reluctance even to consider their use.

In the management review questions at the end of Part one, readers were asked if they could state, in percentage terms, what their organization's absence rate was. In addition, those who did collect absence data, were asked if it was analysed regularly. Scott and Markham's study showed that 30% of the managers responding to the study could not quote their absence rate. Of the companies who said that they did collect absence statistics regularly, only 57% actually went on to analyse them.

While this absence control programme ranking is an interesting addition to our knowledge, it does not represent a good basis for selection. It is too narrow and specific. In this chapter therefore, we will describe three broad strategies to deal with the absence problem. The aim is to garner and classify the hundreds of quick tips that have been suggested about how management might deal with it. A range of productivity experiments from Britain and the United States were analysed to build up the classification. The chapters in this section will consider three absence control strategies, and defining the underlying features and implicit assumptions of each.

Deciding on absence control techniques

Some writers have recommended that absence control approaches should be consistent with, or be in response to, the underlying absence causes[9,10]. However, much of the literature makes little attempt to link absence control methods with absence causes. It has been claimed that there is no practical theory which links the latter with absence interventions[11].

A second aspect of the topic which has received surprisingly little attention is the question of the philosophics or assumptions that underlie the different absence control approaches. Management consultants and personnel managers regularly recommend different absence control techniques. However, when the results of the interventions are reported, little if any consideration is ever given to any of the underlying issues involved. Yet these factors are important. Which absence techniques are appropriate in which circumstances? Why should this be so? Are there any 'families' or groupings of absence control techniques based on similar underlying assumptions, concepts and principles? These are some of the relevant questions which, to date, have not been answered. Our objective is to bring some order into the plethora of ideas and suggestions offered to managers about how they can reduce their employees' absence. One observer has warned that one company's solution can be another's disaster. If this is so, managers need to overview the absence control techniques available to them, so that they can choose the most appropriate one.

A survey of the professional and research literature on absence control techniques reveals three distinct and separate strategies. These are arranged in terms of their focus or the target of the intervention, and the underlying problem diagnosis that they contain or assume. The three are labelled

- *people techniques*,
- *work techniques*, and
- *organizational techniques*.

One chapter will be allocated to each of these types of technique.

Chapter 10 will examine those absence control techniques which seek to improve employee attendance directly. Since absence is a human action, these techniques focus primarily and directly upon the people involved. They seek to modify the behaviour of employees in response to the work circumstances in which they find themselves. Thus, the people techniques do not address themselves to any of the underlying causes of absence at work, nor do they necessarily seek to understand them. From their perspective, what is important is that the desired change in the *attendance behaviour* of the individual is achieved. The three main categories of people techniques are:

Negative incentive: control systems, discipline, punishment centred.

Positive incentive: based on positive (reward) incentives to attend.

Mixed consequence: containing a combination of positive incentives ('the carrot') and negative consequences ('the stick').

Chapter 11 will consider the work techniques to absence control. This group of strategies seeks to influence individual attendance behaviour indirectly by making changes or adaptions in the *nature of the work* which employees carry out, or the environment in which they do such work. Three work techniques which can be considered are:

Job enrichment: including group work design.

Employee policy: changes which permit flexible attendance.

Work environment: changes in the physical conditions in which work is carried out.

The use of job enrichment[12] and flexible working hours[13] has been extensively documented. Many of these work techniques are not solely targeted at attendance behaviour. While some may indeed have attendance improvement as a primary objective, others may be directed at an entirely different area of performance. For example, a programme of goal-setting and feedback in a pulpwood factory was aimed primarily at improving production output. However, as a side-effect, it also produced a significant improvement in employee attendance[14].

Chapter 12 will focus on those approaches to absence control which involve the use of a *co-ordinated programme of activities*. A number of techniques come to be used either in parallel or sequentially. This strategy is based on the belief that absence from work is the result of the interaction of a number of factors related to the individual, the organization, and the environment. Whole organization approaches would also be a good way to describe these.

Increasingly, companies are moving away from traditional bureaucratic forms of organization, and are experimenting with new and more flexible organizational structures. The changes that are taking place are largely in response to the challenges of the market-place, and new technology[15]. These have led to the creation of adaptive organizational designs aimed at creating committed employees. Like many of the work approaches, these fundamental organizational programmes are not targeted specifically at absence, but have been shown to have had a major effect on absence reduction[16]. Each of the three strategies – people, work and organizational, will be examined in turn.

Chapter 10
People techniques

People techniques focus primarily on the behaviour of employees. There are three ways in which one can encourage the desired attendance behaviour. People can be *punished* for being absent, they can be *rewarded* for not being absent, or the company can use a *mixture of both* punishments and rewards. Let us consider each of these three approaches.

Negative (punishment) incentive

Punishments come in all shapes and sizes. Baxi Heating, located in Lancashire is a partnership with a minimum of 51% of its shares placed in a trust, and the remainder distributed amongst employees. As part of its 'equal status' package, the company has harmonized its sick-pay scheme. The control of absence is linked closely to the administration of this sick-pay scheme. The company has 6 sick-pay committees, made up of employees and management, which determine who will receive this benefit. The withholding of sick pay, and suspension from the sick-pay scheme are 2 actions that the committees can take, before referring the absentee to the disciplinary procedure.

In the United States, the Ford Motor Company's absence control approach stresses disciplinary action. In a procedure agreed with the local unions, progressively stricter disciplinary levels are set, and the severity of punishments is based upon the employee's seniority in the company. A warning is followed by successively longer suspensions until the employee is deemed to be 'incompatible' and is discharged. In contrast, General Motors' approach is not to discipline employees directly. Instead it punishes them by reducing the benefits it gives to them in proportion to their absenteeism. Benefits that are reduced include holidays, holiday pay, paid absence allowance, bereavement pay, supplementary unemployment benefit, and profit-sharing. What is the thinking behind this approach?

The approach is based on the view that casual absence by employees represents a rational decision by them to stay away from work. The chronic absentee prefers leisure to a greater extent than the employee with good work habits. While it is not authorized by the contract of employment, additional leisure is one of the options that is available to the worker. The way that the hourly-wage employment-benefit package is structured, gives employees an incentive to take extra leisure, because their fringe benefits are not related to the hours they work.

If employees do react to the incentives given to them in a rational manner, and if the company's compensation policy allows them to draw up to perhaps £20 per week in fringe benefits without having to work, then they can reduce the costs of their leisure time, and increase their effective hourly rate, by not coming in to work for the full 40 hours. This is especially the case when the disciplinary procedure is not effective in reducing absence. If absence is to be controlled, say the proponents of this approach, absence behaviour must become costly to the employees, that is, employees have to 'pay a price' for their absence.

The traditional price paid is the disciplining of employees. The underlying theory is that they work to obtain an income and the loss of work means loss of income, and if absence continues, it results in the eventual loss of employment. The problem with this is that while absences mean the loss of income, employees have already demonstrated their willingness to pay that price in return for being away from the job. If they are not sacked for absence, and if they have a strong preference for leisure, disciplinary suspension may actually be seen by them as a reward for excessive absence.

For this reason, managements like that of Ford, use the strategy of removing the incentives for absenteeism. They ensure that absence is punished and not rewarded. The firm pays employees fringe benefits on the basis that they work a 40-hour week. The hourly wage rate will increase as unauthorized absence increases. Employees lose their hourly pay when absent, but continue to receive all the fringe benefits that they would have earned had they worked the required hours. If employees have to *reimburse* the employer for the costs of the unearned fringe benefits, they are given an incentive to come to work rather than to be absent. In such circumstances, disciplining workers becomes a last-ditch resort.

All approaches described under the heading of negative incentive, seek to reduce absence by punishing the absentee. Many authors, particularly those writing in the popular business and management journals, and presenters on the lecture seminar circuit, take a strong managerialist line with respect to the question of controlling absence. They recommend control approaches that are essentially administrative in that they recommend setting standards, monitoring and measuring absences, giving feedback, and taking corrective action.

Few writers, however, advocate solely the 'big stick' approach. Instead, they recommend a co-ordinated programme of improvement, often with a different emphasis. The Industrial Society[1], for example, stressed the importance of communication, employee involvement, and the role of first-line supervision. This reflects its own philosophy and interests. Other writers see effective monitoring and measurement as being of particular importance[2]. Still others emphasize the particular need for fair, well-defined, progressive sanctions which are both understood and accepted by all employees[3].

If one examines the basic requirements of a programme, based on discipline and authority, to alter the behaviour of absentees, one can see that the differing emphases are not in fact mutually exclusive. Research has shown that absence control programmes which involve procedures and sanctions, are most effective when they are based on motivational patterns of 'legal compliance'. That is, people act in certain ways because they believe it to be right to do so[4,5].

This state is achieved when management's legitimacy and authority is accepted, when rules are agreed, and when adequate sanctions are consistently enacted. According to Rosenthal[6], the main requirements for this to happen are the following:

- The rules regarding an attendance policy must not only be published, but they must be communicated directly to employees

- Clarity is essential

- It must be clear that the rules will be enforced

- Management discretion must be minimized

- Consistency must exist

- Progressive discipline steps should be followed, such as oral warning, a written warning, and a suspension before dismissal occurs.

Clearly then, a key factor in this process is the perception of fairness amongst organizational members. A number of writers have proposed the use of statistical analysis techniques in order to provide an impartial identification of fair standards[7,8]. Some of these techniques are attractive to managers, perhaps reflecting their comfort with the idea of converting managerial problems into measurable relationships. However, there is a danger that some line managers and supervisors may insensitively regard the statistical results as what one personnel manager vividly described as a 'licence to kill'.

It is important that supervisors should be adequately counselled on how to ensure that compliance with company policy occurs. Badly managed attendance control plans, such as sudden clampdowns, have been found to be ineffective. Often they cause new problems, or they result only in a change in the *form* of absence, rather than in its absolute level[9]. For example, employees have shorter but more frequent absences, instead of a small number of long ones.

From the review of the disciplinary control literature, one might conclude, as Latham and Napier[10] do, that 'It would appear that an attendance control policy, established by a legitimate source of authority, and implemented with clear-cut, progressively enforced legal sanctions, should lead to significant improvements in employee attendance'. This theme is echoed in the writings of other authors. It is appropriate to examine the elements necessary if a negative incentive approach to absence control is to work fairly and efficiently. The aspects to be considered are:

- deciding on clear expectations of attendance;

- record keeping;

- achieving consistency of approach;

- management will;

- absence procedures; and

- absence rules.

Deciding on clear expectations of attendance

Any punishment-centred approach must, of necessity, be based upon clear managerial expectations of attendance. When there is a dispute, and if disciplinary action may be taken, reference is made to the contract of employment. The employer and the employee agree the terms of the contract of employment. The written particulars of this statement must contain terms and conditions which relate to three points:

- the hours of work (including any relating to normal working hours);

- holiday entitlement (personal holidays, public holidays, and holiday pay);

- incapacity for work due to sickness or injury.

Unless management makes it clear to employees when they are expected to attend, it has no chance of identifying either lateness or unauthorized absence, let alone disciplining employees for it. While the place of work need not be specified, failure to do so may cause problems as in the case of salesmen, some of whom may claim that they can work adequately well from home. Companies identify numerous instances of when staff are permitted to be away. These are the statutory rights of absence which include pregnancy and maternity time.

In recent times there has been a renewed interest in *special leave*, since it represents a grey area of what is to be expected. Special leave is defined as time taken off work, in addition to annual leave and public holidays, which is initiated by the employee and granted by the employer. Such leave is taken to meet both private needs (for example, family illness, bereavement, paternity, medical appointments), and public duties (such as those of JPs, local councillors, school governors, military training, jury service). In 1988 a survey was conducted amongst 65 organizations by Long and Hill[11]. They were able to compare their results with a previous study on the same topic which had been conducted in 1980.

Their main finding was that in the 8-year interim period, there was a growing trend away from a traditional, flexible, and discretionary response by employers to special leave requests, and towards a greater formalization of procedures. The reasons for this shift were held to be threefold. First, employers considered that by providing employees with a more generous annual leave provision, it was appropriate for them to use part of that to deal with their short-term domestic problems. Second, organizational rationalization, the growth of employment legislation (Statutory Maternity Pay), and the defeats in unfair dismissal cases caused by untidy procedures, have all prompted employers to tidy up their procedures, including those relating to special leave provision. The final influence has been an increasing trade union interest in special leave, which is seen by the unions as an aspect of employee benefits.

The survey showed that employers granted less favourable paid special leave to manual workers, than to non-manual ones. The authors argued that they did this to control the perceived abuse of such leave (for example in cases of medical appointments). Amongst the four main findings of the study were the following. First, Long and Hill found that a third of employers gave no leave for family sickness, a 22% increase on 1980. Second, the granting of marriage leave had declined. Third, while 70% of companies had maternity leave policies, only 22% went beyond the statutory requirements. Fourth, while 12% did not grant paid leave for public duties, a large amount of management discretion was still exercised in this area.

Record-keeping

The second requirement for an effective punitive consequence system is an adequate database. Many writers consider that keeping proper records is a vital factor in overcoming an absence problem. Record-keeping can be a way of telling the employee that he or she is being noticed. Some commentators believe that the majority of employees will opt in or out of work depending on how important the company makes them feel. This is where record-keeping is so vital. If a supervisor does not notice that someone has always two days off a month because he or she does not keep a record of attendances, most employees will simply think that they are not missed, and that their presence is not important to the business. They will therefore continue to absent themselves.

Record-keeping is at the heart of any absence control procedure. It allows a company to zero in on the regular absentees and to institute disciplinary action. In one of our interview companies, the management decided that any absence was unacceptable. They moved from a 'frequency' base of absence calculation, to a 'duration and percentage of the working year' and a 'reason' base. By defining the problem in this way, they were able to remind their employees that they were supposed to be there 230 days a year, and if they had missed 10%, to ask why.

The study by Scott and Markham[12] cited in the last chapter indicated that companies which had a personnel department that kept absence records and analysed the daily attendance figures at least once a month, had significantly lower absence rates. What was not found to be effective was the practice of supervisors keeping such records. Apart from the chore of the task, the supervisors felt that a strong central system, guided by the personnel department was necessary. Only in this way could equity and consistency be achieved. The supervisors felt that they lacked the resources to communicate and update the situation continually. Union shop stewards often challenged the reliability of the records kept by the supervisors, and could confront them with statistics kept by others.

The 1987 Industrial Society's survey of absence[13] found that absence records were kept by the personnel department in 81% of the companies that responded. However, it appears that absence records are held at several levels in the organization at the same time. The survey revealed that amongst the people holding such records were managers, supervisors, the wages department, the medical centre, the company secretary and the industrial engineer. The larger the company, the more likely it was that either the personnel department or the manager would be responsible for keeping an eye on absence.

Statutory self-certification which was introduced by the government in 1982, virtually killed off unauthorized absence in most companies. Instead, they were faced with so-called sickness absence. Many organizations had to build up attendance records, which they have kept running non-stop. Every month, each individual's attendance figures are looked at, and a check is made to establish the frequency and duration of his or her absence over a long period, usually a year. In some organizations, people who break the absence rules are interviewed and either given a warning or else counselled.

Large organizations often have records sections in their personnel departments which pick out people who have been repeatedly late or absent. Offenders are identified, and their line managers informed of their absence or lateness records, and whether they are due for a warning. When the warning has been issued, the information is logged into the computer. On the next occasion that an offender is absent, the computer will identify whether a final written warning is due or a dismissal. The attendance record-keeping systems are easily computerized and form the basis of many of the punitive approaches to the problem of absence control. Many observers would disagree with Sargent in seeing record-keeping as a punitive device. They would argue that it is a way of positively acknowledging an employee's presence and contribution. Nevertheless, most managers would concur with the need to keep and to use absence records.

Achieving consistency of approach

The third prerequisite for a negative consequence system is achieving a consistency of approach. Some absence policies, particularly those which include provisions for excused and unexcused absences, often force the supervisor to judge the legitimacy of whatever excuse the employee offers for not showing up for work. Because specific guidelines to cover all conceivable reasons for employee absence are impossible to write, supervisors must apply their own criteria to the situation. This can create inequities in the way the system is administered. Inequity in the administration of the absenteeism policy tends to aggravate conflict between management and employees.

The managers whom we interviewed expressed a variety of problems which related to different facets of the administrative aspects of absence control management. The achievement of this consistent approach was one of the priorities mentioned. A personnel manager explained the situation, 'We have 12 supervisors, running 12 groups of people. The task is to standardize. Our supervisors range from right-wing fascist, to lefty liberal. The problem is that some are too hard while others are not doing anything at all'. (*Glass manufacturer*)

Because of this problem of achieving consistency of approach, one absence control plan has been favourably viewed as offering a solution to the shortcomings of traditional absence policies. It is called the *No-fault Absenteeism* approach. Under this type of plan, management recognizes the inevitability of an occasional absence and avoids the common tendency to blame the employee for not coming to work. There are no excused or unexcused absences. Employees neither have to prove the legitimacy of an absence, nor are managers forced to differentiate between acceptable and unacceptable reasons for absence. No-fault absence monitoring records each *occurrence* of absence, which may be one day or five continuous days. This aims to avoid penalizing the employee who is genuinely and infrequently ill, and forced to remain away from work for 2 or more days. Second, it seeks to catch the absentee who claims large numbers of single days' absences, usually on Mondays, Fridays and days following and preceding holidays[14,15].

In our own study, we found that on occasions, the absence control rules and established procedures that had been established turned out to be counter-productive. They were so long and extended, that they failed to achieve their objective.

'Our first absence procedure was a weak one. It had lots of caveats built into it. It indicated to the workforce that we were concerned about absence but did not really want to fire anybody for it. It was extremely difficult, even with people with a very bad absence record, to do anything about it. They got warnings and things, but the procedure was so extended that nothing much happened. In the early years, only one person ever got dismissed for absence.' (*Electrical components manufacturer*)

Often companies learned by their mistakes, and were able to achieve some of the objectives identified earlier by Rosenthal[16]. They did this, for example, by clarifying the rules, and by demonstrating management's willingness to enforce them. However, as previously mentioned, such clampdowns can change the form of absence rather than its absolute level.

'In 1983 the safety clauses were knocked out. The procedure has stayed basically the same. It is quite a long procedure, but it's easier to move bad absence people through it. We have used it. There was a greater willingness by management to take the disciplinary route which would mean dismissal. The 1983 amendment basically made it dangerous for you to be off for short periods, but if you got beyond four weeks, the procedure assumed that you were terminally ill and protected you. We found that short-term absence dropped off, and people were off for nine, ten and eleven weeks with colds. It's a tough procedure now, reviewed again in 1985–6. You get penalized for a lot of frequent, short-term absence now. But it works.' (*Whisky bottling plant*)

Discussions with different companies indicated that once the decision to establish a procedure was taken, then two, three and maybe more revisions might be necessary before it was finally found to be satisfactory. An additional point is that the procedure which is initially adopted by the company may appear to be very harsh. Often however, its aim is to weed out the worst transgressors, and leave room for the company to operate the procedure differently at a later date.

'We ended up firing a lot of people. They were the people whom the bulk of the shopfloor felt ought to go anyway. Everyone wondered why it took us so long to do it. Having got over the "night of the long knives", you find that the procedure can be operated in a much more humane fashion now'. (*Electrical products manufacturer*)

Management will

Any successful punitive absence policy needs to be backed up by management conviction. This is why this is the fourth crucial element. Most of the writing on absence control assumes that once the extent of the problem is known, action will inevitably follow. In fact, some commentators suggest that management has to be motivated to take action with respect to absence. Cecchi and Plax[17] described an absence control programme at Rockwell International. It was called, 'Absence Control Through Sensitive Employee

Monitoring'. It involved upgrading the skills of supervisors in dealing with the company-wide problem of absence generally, and with 'absence abuses' in particular. What was significant about this programme was that a major part of the training for it involved human resources department staff running briefing sessions with all levels of management. The aim of these sessions was to overcome the managers' views that absenteeism was a 'fact of life' (even amongst salaried employees), and that nothing could be done about it. The trainers sought to create a *will* amongst Rockwell's management to take action over the absence problem.

The discussions that we had with managers in our study, gave us the impression that while the problem was known, and was getting worse, management was reluctant, in some instances, to grasp the nettle. When action did occur, it was often because the absence problem was getting completely out of hand. Thus it seems to us that much of the question about absence control relates as much to management, as it does to the workforce. Does management have the will to take action? Is it prepared to live with the short-term hostility that is likely to be generated? Are the managers prepared to support one another?

Our discussions were peppered with references to supervisors who took disciplinary action leading to dismissal, having to be backed up all the way. Comments about, 'being ready to ride out the storm' were also common.

'With absence running at 17–18%, and sometimes even 25–28%, we realized we would have to do something. I got agreement from the director that things would have to be upset. Using a staged approach, I wrote to each bad attender personally telling him that if there was no substantial and sustained improvement that I would invoke the disciplinary procedure. It was important for us to act. When the first step of the disciplinary procedure was put into action, it was as if all hell broke loose. As soon as they got into my office, the shop steward fought for them. But I did not back down, and with the management team's support we pursued the thing for the next 18 months.' (*Whisky blending plant*)

In that case, the effect was to reduce absence from the astronomical figures quoted, down to the middle teens, before finally bringing it down to about 5%. Repeatedly we saw a lack of management will to act on absence, even though the procedures might be there.

'We said to the workforce, if you don't stick by the rules, we'll do something about it, which is what we weren't doing. We had a disciplinary procedure but weren't using it.' (*Whisky blending plant*)

It has been reported that since 1986 Vauxhall has actively sought to curb unwarranted absence at its Ellesmere Port and Luton plants. At Luton, total absence including holidays, had been running at 15.5%, and had peaked at 22% on Mondays and Fridays. In the autumn of 1987, it was down to 12%.

Sickness absence had been reduced from 13.6% to 6.5%. This turnaround at Vauxhall was achieved by nothing more than a radical tightening of absence procedures, identifying persistent absentees, counselling them, and ultimately giving them between five and eight weeks to improve their record. The management has not shirked from the final sanction. A total of 130 employees have either resigned or been dismissed during a ten-month period. This progress at the Luton plant means that attention is now being turned to Ellesmere Port. Further improvements at both plants are being hoped for by reducing the period allowed for the improvement of poor individual attendance records from 5 to 3 weeks[18].

Absence procedures

A fifth important consideration when implementing a punishment-centred absence is the content of the procedure itself. An inadequate procedure, while it may not actually encourage absenteeism, may do little to reduce it. In these circumstances, it is a question of amending or revising the procedure. A number of examples can be given. The acceptance of doctors' certificates is one case in point. The value of a doctor's certificate was generally held to be very low amongst the respondents in Scott and Markham's study. This same view was confirmed in the discussions with personnel managers in our study.

'Before self-certification, about 3 years ago, you could get a doctor's note by paying 50p. I believe that a lot of these were signed by receptionists. It's so easy to go into a doctor's surgery and get a medical note, often the day after you've recovered. That has gone now, and it's not such a major issue. I do feel that the medical profession gives sickness cover too easily to individuals who say they are ill.' (*Bakery*)

This being the case, the weight given by the company to the doctor's certificate was greatly altered.

'After the introduction of SSP we put in a new absence/discipline procedure which contained some fundamental changes. We used to take the view that if a person was absent, and the absence was covered by a doctor's certificate, then we couldn't touch that – that it was sacrosanct. Now that has ended. We now discipline people for absence, except in cases of serious illness, where we don't take action. Whatever the amount of time off, whether it's covered by a doctor's certificate or not, we will take action on it and will issue a warning.' (*Electrical products company*)

The personnel managers interviewed each had their own horror story about doctors and sick notes. One recounted the following tale, 'We had a classic case where a GP gave one of the girls a medical certificate for one year for a cold. We took it to our company doctor who telephoned her GP. He said that he was fed up with her coming to the surgery, so he just gave her a note for a year'. With the advent of self-certification, the policy of many companies has been strengthened in a way that puts the onus on the absentee to show that he or she has in fact been absent for medical reasons. As one personnel manager put it,

'If a guy's self-certificated and he hasn't been to a doctor, we say we don't believe you. We can take steps to issue warnings, and if he has too many warnings we can dismiss him'.

A second important area of procedure concerns the payment of sickness benefit. There was a case of the company procedure allowing a person who was being disciplined for unauthorized absence to continue to be eligible for sickness benefits.

'Since revising our absence procedure, when a person goes past a verbal warning to a written warning, we remove them from the sick-pay scheme. In the old procedure, even when they were approaching dismissal, and they were absent, they still got sick pay. Now, as soon as you get a written warning from the company regarding absence, for the duration of that warning, you will not get sick pay, if you're absent. That change has hit people in the pocket.' (*Whisky bottling plant*)

One important area of any absence control procedure concerns the reporting of sickness absence by employees both when they are away and when they return. On both these occasions, the role of the supervisor seems to be crucial. Ford[19] reported the case of a negative (punishment) procedure in a company that he studied. Traditionally, when employees reported in sick, they would telephone a supervisory employee in the central administration. This was a person whom they did not know. They were not required to communicate directly with their immediate supervisor regarding their absence. The change in the absence control procedure that was instituted required absentees to report each sick leave absence by telephone to their immediate supervisor. They were also required to report the nature of their illness, its estimated duration, their estimated return date, their plans to see a doctor, and the name of the doctor. During this telephone conversation, their supervisor gave them information about the number of staff who had previously been scheduled to take holiday leave at this time, and the number that remained to meet the work area responsibilities. The effect of this experiment was to produce a significant reduction in sickness absence.

A second aspect of rules, is the requirement for the employee to report to his immediate supervisor on his return to work. In 1974, Sandvik, the Swedish specialist steel manufacturer had an absence rate of almost 22%. As part of this company's absence control programme, interviews were held with employees. One of the significant findings was the existing attitudes that employees had towards absenteeism. Many workers told the interviewers that they had been absent without a valid reason for many days. Their attitude was, 'Why shouldn't I do this? No one has bothered to contact me when I am absent. No one asks me what happened when I return to work. No one, in fact pays any attention'[20]. Sandvik responded by training supervisors in communication. They were also instructed to contact employees after one day's absence from work in order to show a prompt interest in the well-being of their subordinates. This, together with improvements in company communications centred around briefing groups and Quality Circle ideas, together contributed to a 65% reduction in absenteeism. An internationally famous garment manufacturer interviewed as part of our own study had, as the centrepiece of its absence control strategy, the post-return interview with the absentee by the supervisor. Many other techniques were used by this organization, including recognition awards and lotteries, but the interview with the supervisor was the central plank of their absence control plan.

Absence rules

A clear definition of unacceptable absence is the sixth and final ingredient of a successful punishment programme. The rules and regulations concerning expected attendance, and how individuals will be disciplined in relation to absence, can cause anomalies unless rules and standards are clearly established. A formal definition of 'unacceptable absence' has been produced by a number of companies. For example, Warner Lambert use the following guide to indicate to their employees that an individual's absence is causing concern:

In a 13-week period – 5 days absence (8.5% absence rate)

In a 26-week period – 8 days absence (7.0% absence rate)

In a 52-week period – 12 days absence (5.2% absence rate)

The aim of such a formal definition is twofold. First, it indicates to employees when absence levels have become too high. Second, it guides supervisors and managers as to when warnings should be issued. The accompanying procedures must also be made explicit, otherwise they might actually encourage absence. In our own studies, we came across a number of examples of this phenomenon.

'We follow the ACAS code of practice. Step one, verbal warning; step two, first written warning; step three, final written warning; step four, dismissal. Each step lasts for six months. People used to go through steps one to three, and then come in for six months until step three had expired. They then started being absent again, and went on to step one. We have now changed it. If a person starts being absent again, he or she goes back to step three. That puts more pressure on them.' (*Whisky bottling plant*)

* * *

'Under our procedure, if you were absent at Easter, but stayed clear of absence for six months, you couldn't get caught at all. It so happened that the holiday peaks coincided nicely with our absence procedure. As an employee, you could have a lot of absence if you took the year in total, but the way the procedure was constructed, you couldn't fall foul of it. These issues became clear when we scrutinized the procedure in detail, and we have made changes to alter the pattern.' (*Whisky bottling plant*)

* * *

'We had an absence procedure where you could have thirteen weeks off in any twelve-month rolling period. We had a woman who was off at least one week per month. It was supposed to be a 'female problem'. She had been with the company for a while, and the records revealed she had been doing this for years. Taking three, or four, and perhaps six days off every month, so she was never without sickness benefit. We tackled her and she said that she had problems. We said that we had a problem because she was contracted to work. Her sickness benefit was stopped, and she was off for five days in the following twelve months. In the following three months she was off for three weeks and she was fired. The company benefits scheme is an *ex gratia* scheme, not negotiated with the unions. The majority realized they couldn't exploit the procedure any more, and the absence rate went down.' (*Whisky bottling plant*)

In our investigations, we found a company which had a rule that five days of absence was the minimum period needed before a person could be paid sickness benefit. Naturally, staff with short-period, even genuine illness, were encouraged to stay out until the five days were up. Given the ingenuity of committed absentees to exploit the absence rules to their benefit, management must ensure that the rules are framed in a way that prevents abuse. The examples just quoted may appear minor oversights. Nevertheless, they were obtained from three different companies. This suggests that the problem may be widespread, and that absence rules need to be devised with much greater care. Unless this is done, an absence control system geared to negative incentives is unlikely to operate effectively.

Finally, we might note that some organizations do not take a disciplinary approach to absence at all. British Rail, for example, views absenteeism as a capability problem, rather than as one of misconduct. Thus, absence control is taken out of the disciplinary sphere. In its code of conduct, British Rail explains that it does not consider it to be appropriate to resort to the use of the disciplinary procedure in cases of persistent short-term sickness absence. It argues that the issue centres on the *lack of capability of an individual to fulfil the contract of employment in regard to regular attendance for duty*. British Rail considers disciplinary action to be relevant only in cases where the employee fails to notify an absence properly, fails to provide evidence of sickness as required by the Board, or if there are sufficient grounds to suggest that the sickness is not genuine.

Positive incentives approach

The second approach under the *people techniques* heading s\
incentives, rather than negative consequences. Instead of t.
punishing undesirable behaviour such as absence, it rewards a
encourages the desired attendance behaviour. The jargon te   ⌐y
psychologists for this is 'positive reinforcement'. The positive incentives
approach has been defined as the 'linking of employee desired rewards to
organizationally desired employee behaviour'[21]. Two main types of positive
benefits are offered, financial and non-financial ones.

Financial benefits

The main type of financial benefit is the attendance bonus. This gives the
employee a financial incentive to attend on a regular basis. Such financial
incentives can take many different forms. For example, attendance bonuses
pay cash and may be calculated on either an individual or on a group basis[22].
Good attenders may participate in a lottery and thereby win cars or holidays
abroad[23]; they can accumulate redeemable bonus points, gain food credits,
or a range of other financial benefits.

A 1985 Industrial Society survey[24] briefly considered the subject of
attendance bonuses. It acknowledged that the practice of paying people
twice to attend work had both supporters and opponents. Some organizations, such as Rank Xerox, are against attendance bonuses. They feel that,
as a company, they offer a good remunerative package with several perks.
They therefore baulk at the idea of paying employees more just to turn up.
Only 10% of the companies surveyed by the Industrial Society had an
attendance scheme. The vast majority of these schemes were run by
manufacturing companies, particularly the medium-sized ones. The oldest
scheme in the survey was one that had been introduced in 1956, and the most
recent had began in 1985, the year that the survey was conducted.
Interestingly, more than 50% of the schemes that were in existence had been
installed in the second half of the 1970s.

Two years later, the 1987 Industrial Society absence survey[25] found that
the number of companies with bonus schemes had increased by a small
amount to 12%. Bonus scheme users were equally divided as to whether
these helped to reduce absence. Forty-eight per cent felt that they did, while
52% felt that they did not. Some of the associated details of this study are
interesting. The survey found that the distribution and transport industries
had the highest percentage of respondents with attendance bonus schemes
(20% each), while financial services had the lowest (3%). Of the different
types of bonus schemes in use, weekly schemes were used by 47% of
respondents, and annual schemes by 23%. Monthly and quarterly schemes
were less popular; each was used by only 10% of respondents. The survey
results also indicated a renewed interest in such schemes. A third of them
had been introduced in the 1985–7 period.

Experiences with paying attendance bonuses varied. The Ford company claimed in a newspaper report that its attendance bonus scheme introduced for blue-collar workers at its UK car plants in 1978 had been instrumental in cutting absenteeism. The bonus ranged from £7.42 to £9.58 according to grade, and it was forfeited entirely if, unless excused, the employee did not work full shift hours for any reason. The company reported that its attendance scheme, which was paid weekly, had reduced unauthorized absence from 2.25% to 0.63%[20].

Since 1986, Austin Rover has operated a form of financial incentive for attendance. As part of its general wage agreement, each plant has been given the right to pay employees with at least three months' service for the first three 'waiting days' of each short-term absence, provided that the plant's overall 12-month unauthorized absence record is at, or below, 5%. The Land Rover division gives its manual workers £7 per week, and its staff employees £5 per week for perfect attendance. Imperfect attendance results in the entire bonus being lost for that week. Such a loss can be the result of sickness, industrial action, lateness, early leaving, suspension for disciplinary reasons, or other unauthorized absence. Criteria are applied rigidly. A minute's lateness results in the loss of £7. The effect of this attendance bonus scheme, together with changes in recruitment methods, supervisory control, and a modified shift pattern, has meant the virtual elimination of lateness, and a reduction in absence rates. Given this combination of changes, it is not easy to single out the contribution made by the bonus scheme in isolation.

Ambivalence characterized the organizational response to attendance bonuses. Companies seemed to be equally split about their merits and effectiveness. Values also played a part. Some companies believed that employees should not receive any additional income to attend work. Observers have commented that many of the attendance bonuses were so small that, 'One wonders at the value of some schemes'. To make it worth while, our interviewed managers noted, one had to set the bonus at a level which would make a noticeable difference to the employee if he or she was absent. The figure quoted was between 5% and 9% of gross pay. That represented a substantial increase in labour costs. In the 1987 Industrial Society survey, 78% of bonus scheme users said that the bonus was a fixed sum and not a percentage of pay. The managers in the companies in our research who did have an attendance bonus confirmed that, over time, it tended to degenerate unless it was regularly updated, with the consequential effects on labour costs.

'Within the plant, we have an attendance pay of £5 per week. It's not much as a percentage of the total wage. But it is lost if the employee has more than two hours off a week for any reason. That wouldn't affect the person who is ten minutes late, but it hits the person who disappears for a couple of hours on a Friday. It did have a benefit in the past but not any more. They would forgo it now because of the amount.' (*Glass manufacturer*)

There are two common features of attendance bonus payments. First, they can quickly become regarded as a right, rather than as something to be earned. They can therefore backfire and act as a disincentive to attendance. Second, bonus payments eventually tend to be become consolidated into the regular pay packet in the annual wage negotiations. Perhaps the main contribution of a bonus scheme may be to change the attitude of workers to attendance in the long term, even though the scheme may be withdrawn in the short term. This is certainly how some of our managers saw it.

'In the recent past, we introduced an attendance bonus system which we worked out. Anyone off does not get the bonus. People were earning £7-12 bonus. To lose it became costly to them. At that time it had the desired effect. It brought our absence rate down from 12% to 8%. We have now consolidated this payment. Perhaps it achieved an attitude of mind that they lost money if they took time off. Even though the bonus has been consolidated, the positive attitude seems to have been successfully ingrained.' (*Whisky blending plant*)

A number of the companies that we studied had withdrawn, or were in the process of withdrawing their attendance bonus schemes. One of these was a high-volume manufacturer of security optics. Its attendance bonus scheme involved paying a 3% attendance bonus for full attendance. If any employee was absent for one day in a month, the bonus was halved. More than one day's absence resulted in a loss of the bonus for that month. The incentive was therefore for the employee to attain full attendance each month, and thus receive the bonus. The company however, was actively negotiating with its trade union to abolish the attendance bonus scheme. It saw the bonus as a 'hygiene factor', that contributed neither to employee motivation, nor to job satisfaction. The company's sister plant had ended its attendance bonus scheme, and had not experienced any significant change in the amount, or pattern of, its absence.

A survey[27] of ten American incentive plans in 1980, concluded that most were shown *not* to be cost effective. In the majority of cases, they had been implemented for only between 2 and 4 months. A study by Schneller and Kopelman[28] reported an incentive plan which actually *increased* overall absence by between 12% and 13%. They analysed this dramatic failure. First, they discovered that the financial incentive offered was too small. The bonus, which was paid every 3 months was equivalent to one day's pay, and was insufficient to affect behaviour over such a long time. It seems that employees can accurately assess the trade-off in these incentive plans, and can quickly spot a 'bad deal'. Second, the three-month period itself was too long, irrespective of the reward. Employees who missed more than the allowable time early in the period, had no incentive to correct their absenteeism for the remainder of that period. The time period seemed to discourage those who would have been motivated to attend. Once dis-qualified, it may even have encouraged them to take additional days off (for whatever reason) before the next three-month period began. Finally, the system offered only rewards, without balancing them against any punishments (as in the mixed consequence system). Hence, having lost the carrot, there was no stick to keep them.

In a recent experiment, Vauxhall, a division of General Motors[29] sought to reduce absenteeism by offering a pay rise to employees in return for a promise of more than 95% attendance at work. In October 1987, at the pay talks, the company offered production line staff an 8.25% rise in basic pay over 2 years. In return, it wanted them to agree to 5.25% absenteeism in the current year, and 4.5% in the year ending September 1988. If workers reached these levels, they would also be offered benefits such as a free sickness and accident scheme. At the time they paid an average of £2.13 per week into the scheme. Absence rates on Vauxhall's production lines in 1987 were 7.3%, down from 13.5% on the previous 12 months. How successful this plan will be is not yet known.

A similar positive consequence strategy, based on the workforce as a whole achieving a reduced target, was tried in a heavy engineering company in Glasgow. The experience of this management's attempt to introduce this change provides some useful insights into the problems of implementation. The company sought to reduce absenteeism amongst its manual workers (and regarded the reduction as a prelude to increased productivity). The manual workers' unions complained that it was unfair that staff union members were paid when absent, while their manual worker colleagues were not. For the shopfloor workers, being paid when absent (as the staff were), was seen as a valuable financial benefit. At the time, the manual worker absence rate was 6.5%, compared with 3.0% for staff. The company instigated a three-year scheme which offered to reward the manual workers by the granting of staff conditions. This involved full pay for absence, permission to come late, pass out, and full membership of the company pension scheme.

In return, the company required that the absence level of the manual workers should be reduced to that of staff employees. The agreement was that during the 3-year transition period, an increasing number of sick days would be paid. This would begin with 50% in the first year, and rise to 100% after 3 years. These payments were dependent on an absence target being achieved. The scheme would be phased in, in line with percentage drops in absence among the manual union members. The lower the absence, the more sick pay would be paid. After three years, manual workers would attain full staff conditions provided that their absence rate had fallen to the staff's level of 3%. The targets for improved payments were as follows:

Average absence greater than 6.5%	Current
Average absence 6.5% and above 5.5%	Stage 1
Average absence 5.5% and above 4.5%	Stage 2
Average absence 4.5% and below	Stage 3

Despite the offer, the absence rate amongst the manual workers did not fall, but remained constant. Company managers offered a number of explanations for this. First, the company was merely asking the workers to reduce absence, albeit by offering them staff conditions in return. It made no effort to try to increase the awareness in each individual employee that his or her absence was disruptive to the work programme, that it cost the company money, and that the absence could affect his or her long-term future with the company.

Second, the details of the new scheme were not presented to the workforce in terms of what it might be losing as a group by not addressing its absence problem. It was the question of individual responsibility that the company failed to communicate to employees. The result was that, if individuals were informed at all, the information was not conveyed directly but through their informal group in which communications were notoriously poor. Information came via the grapevine, often inaccurately.

Third, and perhaps most importantly, so far as the managers were concerned, since absence was a group problem it needed a group solution. It was difficult for individual employees to see how their personal responses could affect the overall outcome. They found it difficult to understand how one person's four-day absence could significantly affect the company's overall absence rate. Communication was urgently needed to emphasize that everybody's individual absence made up the total.

Shopfloor operators saw other people taking paid days off and wondered why they should bother coming in every day when all their mates were taking advantage of the paid sick days offered. In other words, the informal group norm was influencing them. Everyone else was having three or four paid days off a year, so why shouldn't they? It became normal to take this time off. The result of course, was that the staff conditions that had been offered would not be granted. When management realized what was happening, it did not work sufficiently hard to break this group thinking by the use of clear and frequent communication.

The strategy failed because it did not attack the basic problem of low worker motivation. Offering people sick pay does not motivate them to come to work or to give of their best. It merely removes the irritation of losing pay, as was the case under the previous regime. If management is to motivate people to feel better about their place of work and their working conditions, it needs to address the higher order needs of people. It needs to make them feel that they are contributing, that they are important, and that being absent is a bad thing for themselves, their work group, and for the company as a whole.

Good communication and real attention to personal feelings, difficult as these may be to achieve, together with the tangible reward of full sick pay, are both required since either solution in isolation is unlikely to be successful. Additionally, the communication must be aimed at the individual level in order to overcome the pressure and influence of the informal group norm.

This particular example highlights some of the basic difficulties in

Table 10.1   Range of incentives used by companies in positive incentive
programmes

- **Monthly lottery.** Employees with perfect attendance records can qualify for a monthly draw. On the last working day of the month, one winner is selected at random from the list of eligible employees. The winner receives a cash bonus or a holiday, and other eligible employees with perfect attendance for the month are rewarded in other ways, e.g. by having their names listed on a bulletin board.

- **Sick-leave bonus.** Under this plan, employers can discourage sick-leave abuse by paying employees a bonus (£5 for example) at the end of the year for each unused sick leave day. No bonus is paid for sick-leave days that are transferred to the next year.

- **Poker plan.** Each employee who arrives on time can choose a card from a deck of playing cards. At the end of the week, those with perfect attendance and punctuality will have five cards. The best hand wins a cash bonus.

- **Profit-sharing.** Based on a company's absence costs, profit-sharing can be adjusted. This plan stresses peer pressure to encourage employees to keep attendance standards high.

- **Sick-leave banks.** Employees can begin a year with an allotted 'bank' of additional time off with pay. This allotment can be reduced, for example, by one hour for each hour of absence on a Tuesday, Wednesday or Thursday, and by two hours for each hour missed on Monday and Friday. Guidelines must naturally be established for excused absence, and restrictions set to curb the blanket use of time off.

- **Well pay.** Under a well pay plan, no one is paid while absent, whether the absence is justified or not. Instead, employees are paid an extra day for each month in which attendance and punctuality are perfect. Thus each day that an employee is absent means loss of both pay and bonus.

- **Multi-lottery.** The company offers, perhaps eight prizes of £50 if absenteeism is held under 8%. For each additional 1% drop, four additional awards are given. This plan fosters a team approach to decreasing absenteeism, and rewards the whole company and not just individuals for low absence.

- **Semi-annual bonuses.** Larger bonuses are distributed twice annually to employees with perfect attendance records.

- **Punctuality plan.** Each day one name is selected at random, and that employee is called on the telephone promptly at starting time. Employees who are at their work station to answer the call are rewarded with money or time off.

- **Trading stamps/coupons plan.** Employees can be issued with 100 trading stamps or coupons each week. For each absence, they must return 100 stamps/coupons; and 50 for each latecoming. Once a year, a bonus of stamps/coupons is given to the employee with the best record. The stamps/coupons can be cashed in.

- **Monday payday plan.** Companies that distribute wages on Mondays find that absenteeism on that day declines dramatically.

- **Retirement bonus.** An extra payment is given to an employee who resigns or retires for the sick leave time that he or she has accrued but not used.

---

adopting an individual strategy to absence reduction. Many aspects of absence behaviour have a group dimension since group norms influence individual behaviour. Moreover, management needs to be responsive to the problems of implementation. Despite the difficulties described, had it intervened at certain crucial times, and provided the information required, it might still have achieved its objective.

The present section has dealt with the two most common kinds of financial inducements used by companies. These are attendance bonuses, and the offer of paid sick leave where this does not already exist. However, there are also a wide range of other money-producing incentives. Critics argue that these have been dreamed up to bribe employees to come to work. Some of these are shown in Table 10.1.

Every manager should be aware of the disadvantages of offering financial rewards. First, rewards tend to motivate workers who already have good attendance records, rather than the chronic absentees. To become eligible for these awards, regular absentees would have to alter their behaviour drastically, which is seldom likely. Second, if an employee is absent, and therefore ineligible for an award, there is little to motivate his or her continued good attendance. Third, any reward system may have an initial appeal because of its novelty. However, once that novelty wears off, the effectiveness of the system may become reduced. Finally, most of these bonus payments tend to become incorporated into basic pay in wage negotiations.

Non-financial benefits

Sometimes, non-financial benefits may be more welcomed by employees than financial ones. Two strategies can be employed here. The first is to identify the perceived benefits of staying away from work, and to design a programme that rewards good attendance by providing those desired benefits. The benefits that have been offered include accumulated free hours, additional holidays (to provide a break from routine), increased leisure time, and the opportunity to attend to personal business. In this last instance, some companies have found that granting time off for good attendance is an effective way to avoid absenteeism. The plan should be structured so as to discourage the taking of extra days on Mondays, Fridays and around holidays. Thus, for example, under the clock system plan, hourly workers who demonstrate punctuality and good attendance, are not required to punch in and out, and are further rewarded with the opportunity to take time off (without pay).

'We give people time off for domestic problems. We will give them time off with pay, for example, in the case of a bereavement. We don't like the casual absence. Special leave has to be based on record.' (*Whisky blending plant*)

Hotpoint at Llandudno Junction in North Wales offers a service-related sick-pay scheme for its 1200 hourly-paid workers. Introduced in 1976, and operated by a joint management–employee sick-pay committee, the scheme has some interesting features. Five 'floating' days are available to all employees in any one year. These have to be earned in the preceding qualifying year. Each full day of absence in the qualifying year forfeits one free day during the following year. Thus, Hotpoint rewards good attendance by extra paid time off.

The Peugeot and Citroen car companies operate a scheme called the Personal Holiday Accumulation Plan. It provides over a million workers with an opportunity to earn extra days off with pay for good attendance. It thus mixes financial and non-financial benefits. The plan is based upon a points system. Wage earners receive 15 points, and salaried employees, technicians and supervisors receive 9 points, for each week of full attendance. Points may also be earned because of special working conditions. By not taking a leave day immediately before or after a holiday, employees earn 700 points. An interesting feature of the programme is that it requires employees to defer a proportion of the leave they earn, based on age. For an employee under 35 years, one-third is deferred for use after the employee is 50 years old, one-third for use between 35 and 50 years of age, and one-third may be used immediately. For employees between 35 and 50 years, 50% must be deferred; and for employees who are 50 or over, all earned days off may be taken at any time. Absenteeism at Peugeot and Citroen had been 11.5% and 7.7% respectively.

A second strategy focuses on the non-financial recognition of exceptional performance. Money is only one of many ways in which individuals can be rewarded. A recognition programme is based around a unified theme using posters, cards and awards. In one company we studied, at the end of every three months, employees with no more than one absence, received a card signed by the manager notifying and congratulating them on this fact. Employees who had a perfect attendance record, or who missed only one or two days in the whole year, qualified for a small gift, such as a piece of custom-designed jewellery.

Rank Xerox gives a, 'Perfect Attendance Award', which consists of a small gift and a certificate. When it began in 1981, 10.8% of the workforce qualified for the award. By 1986, 31% were qualifying. Building on this success, the company has instituted a 3-year award (won by 12% of the workforce), and is thinking of instituting a ten-year one. In 1981, its absence rate was 5.5% and by 1987, it had dropped to 3.0%.

In a British garment factory that we studied, the management had established levels of performance for each of the female machine operators. These performance levels were set in terms of the quantity of output, quality of output and absence record. If the women exceeded the basic performance set, they received various token gifts in the form of pens, badges, watches and certificates. The very top performers for each month were taken out to a slap-up meal by the management, and received pennants to hang above their machines which recognized and signalled their achievements to the other machinists. Although the top performing girls became eligible for additional financial benefits, in the form of an entry for a lottery to win a holiday abroad, the main thrust of the scheme was to reward the women non-financially by recognizing and publicizing their achievements.

Another piece of research was carried out in an American garment factory composed of 94% women[30]. The company used a range of different absence improvement programmes and controls over a one-year period. The findings showed that, of the techniques used, the personal recognition plan had the most dramatic effect on absence. It reduced it by 37%. The next most effective method was the lottery, in which $100 could be won. An employee's name was entered in the lottery if he or she had a perfect or near-perfect attendance record. The company's recognition programme cost $10 000 to implement, and saved $58 000 in direct costs. Recognition had the greatest impact in terms of reducing absenteeism, changing attitudes and saving money. Although only those employees with two or less days of absence were rewarded, attendance improved across the entire spectrum of the workforce. The features which contributed to the success of this programme were the following. First, employees who had a perfect or near perfect attendance record were publicly recognized each quarter by having their names posted on a bulletin board. In addition, a card was sent to the home of those with good attendance records. Second, the programme was professionally designed and customized to meet the needs of the plant. Third, the personal nature of the small gift created enthusiasm among the (female) recipients.

To conclude this particular section, one can say that the range of studies that have been carried out on these positive reinforcement programmes have all indicated beneficial results[31]. Indeed, it has been argued that the value of these approaches has been underestimated, and that they have had an important influence on reducing voluntary casual absence. Nevertheless, the contributory effect of related factors may also have had an effect, i.e. factors such as feedback to employees, the heightened supervisory focus on attendance, verbal praise and so on. In Britain, financially-focused positive reinforcement techniques became particularly popular during the late 1970s. This was when the third and fourth stages of the then Government's incomes policy were in operation. Some observers suggest that many of the schemes which were designed to positively modify the behaviour of people were successful in their early years, and did achieve their objective[32]. However, it is noticeable that by about 1982, a number of such schemes had been consolidated into basic pay.

One can therefore conclude that the use of these positive reinforcement techniques can help to reduce absenteeism, especially in the short term. Results have been particularly positive where the design and implementation of the programmes has involved significant employee participation[33]. However, many managers are fundamentally opposed to the notion of providing

financial incentives for attendance. Some have queried whether they are
cost-effective. Bonuses have to be paid to individuals who were never part of
the absence problem. The 1987 Industrial Society survey quoted earlier,
found that, of its responding companies, 88% did *not* reward perfect
attendance. Perhaps therefore, these are best used as part of a co-ordinated
strategy to reduce absence, rather than as a one off, 'quick-fix' solution
intended to cure all ills.

Mixed consequence system

It may appear that the choice for management is between a negative, 'knock
'em on the head' approach and a positive, 'bribe 'em back to work' strategy.
Increasingly, however, there has been an interest in integrating the two
approaches by using absence control policies that combine punishments
(based upon legal compliance) with the rewards described in the previous
section. Significant decreases in absence levels were found when production
workers in two plants were rewarded with non-monetary privileges for good
and improving attendance[34]. These same employees were subjected to
progressive disciplinary warnings for excessive and worsening absenteeism.
Similar results were achieved when financial rewards and punishments were
given for attendance and absenteeism respectively[35].

A successful mixed consequence system was introduced into an electronics
factory in Central Scotland. Confronted by unacceptably high absence
levels, especially amongst the production workers, this company introduced
such a system in joint consultation with the factory unions. The scheme
comprised fairly modest attendance bonuses of a few pounds per week.
These were given when targeted improvements were achieved at factory
level. The rewards were accompanied by a relatively severe system of
punishments at the individual level for unsatisfactory attendance. In the
five-year period over which the scheme operated, absence levels were
progressively reduced from 8.5% to under 4%.

This case suggests one additional attraction of the mixed consequence
approach. It would appear that the introduction of an attendance incentive
may act to create a company climate where reasonable sanctions are also
accepted by the workforce as a legitimate management requirement. Thus, a
state of legal compliance can be achieved in a situation where the unac-
companied introduction of sanctions would perhaps have met with serious
employee resentment or resistance. In conclusion, there appears to be
reasonable evidence to support the view that within the range of people
techniques, the mixed consequence systems can be a particularly powerful
method of dealing with an absence problem.

Chapter 11
Work techniques

Work techniques are the second important means of controlling absence. As the label suggests, the main focus is not primarily directly upon the individuals involved, but rather upon their associated work situation. There are a number of areas at which work-focused techniques have been targeted. These include changing the job situation of the employee; changing employees' values and job expectations; seeking to affect individual behaviour through changes in selection and training; influencing attendance through supervisory action and group norms; and increasing the ability of an employee to attend. The various work techniques are listed in Table 11.1.

Table 11.1 Examples of work techniques for influencing attendance

Associated absence factor	Technique
2.1 Job situation	Job enrichment
	Work rotation
	Group work design
	Employee participation
	Changing physical working conditions
2.2 Employee values and job expectations	Behaviour modelling
	Matching people to jobs
	Self-management
2.3 Individual behaviour	Stress management
	Selection
2.4 Influencing attendance	Supervisory interviewing
	Group norms
	Counselling provision
2.5 Ability to attend	Medical services
	Company crèche
	Flexible working hours
	Employee-sponsored child care

The work techniques selected by a company will reflect management's explicit or implicit assumption about the cause of the absence problem. The above list has been structured by categorizing each intervention technique in line with the classification system of the major absence influences which were introduced in Chapter 4 as the Steers and Rhodes[1] model.

Job situation

Many of the work-focused techniques that do exist are directed at aspects of the job situation. They have been shown to produce favourable results. Many writers have noted the excellent attendance levels of such employees as managers and professional and skilled workers[2]. Throughout our own investigations, the differences in absence rates between personnel in staff and management grades, and those working at shopfloor level, were found to be significant in all cases. Examples of these differences are shown in Table 11.2.

These figures support the 'absence rule of thumb' quoted in the 1987 Industrial Society absence survey[3]. This was that with all three types of absence – medically certified, self-certified, and uncertified – manual workers are absent almost twice as much as staff, who themselves are absent almost twice as much as management. Supervisory absence almost fits exactly half-way between staff and managerial absence.

Of course, one needs to take account of genuine illness caused by differences in working conditions and accidents. Nevertheless, commentators have suggested that what distinguishes the managerial and staff groups from the manual shopfloor employees is that the former have 'job identification' while the latter do not[4]. They argue that, in order to arouse and maximize job identification in others, management must ensure that the job itself provides sufficient variety, complexity, challenge and the exercise of skill to engage the abilities of the employee. One would expect that work groups whose jobs possessed these characteristics would have lower absence rates.

Table 11.2 Typical absence rates for different levels of employees

Company A: Shipbuilding company	Absence rate
Staff	3%
Manual	11%
Company B: Bottling plant	
Staff	3%
Engineering craftsmen	less than 5%
Building trades craftsmen	less than 5%
Supervisors of general workers	5-10%
General workers	16%

'The coopers are not problem attenders. They're not an unhappy group. Although it's physical work, their job is a more interesting one than that of the others. It's repetitive, but skill is required.' (*Whisky blending plant*)

* * *

'One can see that we had lower absence when we had a small domestic appliances division. This involved mainly handwork in teams. You could make the whole thing yourself, or opt to be part of a conveyor-belt system. There was a certain amount of choice about how you organized yourself to work. Now we see lower absence in the fittings division where it's a handwork area, compared to the machine area. We have moved in the same sort of philosophy there. It's an "I made that fitting feeling", rather than the more impersonal world of the relay machine that is chucking parts at you at the rate of one a second. It may be that the working conditions and environments may be better, it may be to do with the work being more personalized.' (*Electrical components manufacturer*)

However, creating variety, complexity, challenge and the exercise of skills is very difficult in many jobs. One can hypothesize that when changes such as job enrichment, work rotation, and group work designs are implemented, they may have a favourable impact on the employee's identification with his or her job and company, and will subsequently positively affect attendance motivation. Additionally, companies may seek to encourage workers to internalize organizational goals so that they will see these as being their own. In this way, they will become less inclined to break the rules[5]. Tactics used by management to achieve this may include allowing employees greater participation, and giving them greater feedback on performance. Job rotation has been a popular approach amongst the manufacturing companies that we studied.

'On the line you have various functions. Quality control, inspection, machine operator, packer and so on. We tend to rotate them on the line to reduce the boredom. We do it systematically. Usually it's one hour on any function, and then a move to another one. Really it's the best we can do.' (*Food processing*)

Steps can be taken to increase the likelihood that employees will be satisfied with the job situation, and consequently will want to come to work. Managers can examine the nature of the tasks to be performed by employees to determine the extent to which such tasks can be enriched. This strategy can be used for both blue-collar and white-collar workers. Simple changes in job design can produce increases in task identity, variety, responsibility and job challenge. For most people, the requirements of a satisfying job (after adequate wages and conditions) are that the work should offer some element of challenge; individuals should know what their job is and how well they are performing; some area of the job must allow them to make decisions; the work should be organized to allow them to get support and assistance from colleagues when necessary; they should have some idea of how their job fits into the overall department or company picture; there should be some element of desirable future prospects either in terms of promotion, security, stable income or increased skills, and there should be some recognized status enhancement. These elements should be kept in mind when assessing policies and techniques to change departments, work groups or individual jobs.

A large insurance company initiated changes in job design amongst one group of key-punch operators, while not making any changes in a comparative group[6]. Prior to the change, both groups had been instructed not to correct errors in cards, 'no matter how obvious they looked'. Instead, the errors would be reviewed and corrected by assignment clerks. To enrich their work, the key-punch operators in the experimental group were allowed to assign their own work activities, and to inspect their own work for accuracy. As a result of this small change in the level of responsibility (job scope), absenteeism in the experimental group declined by 24%, while it increased 29% in the group that had not had its work changed.

Changing the physical conditions in which work is carried out is another aspect of the job situation that can help to reduce absence. Psychological disorders at work have been identified in the United States as one of the top ten occupational diseases. Poor working conditions, and the presence of physical danger, can be the key causes of such distress. Work environment strategies involve improving the physical conditions in which employees work. Apart from causing absence through physical accidents, poor working conditions can contribute to stress at work. One study suggested that the design of a control room was itself a variable in the stress experienced by nuclear power plant operators[7]. The authors referred to a stress factor highlighted in the Three Mile Island accident which was the distraction caused by excessive emergency alarms.

Reducing high levels of noise is one strategy that management can adopt. In certain types of manufacturing companies, noise has a detrimental effect on health. In high noise areas of shipbuilding companies for instance, the absentee rates can be very high. Changes in the use of noisy tools can reduce the worst effects of noise. In closed working environments, noise can often get trapped. Fumes, and lack of ventilation are further hazards. The provision of protected work areas for staff who have previously been expected to work outdoors can be a help, as can a systematic policy to reduce accidents, for example, by ensuring that people wear the eye-goggles and ear-defenders with which they are provided. There may be a need for more education about, for example, wearing ear-defenders. A study in a steel-manufacturing company which made castings revealed that poor working conditions, due to excessive heat and danger, were major stressors which led to poor individual health and performance[8].

A study which we cited earlier showed that better-maintained machinery not only increased productivity and reduced injuries, but it also reduced employee absence. Our own investigations of a shipbuilding company revealed how management refurbished work facilities, reorganized work groups and provided better working conditions for individuals. It provided separate, well-maintained booths for welders which meant fewer distractions and less frequent breakdowns, resulting in increased productivity. In the machine shop, acoustic walls were erected between machines, thereby providing a quieter, more habitable environment for each operator. In addition to increasing productivity, absence sickness was also reduced.

The most effective refurbishment strategy, however, was implemented in the company's design office. Better natural daylight was made available, and more individual space was provided. The overall effect was the provision of a brighter and more receptive facility. The consequence of this was that a management initiative to introduce new technology in the form of computer-aided design was readily accepted without the usual opposition. The implications for absence were equally significant. The staff in the design office had, up to that time, considered themselves to be second-class employees. This had engendered negative work attitudes in them, and a work ethic that a level of performance just above the minimum was sufficient. The change in the physical environment acted to enhance their self-esteem and the overall perception of their role, and altered their attitudes both to the technical changes and to the behaviour of other functions. Since the decision to be absent is, in many cases, an attitudinal one, anything that can be done to develop a positive picture of self and the organization, is to be welcomed. Simpler, and less dramatic physical changes can also have a benefit – for example, putting new desks in offices, providing better communication systems (notice boards, tannoy speakers, dot matrix signs), new lights over work benches, and installing new heating systems. While perhaps trivial in themselves, each improvement has been shown to alter the employees' perception of their work environment, and their attitude to their jobs.

Employee values and job expectations

It must be recognized that not everybody will either want enriched jobs or an increased degree of involvement. Some people are satisfied with job security and would prefer to foster allegiances outside the workplace.

'We did consider job enlargement and job enrichment. The response of the unions was, "our people are happy doing what they're doing, and don't want to be moved around". One group of trade unionists suggested job rotation as a result of a shop stewards course, but they got little support. There seem to be people who just like to come in, do what they're doing, and go home at night.' (Bakery)

This realization leads to a different type of intervention which is related to managers' and employees' values and their job expectations. Bula[9] studied a hospital and asked the managers why they allowed employees to abuse sick-leave provision. The managers replied that they condoned it because they felt that it was natural that people would be sick from time to time; that there was nothing they could do about it, and that they themselves believed that paid leave was a benefit. Following this disclosure, a direct approach was made by senior management in order to change supervisory and employee values and expectations of sick leave as a fringe benefit. Management wanted them to understand that a benefit was something that was granted to all employees as part of their employment. In the case of holidays, employees were expected to use the benefit to the full. However, sick pay was not, and in management's view, should not be considered as, a benefit in the same way. It was more accurately described as an insurance policy to protect employees' wages in case of emergency. The employer did not expect the employee to use all the available 'sick time'. Instead, it was to be used when needed.

Employees can, however, have or develop the view that sick leave does represent a fringe benefit the same as a holiday. Bula argued that sick leave can become a self-fulfilling prophecy. Employees live up to management's expectations. If management expects them to be sick, they will take sick days off. Instead, he recommends that management should expect all employees to be available on schedule. To reinforce this view, management's expectation should be stressed at the job interview. Prospective employees need to be informed of management's expectations for being on the job. Once hired, the department supervisor should emphasize the importance of attendance. The same point is taken up at the performance appraisal meeting, where the employee's attendance record forms part of the appraisal criteria. Constant reminders, backed up by a procedure that rewards attendance and not absence, can act to establish the importance of attendance in the employee's mind.

Individual behaviour

In the area of personal characteristics, it has been found that employee stress is correlated with absence levels. There are two possible work-focused solutions to this problem. If the stress-producing characteristics cannot be changed (for example, because the technology or the procedures are fixed), then careful staff selection may be needed in order to identify those people who will be least affected by the stress-inducing circumstances. Some writers have suggested that employees should be assigned to the jobs with which they are 'psychologically compatible'. This task involves making job content congruent with the employee's needs and goals. For example, careful matching at the selection stage, can reduce employee turnover later, as well as increasing the employee's work attendance motivation[10]. If this is not possible, the persons involved in the stressful situation may have to be helped to manage their stress. In this context, absence can be seen as a response by the employee withdrawing from a situation which causes discomfort.

So far as selection is concerned, a great interest has been shown in what are called *realistic job previews*[11]. These represent an organizational attempt to provide the employee with an objective view of the features of the job in question. Such previews allow the candidate to ascertain the perceived probability of a satisfying and productive experience in the job. They permit the accurate matching of an applicant's capabilities and needs with the job requirements, and with the organizational climate. This is achieved by describing both the positive and the negative aspects of the job. These descriptions are obtained by management from exit interviews, and from attitude surveys conducted amongst current employees. Each applicant receives a half-hour presentation of the results of the employee survey which describes the job in relation to customer relations, co-workers, supervisors, duties, policies and hours of work. That person may also have a talk about the job with a current employee. Applicants are given information upon which to make an informed decision about whether or not to accept the job offer.

It is hoped that the person who finally accepts the job will have a greater commitment to that choice than someone who, perhaps, may have received a false impression about what the work entails, and particularly what pressures are likely to be applied. Realistic job previews have been conducted successfully with part-time checkout operators in a supermarket, with technicians working in an institution for the mentally ill, and with telephone operators. This clarification of expectations, especially at the employee's point of entry, and the explanation of the potential rewards of attending satisfactorily, was a strategy used in the Oldsmobile plant of General Motors. Prospective engine and assembly employees were shown a film demonstrating realistically the type of operations to which they would be assigned.

How does one deal with employees in the job who are already experiencing stress that is reflected in absences from work? If it is obvious that there is a continual work overload, the job may have to be changed to reduce the workload to a tolerable level. Additionally, job training may be provided by management, and a set of clearly written instructions for performing the task requirements of the job may be necessary in order to reduce role ambiguity. Similarly, managers may take steps to reduce role conflict by, for example, clarifying reporting procedures.

A small but growing number of companies encourage healthy life styles amongst their employees. They provide fitness and health facilities for their staff, and operate wellness programmes[12]. Pepsico Inc. provides a comprehensive wellness programme at its world headquarters in Purchase, New

York. The facilities include a running track, stationary bicycles, massage facilities, baths and saunas. Full-time therapists and doctors are on hand to tailor-make fitness programmes for interested employees. Initially reserved for managerial staff, this facility has now been made available to all employees[13].

However, it is not just in the United States that such facilities are offered. Scotrail, the Scottish division of British Rail has, since 1984, initiated a major organization-wide programme of change[14]. The introduction of an employee health education programme has been a small, although important part of Scotrail's approach to absence control. All employees, including station personnel and loco drivers, are given information about diet and healthy eating. Heart attacks, especially in the west of Scotland, are a major cause of disability and illness absence. Mini-gym facilities have been established at a depot in Glasgow (Yoker) with another planned for Motherwell. As part of this same strategy, rest-room facilities for staff have also been dramatically improved. For example, the facilities for Scotrail personnel at Glasgow Central Station have been completely refurbished, and are now unrecognizable. They contain comfortable furniture in which employees can relax, watch television or play snooker during their breaks when they have finished their tasks. These pleasant surroundings help to relieve the tensions of stressful jobs such as train driving.

In an increasing number of different companies, a great deal of effort has begun to be put into providing emotional support for staff. Whereas before, such support was obtained by employees informally, management is increasingly prepared to provide counselling and other advisory facilities for employees. Their problems, while they may stem from their home environment, nevertheless affect their work performance. This new preparedness, argued Cooper, was the result of two developments. First, it was the result of increasing litigation in the United States by employees against companies, for the stress that is alleged to exist at places of work. Second, it is caused by an increase in stress-like epidemics which adversely affect absenteeism amongst the employees working in factories and offices[15].

In practical terms, employee support has been provided in different forms. A copper-processing company provides counselling facilities for all home and work-related problems, and has helped to organize an Alcoholics Anonymous group[16]. The Converse Corporation of Wilmington, Massachusetts, provides a voluntary relaxation programme for its staff[17], allowing them to take breaks during the normal working week. These have led to improvements in health, job performance and well-being. All of these factors are aimed at reducing the likelihood of absence. A large chemical company in Britain offers an employee counselling service to provide stress counselling for staff. After four years of operation it has been used by 10% of the staff. Finally, employees may be offered the service of companies such as Stress Management Ltd. This company claims substantial success in reducing absenteeism through stress alleviation techniques. In addition, there are an increasing number of stress consultants who offer courses on managing stress at work.

Influencing attendance

A number of influences have been brought to bear on employees to improve their attendance. Some of these emanate from the employee's immediate supervisor; some relate to the force of group norms operating within the work group; and yet others are derived from company-wide counselling. We will consider these three influences in turn.

Role of supervisor

Much of the popular literature on tackling absence emphasizes the importance of the role of the first-line supervisor. This suggestion does have an intuitive appeal. Surprisingly, research on this topic has not found a consistent linkage between supervisory practices and employee attendance[18]. Most writers, however, believe that supervisors can be effective. Scott and Markham's[19] survey highlighted the role of the supervisor in the absence control process. He was involved in activities such as the maintenance of daily attendance records (ninth most effective control method), and the interviewing of employees after they had been absent (rated eleventh most effective). See Table 9.2.

Interviewing all employees on their return from a period of absence, however short, is now a common feature of many absence control strategies. The purpose is partly to discover the underlying reasons for absence, but perhaps more importantly, to indicate to the employee that his or her absence has been noticed. At Warner Lambert, for example, all employees returning from a period of sickness absence have a talk with their supervisor. The discussion focuses on the employee's health, and on the identification of any assistance that the company can offer. At Land Rover UK, the control of absence is the responsibility of supervisors. It is they who apply the procedures within the disciplinary code. Their tasks involve monitoring attendance records, and initiating disciplinary action when this is deemed to be appropriate. The personnel department maintains an overview of the situation.

Of the companies surveyed by the 1987 Industrial Society study[20], 45% said that absentees were always questioned on their return to work, and 62% of respondents said that it was the supervisor who conducted the initial interview. The larger the organization, the more likely it was that the absentee would be questioned on his or her return to work, and that the interview would be carried out by a supervisor.

Supervisors have an important role to play, under both the negative approach and the positive reinforcement approach to absence control. A major theme is that of line managers and supervisors taking responsibility for the absence problem. One personnel manager put it bluntly, 'It's really got to happen out there. We in personnel can enforce it, make it happen, but we need the supervisors on the continental shifts. They've got to pick up the absences, and act on them'.

Many companies have delegated responsibility for absence control down to supervisors, while centralizing the keeping and analysing of attendance records. Responsibility for action has therefore been taken away from the Personnel Department where it was remote, and where reactions to situations tended to be slow.

'We operate our procedure in the following way. As a result of this self-certification, the employees who take a few days off on a regular basis, have to go to their supervisors, and say why they were absent. That can act as a great deterrent because people don't like going up in front of supervisors or management to fill in a form to say they have been absent. It stretches their imagination to find reasons.' (*Whisky bottling plant*)

However, there are problems in delegating responsibility for absence control to supervisors, as was discussed earlier under the issue of the standardization of responses between the different supervisors. Hence the importance of the continuing role of the Personnel Department to provide the basic statistics, and ensure equity of approach, without, at the same time, reducing the supervisor's role in the absence control process.

'When anyone has been absent, their record goes to the Personnel Manager on the day of their return, together with their historical record over the past ten years. The Personnel Manager looks at them, and then decides if a warning should be issued. If yes, he passes it on to the supervisor who will issue the warning. If it gets to a dismissal situation, it would be the line manager and the Personnel Manager who would do it jointly. The initial warnings are issued by the supervisors, having first been vetted by the Personnel Manager so as to ensure standardization.' (*Glass manufacturer*)

Where such a standardized approach is lacking, the problem is easy to see. One personnel manager recounted the situation when the production managers, rather than his department were issuing the warnings. He described it as an absolute shambles. One manager was as hard as nails, while another would let anybody through. When these cases ended up going through the grievance procedure, it was the Personnel Manager who received the criticism. He was asked why, for the same offence, one person had received a warning, while another, whose absence was ten times worse, received nothing. In the end, the Personnel Management department had to take over. Frequently the problem is solved by a computer monitoring system picking up the persistent non-attenders, checking past absence data, and recommending the appropriate action to be taken by the supervisor. This method combines equitably the benefits of central monitoring and supervisory action.

The strategy used most frequently to overcome the reluctance of supervisors to take responsibility for controlling absence is communication and education. Communication involves explaining to them the importance of controlling absence, and emphasizing both the benefits of cost reduction to the company, and the benefits to the supervisors themselves. Reduced absence allows them to carry out their supervisory duties with less fuss.

'Often the Personnel Manager is the person who collects and issues absence figures on a weekly basis. If he identifies certain people, he gets on to the supervisor to find out what he is doing about it, because he ought to be acting. The supervisor will speak to the individual, show him the problem pattern, explain that the issue could become a disciplinary one, and identify if a personal problem is involved. On a monthly basis, this reporting pattern will show up a profile for every employee in the plant. Personnel will therefore support the supervisor with information.' (*Glass manufacturer*)

Effective supervisory action is based on adequate training. Many American companies offer supervisory training programmes which specifically focus on attendance control. In these courses, the supervisors are trained with the use of behaviour modelling techniques that were originally developed in clinical psychology.

Supervisors are trained so that they can undertake a counselling as well as a directing role. The management style currently used by many supervisors may not only ignore the employee's intrinsic motivation, but may actually inhibit it. The style might encourage absenteeism amongst employees if they felt that the penalty from the supervisor for being away was less than for being late. When employees feel that the organization does not trust them to be responsible adults, there is no reason for them to reciprocate by trusting the company to act more responsibly towards them.

The education and training of supervisors is therefore most important. Courses teach positive reinforcement techniques which help the supervisor get across to absent employees that they have been missed. Assembly-line workers can feel anonymous, and think that no one will notice if they go missing. This was the message of the Sandvik company example mentioned earlier[21].

'We have an agreement with the hourly-paid unions. There is a disciplinary procedure, we train supervisors as to how to operate the procedure. We train them with video. The objective is that where there are instances of the occasional absent day, the supervisors will nip it in the bud at their level.' (*Glass manufacturer*)

Encouragement of desirable group norms

The second major source of pressure on the individual to attend is his or her work group. Group norms play an important part both in encouraging employees to attend, and in making them feel guilty about being absent. Management has therefore to encourage the development of positive attendance norms. Group norms which support regular attendance are more likely to develop in small work groups in which there is considerable task interdependence between members. Additionally, the more the responsibility for task completion is felt to be in the hands of the work group, for example, as in the case of an autonomous work group, the more likely it is that the group will exert pressure on its members to attend. Thus, the design of the work group and its size can affect attendance motivation because it increases an employee's satisfaction with his or her job, as well as increasing the pressure to attend. The management of group norms therefore, can be a particularly effective control method for management.

One of the problems reported by personnel managers in our study was that the production technology used in the company, often made the employees operate as *individuals*. Thus they did not feel themselves to be the members of a *group* and hence were not subject to any form of group pressures[22].

'If you're one in 150 and are flexible and interchangeable with all of them, you can have a day's absence and know that someone will cover for it. The worker doesn't think he's leaving someone in the lurch. In fact, with the overtime provided, he might feel that he's doing someone a favour.'
(*Garment manufacturer*)

Where employees do not see themselves as part of a group, being absent becomes part of a company's culture. This can have a negative influence on attendance, as one of our respondents explained. 'It's almost become a part of life and accepted that shopfloor operatives are absent most often. The point is brought up that they get away with murder, and that it is the staff and management who are the loyal workers. This causes resentment at times.'

Some companies purposely create work groups in order to foster circumstances in which attendance norms favouring regular attendance can develop and become institutionalized. In contrast to the circumstances quoted earlier, if there is no overtime, if the work is made intrinsically more interesting, and if employees know that their workmates will have to do extra work to cover for them, there will be a greater incentive for them to come in.

'We had a crackdown on absence. The general level of absence went down. The people who didn't exploit the system were happier that those who did abuse it were getting caught. You got the aside from the shopfloor – "well done, it's time somebody did something about X." It had a beneficial effect throughout the workforce. They realized, "I'm the honest Joe, why do they get away with it?"' (*Confectionery manufacturer*)

* * *

'There were a core of people who abused the system, and a majority who felt that they were working for a very good company. One of the things that helped in the implementation of the new absence control procedure was the help from those who were good attenders dealing with those who were not. That ended up raising morale.' (*Metal products factory*)

Keeping groups sufficiently small to permit cohesion and good communications is therefore another thing that management can institute in line with the recommendation that there should be less task specialization. This factor has constantly been found to increase employee motivation on the job. Taylor[23] described a case study in which moral pressure on employees affected their absence behaviour. The situation involved lateness, but the implications for absence are clear. The lateness behaviour of day workers and continuous three-cycle shift workers was measured. Under the factory rules, day workers lost pay for any lateness over two minutes. In contrast, the shift workers had a 30-minute time allowance. It was found that day workers of all ages were late twice as often as shift workers. It appeared that shift workers (but not the day workers) had to remain at work until they were relieved by their replacements. This moral pressure between employees, argued Taylor, far outweighed any financial disincentive.

When considering the notion of groups more broadly, the key formal group whose agreement needs to be obtained is that of the trade union. In many of the companies that we studied, when union representatives realized the problems that absence caused, and how it endangered the profitability and competitiveness of the company, they were generally willing to support fair management procedures to reduce it. The elimination of absence, after all, represented a way of reducing costs that did not involve redundancies.

'Also essential from the company's point of view, was the complete agreement of the unions, the AEU and TAS. They recognized that a high level of absenteeism was bad for everyone in that it undermined the future of the company, so that we got them to agree to an overall site target of keeping absenteeism below 3%.' (*Electrical products factory*)

Writers have recommended getting the unions involved at an early stage. If they are consulted, they often recognize that involvement is in their own best interest. In one study conducted in General Motors[24], the company negotiated with its union (the UAW) an agreement which tied fringe benefits to the hours worked. Employees who were absent for 10% of their scheduled hours during the first six months of their contract were placed on a list and warned that any further such absenteeism would result in a loss of fringe benefits for the next six months. As a result of this scheme, absence fell from 18.3% to 13% within a two-year period. General Motors estimated that the overall cost saving per year throughout the company was millions of dollars.

'We've had a great deal of co-operation from our trade unions. We are in a very price-competitive situation with most of our products. They accept that anything that you can do to cut costs can protect some of their jobs. They saw absence as an avoidable cost. We got a tremendous amount of co-operation from the trade unions to get the figure down.' (*Electrical company*)

'It is always the minority who are absent; the majority are happy. Even the trade union representative asked the company to take action against the worst offenders. There is an unspoken acceptance. You might say it helps morale when they see absence is low and that the company's keeping it under control.' (*Electrical company*)

* * *

'The first real analysis of absence was in 1985–6. The review was done with a great deal of co-operation from the trade union against the background of the business getting more competitive. They were really frightened of their future at that time.' (*Electrical company*)

Company counselling

The third and final strategy used to influence good attendance is counselling. The 1987 Industrial Society study[25] showed that 63% of responding companies provided a counselling service for employees. The larger the organization, the greater the likelihood of there being a counselling service available. In half the cases, this was provided by the Personnel Department, and in 30% of companies, by the Occupational Health Department. The provision of counselling was the third most quoted reason given by managers to explain a reduction in absence. Clearly therefore, many companies provide this service, and believe that it works.

Ability to attend

The work-focused techniques in this strategy seek to reinforce the employee's ability to attend. Practices include:

● setting up crèche facilities for young working mothers
● flexible time working

Crèche facilities

It has been argued that the provision of crèche facilities can counter the fact that women have more days' absence than men, especially during the childbearing and rearing years. There is a belief that child care responsibilities account for women's greater absenteeism. Hence, the provision by the employer of quality child care can reduce such female absenteeism. Many companies in the United States claim that such programmes also increase the ability of the firm to attract better employees, improve employee attitudes, generate favourable publicity for the employer, and improve community relations.

Flexible time working

Another thing that has reduced absence is the introduction of flexible working hours (flexitime). This enables employees to balance better their non-work demands against their working time responsibilities. A number of studies have shown that this can be an effective intervention in reducing absence[26]. In two instances, moderate declines in absenteeism were reported after the introduction of flexitime. The use of a four-day, forty-hour week (known as the 4–40 hours approach) is a variation on this theme. Krausz and Freibach[27] studied the application of flexible time schedules. They found that absenteeism was significantly lower under a flexible, than under a rigid, work schedule. Moreover, married women and mothers were found to have the lowest rates of absenteeism when employed under such schedules.

Flexitime has been widely used in Europe, particularly in West Germany since 1967. By the early 1980s it had been adopted by over 5000 firms throughout the Continent. In use, flexitime has nearly always led to improved morale, reduced absenteeism, and improved productivity. It seems to work because it represents a response to an important need of workers. This is that, given the opportunity and the responsibility to modify a work schedule, all workers (and in particular the younger ones who are particularly sensitive to free time), can be educated to plan for absences in a way that does not adversely affect the company's operation.

Some companies allow their employees to take one day or a half-day holiday to attend to urgent business in order to avoid casual (and therefore unscheduled) absence. Others work *short Fridays* as part of a four-and-a-half-day working week. The employees of Lambert Warner complete their 37.5–40 working hours in 4.5 days. Their short Friday finishes at 1.30 p.m. Single and half-day holidays can be taken by employees. During 1987, the company's absence rate fell from 7.5% to 6.5%, and fluctuated between 6.5% and 4% in the six months following the implementation of the new absence control plan.

At Baxi Heating, the approach is the same. Employees work a 37.5-hour week. They receive 8 statutory days' holiday, and 27.5 days' annual holidays. Of the latter, 9.5 days are *floating* and any number of these can be taken as half days. Their four-and-a-half-day week finishes at midday on Friday. Thus the same number of hours are worked in a shorter period. In 1987, Baxi Heating's company-wide absence rate was 3.7%. This was composed of a 4.5% absence rate for manual workers, and 1.7% rate for staff employees. It presented a significant improvement on previous levels.

Chapter 12
Organizational techniques

The third and final family of absence control techniques focuses on company-wide interventions. In the previous chapters, a number of these techniques were described. Some of them sought to change the behaviour of employees directly (by punishing or rewarding them), while others did it indirectly (by changing their work situation). However, these different techniques need not be introduced in isolation. Writers often recommend the adoption of a co-ordinated programme of change techniques which embraces several strategies. The mixed consequence approach described previously, is one example of such a strategy. Where the proposed set of interventions are sufficiently comprehensive and integrated, the 'package' may represent an organization-wide change strategy. It may be directed specifically at absence control, or it may be targeted at a range of productivity and quality improving goals of which absence reduction is only one.

An organizational approach that is directed specifically at absence control recognizes that employee absence is the result of the interaction of a large number of different variables. These relate to the individual, the company, and the environment. Consequently it is held that overemphasis on any one aspect can lead to a sub-optimal solution to the absence problem. This, in turn, can cause new problems to emerge elsewhere in the company. For example, a clampdown on unauthorized absence may lead to an increase in 'certified' sickness absence. Alternatively, an increase in punitive measures may result in a deterioration in the climate of industrial relations. These dysfunctional consequences can be avoided if one constructs a comprehensive programme of changes.

Nissan's UK car plant in Washington, Tyne and Wear, uses just such a range of approaches. Attendance lists are displayed in the plant, identifying absentees of a particular work section by name, and by the dates on which they failed to attend. The implication is that they let down their colleagues by their failure to turn up to work. At first sight, it would appear that this absence control technique should be listed amongst the person-focused (negative consequence) ones. However, the idea itself came not from management, but from the shopfloor employees themselves. It is not a universal practice throughout the plant, as it has been adopted by some sections and not by others. Management's contribution has been to take a broad organizational view, and to create an atmosphere within the plant, where such a thing is possible, but not insisted upon. Management has paid attention to creating motivation, job interest, and the provision of a reasonable working environment. Nissan is seen as a success story, with a major plant investment and expansion announced in December 1987. Their overall absence rate is less than 3% which is recognized to be a remarkable achievement in the motor-car industry.

The Advisory, Conciliation and Arbitration Service[1] has stressed the need for a broad approach. It might require significant procedural changes which are likely to include employee involvement at an early stage. Its other recommendations include:

- good working conditions and high safety standards

- adequate training and the early encouragement of good work habits among new starters

- optimal group work design

- job satisfaction achieved through job design, training, career prospects and communication procedures

- supervisory training and concern for employees

- adequate recognition of individual circumstances of employees through facilities such as flexitime, crèches, special leave and so on.

The Industrial Society's booklet[2] on absenteeism recommended a similarly comprehensive approach. It emphasized that any plan for absence control must consider both group absence behaviour and individual absence behaviour. A number of strategies were therefore proposed.

At the *group* level, it recommended creating a climate of concern with visible senior management support, the provision of adequate, meaningful and well-communicated statistics on absence and its effects, and the development of policies which maximized job satisfaction through:

- the creation of an open and participatory atmosphere

- proper training and selection of supervisors

- paying adequate attention to job design, group interaction, prospects for advancement, and to employee recognition.

At the *individual level*, the Industrial Society booklet suggested the development of specific tactics for absence control. For example:

- ensuring that medical, personnel and supervisory staff work together to address key issues

- using trial periods effectively with regard to new employees

- considering some form of incentive scheme, while recognizing its short-term value

- carefully applying a fair system of sanctions

- using a rolling programme of absence control measures to maintain attention to the importance of good attendance.

In order to give an example of an organizationally-focused approach, we report in detail upon the steps taken by one manufacturer in the electrical products business. It should be noted that, in this example, absence reduction was a means to a wider end (greater competitiveness), rather than an end in itself.

Diamond Measurements Ltd: a case study of the application of organizational techniques

An important and recurring theme in organization-wide attendance improvement programmes is the achievement of heightened employee commitment. Since this aspect is also basic to the broadly based activity of organizational change, it is appropriate to consider it in some depth. The organizational strategy pursued by one of the companies in our own study, can provide an illustration of what we recommend. For confidentiality, we have called the organization Diamond Measurements Ltd.

Diamond manufactured electrical protective devices. It used a technology that was old, but whose process was complex and intrinsically difficult, even though the product itself was simple. Because the technology was old, there were inherent problems in actually operating it, and making thousands of electrical units, all to the same standard, week in, week out. The factory employed 750 people, and had a payroll cost of £6 million. In the past the company had budgeted for a 9% absence level (which cost it £540 000), but it had now reduced that figure to 7% (which cost it £420 000). The company's actual absence rate, at the time of the study, was 5.6%.

Over two-thirds of the employees were production and process operators. The factory was organized into 4 work areas. The first produced household electricity meters using high-speed automatic and semi-automatic equipment. The machine-controlled environment was very noisy and the work was repetitive. A second area produced protective relays at a slightly lower speed, although the environment was similar in that it was machine-controlled. The third area produced hospital bedsets each of which included a radio and a unit for summoning the nurse. Manufacture of this equipment called for a mixture of hand and machine work. Finally there was the area which manufactured high-voltage protection relays.

The 4 work areas were physically separate, although the protection relays and the hospital bedsets areas were made in the same building but at different ends of it. In the past, employees in one work area stayed in that area until they were promoted. Some of the jobs were inherently interesting, but many more were not.

Traditionally the company had a long-standing absence problem for which it was unable to identify the specific causes. The absence figure used to be in the 12–14% range. People used to shrug their shoulders and claim that it was endemic to the area and to the technology. The company has, however, been able to reduce its absence rate to 5–6% over a ten-year period. The approach used has increasingly been an organization-wide one, which has broadened out over time. This strategy is partly based on the belief that there is no one single cause of absence. If the causes are many and varied, the control strategies must be similarly diverse.

Philosophy

A starting point for the absence control programme is the establishment of an objective or goal. That objective needs to be determined by circumstances and personal values. Some respondents felt that any level of absence which impeded getting the budgeted production out could not be tolerated. Diamond therefore took the view that any absence was unacceptable. They said to their employees, 'You're supposed to be here 235 days a year; you've missed 10%, and that's unacceptable'.

They began by zeroing in on individuals who were bad attenders. Absence records were changed from a frequency measure, to a duration, percentage of the working year, and reason basis. Record-keeping became more sophisticated and comprehensive. The first tactic was to revise the absence procedures. To put these activities into perspective, it should be noted that the reduction of absence by Diamond was part of a broader and wide-ranging strategy that was designed to make the company's products more competitive. Thus, they were not solving the absence problem *per se*, but rather seeking to reduce absence (along with making other changes) in order to achieve competitiveness.

Underlying the strategy was the belief that, outside the factory gate, the employees were considered responsible enough to have families, take on mortgages, and enter into hire-purchase commitments. However, as soon as they came through the gates, and punched the clock card, the company treated them as idiots. The view was taken by Diamond that if you treated the employees like adults, the vast majority would respond as adults. People wanted to be treated as responsible members of the community. The changes that Diamond has implemented can be considered under the broad headings of absence procedures, union representation, flexible manning, flexitime, communication, training, and job enrichment.

In implementing its strategy, Diamond provided increased amounts of information to its employees. Management found that if a sensible and logical view was taken of the data, employees and their unions often came to the same conclusion as the management. This was because the number of available options at any one time was fairly limited. In the past, management had felt too afraid to let employees have this information. However, it found that once they did get it, their response, to quote the personnel manager was, 'Yes, that's what we've got to do, and they rolled up their sleeves to do it'. Indeed, the company acknowledges that the management has been slower to adapt to some of the initiatives than have the shopfloor. Management tended to look at the problems, whereas the shopfloor was much more willing to give new ideas a try, and to stop them if they did not work. Inevitably many of the changes were difficult for managers and supervisory level staff to come to terms with. Many felt tremendously threatened by them. Indeed they admit that they do not like them. The logical consequence of the changes now being initiated is that managerial jobs will disappear as managerial functions become absorbed by the work groups.

The major change, and hence the greatest pressure has been put upon the middle managers. There has been a tremendous requirement to keep people informed. Moreover, employees now want to debate things more than they did in the past. For some managers, this 'management by committee' is something of a nuisance. Overall however, Diamond's managers have responded well to difficult circumstances. As the process got going, people came to know more, and everybody started arriving at the same conclusions more quickly. Initially there was resistance to the new ideas, and managers disliked the requirement to communicate quite so much. Now, however, such communication is seen as being beneficial in the long term, since it makes the factory easier to run. The change process is more difficult for management than for the shopfloor because the former has more to lose. The effect of the changes is that the shopfloor staff see their jobs as getting more interesting, their pay increasing, and they receive a number of other tangible benefits. In contrast, the managers may feel that the place is becoming unmanageable.

Changes in the absence procedure

Recognizing that the absence figure included an element of malingering, the company instituted a staged revision of its absence procedure. The initial procedure indicated to the employees the concern with which management viewed absenteeism. However, because management's message was weak about the issue, it also signalled its reluctance to do anything about it. Management did not seem to be sufficiently concerned about absence to fire anyone over it. As the revisions of the absence procedure occurred, the so-called safety clauses for employees were progressively removed. Diamond's current procedure is now tough, and it penalizes employees for short-term absences.

It is important to make a number of observations at this point. First, management's act of establishing or revising an absence procedure represented a public signal to employees that absence was considered to be a problem. Second, the revision was followed by action. That is, management showed itself to be willing and able to implement the disciplinary procedures, and ultimately to be prepared to dismiss those employees who fell foul of the revised absence rules. Third, the absence procedures were necessarily designed with the worst absence offenders in mind. After the initial 'night of the long knives', during which the worst absentees were dismissed, it was possible to implement the revised procedures in a more relaxed way, while continuing to indicate that the absence problem was considered serious.

Changes in union representation

At Diamond, the review of the absence procedure was done with a great deal of co-operation from the unions, as it was important for the business to become increasingly competitive. At the time, both the union and the employees were worried about their future. Both had realized that jobs were precious, and were not to be toyed with. This view played a significant part in the implementation of the various changes. In this context the quality and commitment of the trade union officials was of crucial importance. The company reduced the number of shop stewards by half, on the understanding that those who remained would be trained properly, and that they would be fully informed. At the same time, the number of unions on the factory site was reduced from six to four. The hope is that ultimately this figure will go down to two. The representative structure of the plant has been rationalized with a view to increasing its quality. Because the quality of some of the senior shop stewards is high, management is now able to talk about business issues and get a constructive discussion.

Flexible manning

Flexible manning is another part of the overall strategy to achieve competitiveness. In the past, people had been trained in one of four production areas, and they stayed in these. Now, a situation has been created where there is a great deal of movement and rotation within, as well as between, the different work areas. To do this, Diamond has developed a team concept. Each team consists of one supervisor and 16 operators, and is responsible for two units or work areas. The members cover each other for breaks. Within these limits, they have quite a lot of flexibility in how they choose to run a particular shift.

This restructuring has meant that Diamond has moved away from the idea of individuals having a specific job. Each person now does a range of jobs within a pay grade. Depending on what is required, employees are expected to cover any or all of these jobs during a shift. If work is not required in any of the jobs in that particular department, they are expected to transfer to another department, and to work there. The aim is for them to be occupied at all times.

Underpinning this restructuring was a productivity deal which was completed a few years before when every employee's rate of pay was enhanced to take account of this new flexibility. When there is an absence, team members are expected to reorganize themselves to do the job. Overtime has not been totally eliminated, but it now represents the last, rather than the first, solution. Supervisors consider how they can reorganize their labour before calling someone in on overtime to do an extra shift.

Flexitime

Diamond adjusted the hours of work to suit its operators. In the household meters division, employees now work long winters and short summers. This meets the company's market needs. Instead of being at work at 10 p.m., they finish at 6 p.m. during the summer. Another department is now part of a flexitime experiment. It works from 7.30 a.m. to 4.30 p.m. and has Friday afternoon off.

What the management found particularly encouraging, over and above this particular innovation, was the preparedness of the workforce as a whole to permit experiments to take place in work and hours in particular parts of the plant without requiring them to be extended to all parts of the factory. In the past, the complaints and moans that management would receive from people who had been excluded, made it reluctant to try something new. As a consequence, everybody would do the same shift hours. Now, a more relaxed attitude has become evident on the shopfloor. As a result, employees are prepared to allow their co-workers various concessions which they themselves might not have, provided that it is explained to them why they may not have got them. People are not now so jealous of each other's perks. Management sees this attitude as being another facet of the feeling that employees have ownership of their jobs.

Communication

The company spent a great deal of time on communications. It communicated what the programmes were, why the changes were necessary, and why it was important to meet the requirements of particular customers. Shopfloor staff now participate in meetings with management, and explain how they think the production process can be improved. In contrast to the past, the communication is now two-way. The change is based on the acknowledgement that it is the shopfloor workers who know most about the process since they spend eight hours a day doing the job.

Customers are now invited into the factory, so that the workforce can meet, face-to-face, those who buy the output. In the past, the employees would not have known to whom their relays, meters or headsets were sold. Now they see the customers and talk to them. The company is proud of its workforce, and is happy for customers to mingle with them, and ask them questions. The management is sure that they will not let it down. A mere three or four years ago, it would have been reluctant to permit this.

Training

To improve its position, Diamond takes the trouble to train people because there is a need to get things right first time. This is a real requirement rather than a platitudinous statement. People respect that they have a job that is worth having, and worth doing, and they respond to it. So far as management is concerned, it is no longer acceptable for a manager not to have a reasonable technical understanding of the manufacturing process. One of the plant accountants was recently sent on an electronics course. It was felt that if he was going to communicate with product managers, and talk about circuits and so on, then he should know exactly what they were, how they worked, and why a certain type might be needed. It is recognized that managers of all kinds need to have a bit of process knowledge in order to be effective. The effect of this is to give managers an increased credibility with the shopfloor staff. When a manager goes down, he can talk their language, and actually understands what they mean, when they discuss the different products.

Job enrichment

Diamond has devolved much of the routine machine maintenance activity back to the workteam. The company says to the employees, 'You fix it – you're competent enough to do it'. The effect of this has been to enhance the job content of many employees. The company seeks to involve employees in its particular brand of quality improvement programme. Improvement teams have been created to suggest ways in which jobs could be improved. They have been given more responsibility for the quality of their output in the general area in which they work. It is not unusual to see a woman painting her own machine. She merely has to ask stores for a tin of paint and she paints it. That was something that was unheard-of three or four years ago. Employees like to see their work areas looking nice, so they take little initiatives like that. The areas around the machines are now also very well kept, and shopfloor personnel take pride in their equipment.

The company found that people were interested in having a say in how the job was done. It is seeking to devolve more and more responsibility to the group. The consequence will be that the groups will become totally self-sufficient. As a consequence, the company is slowly doing away with the chargehand level, and devolving those management tasks back to the groups. Each group has its own leader or spokesman. These people may rotate in the role. The groups will, ultimately, take on the responsibility for monitoring their own scrap levels and materials, and will be responsible for making their own repairs. Diamond hopes to reach the stage where it can do without foremen altogether. It will then have achieved the goal of having an unsupervised workforce. The employees will all know what the product targets are that they have to meet, as well as the scrap standards. Essentially, the company contracts with them for what it requires.

The effect of these changes is that employees now feel a greater sense of involvement in their work and with the company as a whole. Diamond's management recognizes the changes in the employees' general attitude to the work environment, and to the equipment with which they work. They feel that there is a new pride in doing a good job, whereas in the past the aim might have been to do as little as possible for as long as possible, while being paid as much as possible. Now there is a pride in meeting the targets, and in generally doing a good job. This has become much more of an accepted attitude. Even small things make a difference, such as giving everybody overalls with the company logo upon them. 'They look like a team now', said the personnel manager, '... and they identify more with the company'.

High-performance, high-commitment organizations

The foregoing description of Diamond's organizational change strategy has made little explicit reference to absenteeism *per se*. This is because nearly all change approaches at this level are concerned with achieving increased competitiveness in the market-place. This means that lower absence is not seen as an end in itself, but rather as a means to a longer-term goal. It is not so much a question of solving an absence problem, as grasping a productivity improvement opportunity. The change tactics described here – increased communications, greater employee interest and involvement, changes in job content and hours of work and so on – are all designed to have an impact upon a number of key variables which will, ultimately, improve the performance of the company as a whole. That improvement is seen as being achievable only if all employees, from the boardroom down to the shopfloor, all use their brains, and out-think the competition. This in turn requires them to give of their best, which is what commitment means. By doing this, it is held, the organization will produce a high performance.

Throughout the 1980s, management writers have focused on the need to create, 'high-commitment, high-performance organizations'. In this search, it is believed that the traditional bureaucratic-scientific forms of organizational design may no longer be adequate to meet these criteria. A number of different writers have suggested that the high-commitment, high-performance organizations of the future will adhere to 3 key principles of organization. These are that:

- the product or service is at the core of the organization;

- the people who know most about the product or service are the employees on the spot, and it is they who are in the best position to manage it;

- in order to be able to manage it, the employees need to understand the overall aims of the organization; understand how these are to be implemented within the mutually agreed organizational norms; be supplied with information on which to base their decisions; and be given the responsibility to take such decisions.

Already a diverse number of work innovations can be identified which illustrate the fundamental shift from traditional approaches. These include the quality of working life programmes at Tannoy in Scotland[3]; autonomous work-group working at Volvo in Sweden[4]; the use of subcontracting groups where internal support services are encouraged and assisted to function as external groups, effectively independent of the organization (e.g. Cadbury Schweppes and its printing services)[5]. These new-style organizations will be typified by an appropriate culture (e.g. high skills, flexibility, employee identification with the business, problem-solving, openness, trust and equity)[6]. They will also be value-driven, that is to say, the values of the employees will be in line with organizational goals. Such an approach would appear to be consistent with the current practices of many successful organizations. Peters and Waterman in their book, *In Search of Excellence*[7] concluded that declining companies manifested overtly rational management principles and practices, while the successful ones were typified by their rigid adherence to only a few key values.

Turning our attention specifically back to the absence question, it may be too early to say what the overall impact of some of these programmes will be. However, Mary Weir, the consultant who was responsible for the Tannoy experiment, reported exceptionally low absenteeism in that particular plant. Other socio-technical interventions identified in US productivity experiments also present a generally favourable absence picture.

Chapter 13

Summary of approaches to absence control

We feel that these are appropriate considerations with which to conclude this part of the book on attendance control techniques. In chapter 10, the attention was focused on *people techniques* which could be introduced within the existing company structure and value system. A wide range of *work techniques* were considered in chapter 11 which could have a varying influence on existing structures, control processes, and value systems. Finally, in chapter 12 the possibility of a major programme of *organizational techniques* designed to effect a programme of planned change were identified, involving a fundamental rethink in areas such as work organization, control hierarchies, employee participation, and management style.

Cecchi and Plax[1] implemented an absence control strategy in Rockwell International's Space Transportation Systems Group. Instead of providing general panaceas for managers and supervisors who attended their courses, they encouraged them to consider how they could use the ideas on absence causes and controls that had been described, 'in the unique context of their particular work environment'. These writers were adamant that there was no universal cure or control programme, and they identified a number of design features of absence control programmes that had a widespread relevance.

First, they felt, a strategic approach to absence control involved defining absenteeism, and identifying accurately its causes. Second, since there were a wide range of absence control measures that could be implemented in any particular situation, management needed to ensure that the one that was chosen reflected the uniqueness of the particular work environment. The strategy should therefore be based on a thorough understanding of a particular organization and its employees. Third, the success of any control programme began and continued with the sincere belief by management that something could really be done to curb absence. Often, they felt, such a belief was missing, and this could contribute to programme failure. In addition to believing in absence control efforts, employers had to be consistent in their absence policy application and implementation. These points by Cecchi and Plax are echoed in our own recommended systematic approach to absence control which is described in the next chapter.

Management review questions

The purpose of this activity is to allow you to identify which absence control techniques your company *uses at present*. This analysis will be used, and added to later when you come to assess the effectiveness of your organization's current absence control programme.

Table 13.1 contains a list of the absence control methods from Scott and Markham's study. Opposite each is a column headed *type*. Each of the methods has been classified using the typology explained in this part of the book. Thus,

P –   person-focused, negative (punishment) approach

P +   person-focused, positive (reward) approach

P – + person-focused, mixed consequence (punishment and reward) approach

W   work-focused approach

O   organization-wide approach

Instructions

● Read each description of the absence control methods in turn, and tick any that are used in your organization at present.

● In the space at the end, add any absence control methods that are used by your organization, but which are not included in the list.

Table 13.1 Revised version of Scott and Markham's list of absence control methods

Absence control method	Type	Used in this organization (✓)
1 A consistently applied attendance policy.	P –	
2 Dismissal based on excessive absence.	P –	
3 Progressive discipline for excessive absenteeism.	P –	
4 Identification and discipline of employees abusing attendance policies.	P –	
5 At least monthly analyses of daily attendance information.	P –	
6 Daily attendance records maintained by personnel department.	P –	
7 Employees required to telephone in to give notice of absence.	P –	
8 A clearly written and communicated company attendance policy.	P –	
9 Daily attendance records maintained by supervisors.	P –	
10 Allowing employees to build a 'paid absence' bank to be cashed in at a later date, or added to next year's holiday entitlement.	P +	
11 Employee interviewed after an absence.	P – +	
12 Flexible work schedules	W	
13 Inclusion of absenteeism rate on employee job performance appraisal	P – +	
14 Perfect/good attendance banquet and award ceremony.	P +	
15 Formal work safety training programme.	W	
16 Screening applicants' past attendance records before making a selection decision.	P – +	
17 Supervisory training in attendance control.	W	
18 Inclusion of work unit absenteeism on supervisor's performance appraisal.	P – +	
19 Wiping clean a problem employee's record by subsequently good attendance.	P +	
20 Improving safety on the job.	W	
21 Public recognition of employee's good attendance (e.g. in-house bulletin board, newsletters).	P +	
22 Job enrichment/job enlargement or rotation implemented to reduce absenteeism.	W	
23 A component on attendance in a formal employee orientation programme for newly appointed employees.	W	
24 Requiring a doctor's written excuse for illness/accidents.	P –	
25 Spot visits (or phone calls) to check up at employee's residence by doctor, nurse, or other company employee.	P –	
26 Operation of day care for employee's department.	W	
27 Substance abuse programme (alcohol, drugs)	W	

(Continued)

Table 13.1 (*Continued*)

Absence control method	Type	Used in this organization (✓)
28 The absenteeism control programme has been negotiated in the union agreement.	W	
29 Employee bonus (monetary) for perfect attendance.	P +	
30 Education programme in health, diet, home safety.	W	
31 Attendance lottery or poker system (random reward).	P +	
32 Peer pressure encouraged by requiring work colleagues to fill in for absent employees.	W	
33 Chart biorhythms for accident prone day.	W	
34 Letter to spouse indicating lost earnings of employee due to absence.	P –	
35 Combination of complementary techniques (those described above plus others) which are part of a long-term, company-wide, absence control and productivity improvement strategy.	O	
36 Other (insert here)	–	
37 Other	–	

Part four

Developing a strategy to control absence

Chapter 14

ALIEDIM: the seven-step approach to absence control

Part four of the book deals with the application of the ideas and concepts presented in earlier chapters, to the solution of practical absence problems in the reader's organization. The management review questions which appeared in each of the previous three parts represent the bridges that link understanding to action.

This chapter provides a description of each of the seven steps that make up the ALIEDIM approach. Each step is described in detail, and sample checklists and questionnaires are supplied which managers can use to work through their own absence problems so as to arrive at custom-made solutions.

Chapter 15 presents a case study of Arlanda Electronics. This is a real company whose name has been disguised. We describe the application of our ALIEDIM approach in this organization.

Previous books on absence have rarely, if ever, tried to help readers to analyse their absence problem systematically, or to assist them in designing an appropriate absence control programme. The aim of this chapter is to bring these different checklists and diagnoses together, and apply them to the task of developing a programme aimed at managing absence in the organization. While much of the description in this chapter is couched in terms of a manufacturing company environment, the steps and principles are equally relevant and applicable to service sector organizations. Indeed, some of our examples are taken from the airline and insurance industries.

Most managers, when faced with an absence problem, frequently reach for the nearest solution to hand. In our view, what they should be doing instead, is developing a systematic approach to controlling their absence problem. In this chapter we explain each of the seven necessary steps that are involved in that systematic approach which we have labelled ALIEDIM. Each step in the ALIEDIM approach contains a checklist to help readers to consider their own work situation. The seven steps making up the ALIEDIM approach are shown in Figure 14.1.

In the next chapter, we shall consider the case of Arlanda Electronics. We shall first describe how it sought a quick solution to its absence problem without a detailed analysis. An explanation will then be given of how, after the failure of a quick-fix strategy to deal with absenteeism, it adopted the seven-step ALIEDIM approach which is summarized below.

Step 1 *Assess the absence problem*: How great is the absence problem/productivity improvement opportunity?

Step 2 *Locate the absence problem*: Where in the organization are the absence problem groups?

Step 3 *Identify and prioritize the absence causes*: What are the causes of absence amongst each group or class of employee?

Step 4 *Evaluate the current absence control approaches*: Given the causes identified, are the current approaches the appropriate ones? How effective are they at reducing absence?

Step 5 *Design the absence control programme*: Decide which absence control approaches are available and integrate them into a custom-designed programme to match the company's needs and circumstances.

Step 6 *Implement the absence control programme*: Prepare the ground for implementation, anticipating and overcoming the resistance to the newly-designed programme.

Step 7 *Monitor the effectiveness of the absence control programme*: Check how effective the new programme is in practice as measured by established benchmarks.

Each of these seven steps will now be described in detail.

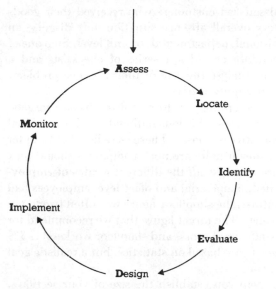

Figure 14.1 ALIEDIM: a seven-step approach to absence control

Step 1 Assess the absence problem

Who is it that decides whether action will be taken about absenteeism? The reader of this book may be a personnel manager, a section leader, a supervisor, a departmental manager, a divisional manager, or a general manager. Employee absence affects many people throughout the organization. However, it is the managerial staff who, in their different ways, are responsible for dealing with the absence problem, and implementing changes. Clearly not all of these managers have the same power to affect change. What is done about employee absence depends on where one is in the hierarchy. Some individuals – the divisional or departmental managers – have the authority to institute company-wide, absence reduction programmes. Other people, for example, section leaders and supervisors, although they may know about the problem, do not have the authority to initiate such wide-ranging action. In order to get something done, they have to persuade others that absence is a problem. Thus, they need tools to help them to influence others, specifically those with the power to make the necessary changes.

As a first step, one must establish whether a significant absence problem exists, and what its magnitude is. The extent of an absence problem will depend on an assessment of the true cost of absenteeism and its operational impact. The true cost involves first the direct, short-term, and easily quantifiable costs such as overtime payments. In addition, it is necessary to add the indirect or longer-term, and less easily assessed costs, such as the lack of repeat orders from dissatisfied customers who received their goods late. An apparently satisfactory overall absence situation may disguise an underlying problem at the divisional, departmental, or unit level. Step one of the ALIEDIM approach therefore provides a series of checklists and a framework to help managers to analyse the size of their absence problem, and assess the productivity opportunity it offers.

Comparative figures of absence are helpful to establish absence targets, and to provide benchmarks for progress. Various national and international statistics can be used for comparative purposes. These were listed in Chapter 1. All things being equal (and they usually are not), companies should seek to achieve a low absence figure amongst *all* the different grades of employees. In the companies we studied, managerial and office level employees had absence rates of 1–2%. In contrast, the shopfloor figure was often two to ten times higher, except for craftsmen. The target figure that we recommend for all employees (management, staff, supervisors, and shopfloor workers) is *3%* *or better*. This is not an average figure based on statistics, but a realistic goal based upon observed best practice.

Here are three activities to help you establish the size of your section's, unit's, department's or company's absence problem and the size of the productivity improvement opportunity that it offers. The aim is to allow you to decide whether, in your area of responsibility, the absence problem/ opportunity is SMALL, MEDIUM or LARGE. To some extent, this is a subjective judgement. However, we hope that these three activities will allow you to make that assessment realistically.

The first activity uses *external* comparisons, while the next two use *internal* ones. The answers to some of the following questions may already be available if responses have been obtained to the checklist questions contained in Chapter 3. If that data has not yet been collected, it may be helpful to assign a junior manager or management trainee to obtain the necessary information as part of his or her own development.

Activity A: external comparisons

In his book, *Thriving on Chaos*, Tom Peters[1] argued that fundamental rethinking is required if companies are to achieve quantum leaps in performance. Incremental improvements are no longer adequate. American car manufacturers take months to reorganize themselves to produce an alternative model. Japanese car companies can reorganize production processes in days. That is the magnitude of the task. Translated into the sphere of absence rates, to remain competitive and establish a leading-edge advantage, it is no longer adequate to seek marginal improvements of 10, 20 or 30%. It is necessary and possible to reduce absence by a factor of two, three or four. Managers need to be talking about virtually *eliminating* significant absenteeism altogether. These are not pipe-dream figures. Who in the motor-car industry would have believed that an absence rate of 3% could be achieved by the Nissan motor-car company in Washington, Tyne and Wear, when the industry average is above 10%?

Here, therefore, we offer an absolute benchmark. We believe that 3% or less, has to be the first target for *all* employees in *all* industries. The following suggested figures are for averages computed over a twelve-month period. One can expect fluctuations within a narrow band. Thus, for example, with a large number of employees, a 3% absence rate might fluctuate between 2 and 4%. But if it goes beyond that band, and if this is not caused by the calculation being based on too small a number of people, then an investigation may be necessary.

Enter your section's, unit's, department's or company's absence level. (See Chapter 3, Question 2, page 26). Write this percentage figure next to the independent external absence benchmark figure shown in Table 14.1. It is useful to recall the description of the productivity opportunity indicated by each of the absence rates. This was described earlier, on page 25.

Objectors often argue that a company's absence figure should be comparative and not absolute, as it is here. They say that a firm should compare its figure with the average for its industrial sector. *We totally reject both the principle and the practice of comparing a company's absence rate with the industry average.* In our view, it is as unhelpful as assessing a firm's current absence rate with its past rate (last year 24% absence, this 12%, means a 100% improvement). In each of the industrial sectors, there are organizations whose absence rate is 3% or less. It is of little comfort to know that your organization's rate is equal to the high sector average when your competitor with a 3% absence rate is winning all your business.

Absence rates for different industrial sectors are generally available. Table 14.2 shows the absence rates for the different industry groups obtained from the *1984 General Household Survey*[2].

We believe that such comparative figures have only a very limited role to play in the task of absence reduction. If a company's absence rate is higher

Table 14.1 Independent external benchmark absence

External benchmark figure	Enter your company's absence figure here	Productivity improvement opportunity
<3% 3-4%		SMALL
5-8%		MEDIUM
9-10% >10%		LARGE

Table 14.2 Percentages of employees absent from work in the previous week for different reasons by industry group (*General Household Survey 1984*)

Industry group	Total absent from work (%)	Employees sample size 100%
0 Agriculture, forestry, fishing	8	143
1 Coal-mining, energy and water supply	26*	295
2 Mining (excl. coal), manufacture, of metals, minerals and chemicals	9	315
3 Metal goods, engineering and vehicles	8	1109
4 Other manufacturing	8	978
5 Construction	6	514
6 Distribution, hotels, catering, repairs	5	1714
7 Transport and communications	8	549
8 Banking, finance, insurance, business services	5	777
9 Public and other personal services	7	2641
Total	7	903

* Affected by miners' strike

than the industry average, this fact can be used to persuade senior managers to take urgent action to reduce absenteeism. If the firm's figure is below the industrial sector average, but not yet at the 3% level or less, then such comparative data should be ignored. Its effect, in such a situation, is to breed complacency.

In our view, comparisons with the industrial sector averages tend to impede rather than encourage the achievement of excellence in absence control. Averages are, by definition, composed of best performance and worst performance. To be told that one's performance is *average* is, after all, regarded as criticism and not praise. The comment implies that one should do better and improve. Improve by how much? Surely to improve in order to rank amongst the best. Why then not say so? Why not establish *the best* as the goal and aspire to that? The same absence goals, in our view, need to be set in absolute terms across different industries and in different geographical areas. To do otherwise is to create a self-fulfilling prophecy. If you believe that it is not possible, then you probably will not achieve it.

Finally, one can note that the target absence levels are based on a projected 3% absence rate composed of rates from different groups of employees. These figures reflect the comparative absence rates quoted earlier:

Employee group	Target maximum absence rate (%)
Management	1
Staff	2
Supervisors	2
Shopfloor employees	3

Activity B: internal comparisons

A second way of assessing an organization's absence level is to conduct a comparison against *internal* benchmarks. This is possible if your unit, department or factory is provided with regular comparative figures. Usually, these figures compare the performance of your unit with that of other similar units, across a number of dimensions. The number 1 ranking is allocated to the best performing unit on that dimension.

In his book, *Moments of Truth*, Jan Carlzon[3], President of Scandinavian Airlines, described a new method of monitoring the performance of the company's cargo operations. Called QualiCargo, the system measured the precision of SAS's service in this field. The following performance measures were used:

— the speed with which telephones were answered

— frequency with which promised deadlines were met

— frequency with which the cargo actually travelled on the plane it had been booked on

— the time lapse between an aeroplane landing and cargo being ready to be collected by the customer

A significant aspect of the QualiCargo monitoring system was the production of a monthly performance ranking. The different SAS cargo terminals were compared, in a diagrammatic form, first against their own individual targets, and then with one another. The monthly graph clearly showed which terminal had the best, and which had the worst performance. Those which achieved their objectives received recognition through the award of a star, and the praise of the operations manager. Those that had not achieved their targets had to explain their poor performance.

In his description of this method, Carlzon raised some general points about the acceptability and value of such highly visible internal benchmarking. Many companies might argue that their culture makes such a public comparison and criticism of employee performance unacceptable. They argue that it will lead to hostility, will reduce morale, and produce an even worse performance. Carlzon recognized such concerns. Indeed, he himself mentioned the general reluctance of Scandinavians to criticize one another in public, and admitted that many of his own colleagues feared that SAS staff would not respond well to such evaluations. In practice, however, there was no problem. Prior to the implementation of the QualiCargo monitoring system, 80% of deliveries had arrived on time. After its introduction, the figure rose to 92%.

Internal benchmarking is also used in an Australian insurance company which has eighteen branches. Each month, each of the branch managers receives a list of rankings indicating where his or her branch is placed with respect to the other seventeen. The rankings are based on the number of new insurance policies sold, monthly revenue, costs and staff turnover and absence. While not receiving the figures for the other branches, each branch manager is told what the overall company average is, and what his or her particular branch's figure is.

If you receive such a comparative ranking with other groups, units, sections or divisions, you can assess your own relative performance. Simply add up the total number of branches/units being ranked, divide that figure into three groupings, and see where you appear on the list. For example, if absence data is available on twelve centres, it could be shown as in Table 14.3. If your department or factory occupies the sixth place on the ranking, it indicates that medium improvements are possible since there are five other centres that are doing better than you. The ranking is relative, in that it assesses performance with respect to other centres within the total organization.

Internal benchmarking can be carried out in a number of other ways:

- different groups of workers can be compared (e.g. directs with indirects) within the same company

- different classes of workers can be compared working in the same area (e.g. craftsmen versus semi-skilled)

- the absence rates of people on different shifts doing the same jobs can be compared.

Similar comparisons can be carried out inside the same organization (and even within the same site). Rather than averaging out and hiding the data, management can identify the differences, and communicate them to the

Table 14.3 Example of an internal benchmark table

Section ranking	Scope for relative improvement
1...............	
2...............	
3...............	SMALL
4...............	
5...............	
6....YOU....	
7...............	MEDIUM
8...............	
9...............	
10...............	
11...............	LARGE
12...............	

groups and individuals concerned using noticeboards and posters. The communication of that data would represent part of an absence control programme design. While a certain amount of work would be involved in obtaining such comparative data, it would be well worth the effort. With the rapid improvements currently taking place in both computer power and software development, it is often possible to get your own data processing department to carry out such an analysis for you simply and quickly. Finally, it should be noted that an analysis which reviews the same set of data using several distinct classifications, can shed light on absence problem areas, and even give pointers to the possible causes of the absences.

Activity C: cost of absence

A second form of internal comparison involves calculating what the true cost of absence is for the unit, section, department or factory. This figure can be expressed in hard cash. It is not necessary to give an exact figure for this. An indication of an order of magnitude is perfectly sufficient. However, this should not preclude identifying actual costs whenever possible, and making realistic *guesstimates* where it is not. Table 14.4 contains some suggestions for computing the true costs of absence, and includes the relevant calculations to be done. These are based on the costs of absence which were identified in Chapter 3.

Having computed the direct and indirect costs of absence, it is now possible to make comparisons, and assess the productivity opportunity that reduced absence offers.

Comparisons

The comparisons used will depend on the measures of performance that are relevant to the company concerned. Organizations differ in terms of their cost elements (labour, materials, and so on). Each organization has therefore to ask itself which are the financial measures that are relevant to it. It can then express absence in relation to those measures. Some examples of measures are shown below.

- Absence cost as a percentage of annual turnover   — %

- Absence cost as a percentage of annual profit (before tax)   — %

- Absence cost as a percentage of total annual operating costs   — %

- Absence cost as a percentage of added value   — %

One can imagine a company for which the bulk of costs are represented by raw materials. In that case, absence measured as a percentage of the added value (AV) would be a more helpful comparison than if it were expressed as

Table 14.4 Calculating the true costs of absence

1 *Direct costs of absence*	£ (annual)
1.1 Sick pay	
1.2 Continued payment of fringe benefits during absence	
1.3 Overtime payments for those filling in for absentees	
1.4 Overtime payments arising out of absence farther down the line	
1.5 Excess cost of temporary staff employed (i.e. employment agency premium)	
1.6 Overstaffing to cover for absence *Weekly wage plus employment cost x number of extra staff x 52*	

2 *Indirect costs of absence*	£ (annual)
2.1 Cost of recruiting and training extra staff *Cost per person x number of persons*	
2.2 Cost of management/supervisory time devoted to dealing with absence-related issues (e.g. revising schedules, disciplining, record-keeping, counselling). *Hours devoted per week x hourly rate x 52*	
2.3 Reduced productivity from work being done by less experienced/more tired employees, from returning workers operating at lower point in learning curve *Excess hours per annum required to achieve standard output x hourly pay rate* *or* *Lost output per annum x profit contribution per unit of output*	
2.4 Lower product quality of work due to replacement of staff *Cost of rejects, i.e. cost of scrap materials* *and* *Cost of rework (i.e. materials and labour costs to put things right)* *and* *Cost of extra premiums to maintain saleable volume (e.g. extra overtime to make up the volume)*	
2.5 Cost of disruptions/section shutdown due to absenteeism Estimate of profit forgone by lost production or financial penalty incurred due to late delivery, cost of feeding other parts of the company.	
2.6 Extra costs incurred to meet slipped deadlines (e.g. freighting by air instead of sea)	

Table 14.4   (Continued)

2 Indirect costs of absence	£ (annual)
2.7 Loss of customers due to failure to meet deadline or to inferior product quality (last financial year) Profit loss from customers who did not reorder as expected (when this can be related to absence)	
2.8 Low morale amongst other employees caused by lax attendance of certain employees (lateness, turnover, failure to work at measured standard performance)	
2.9 Imagine that your company did not have an absence problem (i.e. that it was less than 1%). What equipment would no longer be necessary, how many absence-monitoring staff could be dispensed with or reallocated to other work? Estimate the cost savings involved in equipment purchase or hire, and wages and employment costs for staff. i.e. what are the excess costs incurred against the best attainable?	
2.10 Insert any other calculations relevant to your organization or section.	
Annual Cost of Absence GRAND TOTAL	

a percentage of total annual operating costs. Added value is generally defined as,

Sales income − Expenditure on materials and bought-in services

That is, it represents the difference between the value of output (i.e. sales), and the costs of the materials and services used in creating those sales. From this added value must be paid all the other costs incurred in the operations such as rent, rates, insurance, depreciation, design costs, administrative costs and capital charges, disposable profits and direct labour.

The use of the AV concept in absence costs analysis allows changes in performance, especially labour productivity, to be expressed as values. For this reason, added value has been used as a productivity measure to indicate the overall performance of a unit. It has also been used as a basis for incentive payments, and can be used for comparison purposes with the absence rates. This is because value can be increased by improving the utilization of human resources, including absence reduction.

Assessments

Finally, we offer a number of suggested assessments that can help determine the potential gains that can be achieved if absence were to be reduced.

- Anticipated profit (before tax) improvement for a 1% improvement in absence   £ _____

- Anticipated profit (before tax) improvement by meeting the targeted external benchmark.   £ _____

Having conducted the analysis, how do you judge your unit's, section's, department's factory's or company's absence problem (and thus the productivity improvement opportunity)? Do you judge it to be,

SMALL?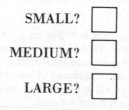

MEDIUM?

LARGE?

Where a number of different measures have been taken, the different results should broadly tally. If they do not, then this could indicate a need for further investigation. The fact that you may have judged the performance improvement opportunity offered by absence reduction to be small does not mean that management action on this is unnecessary. Pockets of absence are likely to exist amongst groups and individuals.

Step 2   Locate the absence problem

The second step in the ALIEDIM approach is to measure and analyse the absence levels in order to locate the major absence problem areas in the company. It may be that the problem groups in the organizations are already well known to you. If this is the case, skip over the next few sections and enter the names of these groups or classes in the space provided on page 167.

If the high absence groups are not immediately obvious, you will need to conduct an absence data analysis, which depends on adequate data collection. You cannot analyse data that you do not have. The analysis can be done manually, and different classes and types of employees can be compared in order to identify the high absentees. Some of the main analyses are suggested below:

Comparison by *employee characteristics* (e.g. age, sex, marital status, length of service with the organization)

Comparison of different *units, sections, departments* (e.g. stores, maintenance, assembly area, repair workshop).

Comparison of different *types of employees* (e.g. direct versus indirect, temporary versus permanent)

Comparison of different *shifts* (e.g. early shift, day shift, late shift)

The investment of time and effort in such an analysis is vital. Unless it is done, the absence control policy may be targeted at the wrong class or group of employees. Too many control policies are already plagued by management's tendency to shoot before it has bothered to aim.

The ease and speed of absence analysis can be increased if the company already has an automated reporting system which can calculate percentage absence, and total *lost days* information for all employee groups. It needs to be able to do this by department and on a regular periodic basis. Where such a facility exists, readers should discuss their data analysis requirements with their data processing manager who can advise them what can be done. Powerful software is now available which can easily and cheaply conduct the analyses required. The necessary tools with which to conduct an absence analysis of the database may already exist in your organization.

Identification

Having obtained and analysed the data, identify those groups or classes of employees who have the highest absence rates in terms of either *lost time*, or *frequency*, or both. Assume that two main areas have been highlighted by the analysis and insert the information in the space below:

Group A ....
(e.g. direct male workers employed on a permanent basis in the night shift in warehouse division)

Group B ....
(e.g. indirect female workers employed on a temporary basis, working days in the assembly testing section).

At a later stage, you will be asked to transfer this information to another checklist.

From now on, these two groups or classes will be referred to as Group A and Group B.

Step 3   Identify and prioritize the absence causes

Having identified the absence problem groups A and B, the third step is to conduct a systematic diagnosis of the possible causes of absenteeism in these groups and then to prioritize them. The Steers and Rhodes process model presented earlier in the book, can serve as an excellent diagnostic tool for this.

We suggest that by working through the process, and asking at each juncture whether this aspect of the model may be causing the problem, it is possible to pinpoint what the causes of the problems are (and indeed, are not). For example, having already identified an apparent problem in relation to a specific group of employees, a systematic analysis should be conducted to assess the significant aspects of their job (e.g. its design, work group, supervisory style), the ability of the employees to attend, their personal characteristics, the pressure on them to attend, and so on.

The reader should be aware that this assessment of the causes of absence is necessarily made on his or her own judgement, albeit supported by evidence that he or she may have to hand. In Part two we noted the benefits of having an attitude survey conducted by an independent, outside consultant who asked employees directly, not about why they were or were not absent, but about their experience of the organization in general, their attitude to different aspects of their work and so on. Indeed, the 24 absence causes contained in this checklist, could be skilfully incorporated into such a questionnaire. Such independently produced data would shed light on what employees really thought, thereby reducing the need to depend on what *managers thought that the employees thought.*

To explain clearly Step 3 of the ALIEDIM approach, we shall break it down into its five constituent stages, and indicate whether each involves the manager working on his or her own or the management team as a whole. The five stages are:

(a)   Focus on the absence problem groups (team)

(b)   Identify the causes of absence for each problem group (individual)

(c)   List the absence causes identified (individual)

(d)   Produce a team-agreed list of absence causes (team)

(e)   Prioritize the absence causes (team)
      — ranking approach
      — comparison analysis

(a)   Focus on the absence problem groups (team)

To begin with, enter the name of the absence problem groups, sections, units, departments, factory to be considered (see page 167 for illustrative examples).

Group A ....

Group B ....

(b)   Identify the causes of absence for each problem group (individual)

To simplify the process of absence cause identification, in Chapter 8 (pages 87–88), the authors translated the Steers and Rhodes model into a set of

24 questions. Readers were asked to indicate, for each of the absence groups or classes of employees, what the likely causes of their absences were, and on what evidence they based this assessment.

If such an absence cause analysis *has* already been carried out, then all that is necessary is for the reader now to transcribe the results directly on to the Table 14.5, and proceed directly to stage (c). If such an analysis *has not* yet been carried out, then readers should do it now. Each manager should, separately, complete the following analysis.

Table 14.5 Absence Cause Analysis Checklist

Absence cause	Group A evidence	Group B evidence
Job situation		
1 The job is boring and lacks challenge.		
2 The job causes the individual stress.		
3 Frequent job moves disrupt employee work patterns.		
4 The organization of shifts and the hours of work contribute to absence.		
5 The quality of supervision contributes to the level of absence.		
6 The physical work environment demotivates employees.		
7 The work-group size is too great to allow individuals to identify with the group.		
Employee values and job expectations		
8 Employees have incompatible values and job expectations.		
Personal characteristics		
9 The length of time employees have been with us seems to influence their absence rate.		
10 The age of employees seems to determine their likelihood of absence.		
11 People with certain types of personalities seem to be off more frequently.		
12 The sex of the employee affects the frequency of absence.		
Satisfaction with the job situation		
13 Dissatisfaction with the job situation seems to affect absence levels.		

(Continued)

Table 14.5   (Continued)

Absence cause	Group A evidence	Group B evidence
Pressure to attend		
14 People are absent less frequently when the financial pressures on them are greater.		
15 Our incentive/reward system contributes to the absence problem.		
16 The sick pay/NHI benefits that employees get do not encourage them to come to work.		
17 The work-group norms either do not operate, or else they discourage regular attendance.		
18 The personal work ethic of the employees does not demand that they give of their best.		
Ability to attend		
19 Genuine illness and accidents at work are a regular cause of absence.		
20 Many employees come from far away, and local transport problems put many off from coming in sometimes.		
21 The family responsibilities of employees often take precedence over work attendance.		
Other		
22 Certain days of the week have exceptionally high absence levels.		
23 Certain employees have a history of poor attendance.		
24 Self-certification has resulted in employees taking extra days off.		
25 OTHER ..... (please insert)		

Consider each absence problem group in turn (first A, then B). Use the *Absence Cause Analysis Checklist* shown in Table 14.5

- For each cause listed, decide if it is relevant to the group being analysed.

- Tick those causes that are considered relevant.

- Add in, at the end, any absence causes not listed.

- Note down the *evidence* for your view in the space provided adjacent to the cause description.

(c) List the absence causes identified (individual)

By using the Absence Cause Analysis Checklist (Table 14.5), each manager in the team will now have separately identified perhaps four or five causes of absence for Group A, and a similar number for Group B.

The causes ticked for each problem group are now listed by each manager on a separate sheet. Three examples of individual managers' lists are shown in Table 14.6.

Table 14.6 Examples of individual managers' causes of absence lists

Absence Group A:

Manager A		Manager B		Manager C	
1	Job boring	1	Job boring	2	Job stress
4	Shift hours	2	Job stress	7	Group size
10	Employee age	7	Group size	14	Money pressure
16	Sick pay	10	Employee age	16	Sick pay
21	Family responsibilities	12	Employee sex	21	Family responsibilities
		14	Money pressure		
		19	Accidents		

(d) Produce a team-agreed list of absence causes (team)

Next, the managers build a team-agreed list of causes. Team members in turn read out causes from their individual lists, together with the evidence on which their judgement is based. The evidence is likely to come from an analysis of absence statistics, an attitude survey, or from corroborated anecdotal data. Each absence cause read out is written on a flipchart with the evidence alongside it. An example is shown in Table 14.7.

Table 14.7 Group-agreed list of absence causes for Group A

No.	Absence cause	Group A Evidence
1	Job boring	Opinion survey
2	Job stress	Discussions with workforce
4	Shifts/hours	Absence statistics
7	Group size	Absence statistics
10	Employee age	Absence statistics
12	Employee sex	Absence statistics
14	Money pressure	Less absence before holiday
16	Sick pay	Temporaries absent less
19	Accidents	Unevenly distributed
21	Family responsibilities	Female absence rate higher

(e) Prioritizing absence causes

Once the team-agreed list of absence causes has been produced, all that remains, is to prioritize the causes of absence in the problem group. This allows the development of an appropriate absence control programme. There are at least two ways in which such prioritizing can be done. The first is called *ranking analysis*, and the second is *comparison analysis*.

Ranking analysis

In using this method, the members individually, and without conferring, rank the team-agreed causes that appear on the flipchart. In this example, there are ten of them. They place them *in order of their importance in relation to the absence problem group being considered*. Thus 1 is allocated to the most important of the ten absence causes, and 10 to the least important. The managers take into account the evidence to which they have just listened, and chart it alongside each cause. An example of one manager's individual ranking is shown in Table 14.8.

In dealing first with Group A, the assessments of the individual managers should now be pooled. This is most easily done with the aid of a flipchart. Managers read out their individual rankings and these are charted on a group ranking worksheet.

A number of points can be made about the group ranking worksheet (Table 14.9). First, since the most important causes carry the lowest number, the *lowest* total value indicates the absence cause considered to be the *most important* as judged by the group as a whole. In our example, the provision of sick pay to employees was considered to be a major cause of absence in the group being investigated. By contrast, employee age was

Table 14.8 Manager A's individual ranking of team agreed absence causes

No.	Group A Absence cause	Ranking 1 = high 10 = low
1	Job boring	9
2	Job stress	5
4	Shifts/hours	8
7	Group size	4
10	Employee age	10
12	Employee sex	6
14	Money pressure	7
16	Sick pay	3
19	Accidents	2
21	Family	1

Table 14.9 Group ranking worksheet

Absence cause	Individual member rankings							Total value of rankings	Group ranking
			Manager						
	A	B	C	D	E	F	G		
Job boring	9	7	3	5	7	5	7	43	8
Job stress	5	4	10	9	4	2	1	35	5
Shifts/hours	8	10	9	4	3	1	9	44	9
Group size	4	6	7	3	2	8	10	40	6
Employee age	10	9	8	10	10	3	10	60	10
Employee sex	6	2	4	1	8	3	8	32	4
Money pressure	7	5	2	2	9	4	2	31	2
Sick pay	3	1	5	8	1	6	5	29	1
Accidents	2	3	1	7	5	9	4	31	2
Family	1	8	6	6	6	7	6	40	6

considered to be the least important. There are two ties in the rankings at positions 2 and 6. Finally, although this system uses a maximum of 10 points, other rankings 1–5 or 1–7 are also possible. The key objective is to establish a priority ranking of causes. The procedure is repeated for Group B.

Comparison analysis

Once individual managers from the team have identified absence causes and pooled them, an alternative procedure for the systematic assessment of these causes is compare one against all the others in turn. Again, the procedure is carried out first for Group A, and then repeated for Group B.

To conduct such a comparison analysis, all the identified absence causes (or their numbers) are listed first horizontally and then vertically on a grid. The resulting grid or matrix is shown in Table 14.10. Each cause is then

Table 14.10 Group cross-comparison of absence causes

Absence cause	1	10	16	19	21	26	Total
1	X	10	1	19	1	1	3
10	10	X	10	10	10	10	5
16	1	10	X	19	21	16	1
19	19	10	19	X	19	26	3
21	1	10	21	19	X	26	1
26	1	10	16	26	26	X	2
Total	3	5	1	3	1	2	15

compared with every other one on the grid. Thus in our example, cause 1 is compared with cause 10, then with cause 16 and then with 21. Next, cause 10 is similarly compared and so on.

Example

The 6 causes identified were:

1   Job boring
10 Employee age
16 Sick pay
19 Accidents
21 Family
26 Absence history

When an item is compared with itself on the grid, an X is put in the space. Thus, beginning with line one, absence cause 1 (job boring) is compared to absence cause 10 (employee age). If it is judged that, of these two causes, for this group, age is more likely to be the cause of absence than is the nature of the job, then 10 is inserted in the grid. The procedure is repeated until all absence causes have been compared with one another.

This process of comparison can be done with all the members of the management team sharing their evidence, and agreeing on the likely causes. The outcome is that the management team collectively produces an absence cause ranking, an example of which is shown in Table 14.11. The same ranking procedure can be used to deal with any number of absence causes. The grid merely needs to be extended to accommodate additional items.

The outcome of the exercise is a clearer and more objective identification of the causes of absence in the organization. This in turn is a necessary prerequisite for the completion of ALIEDIM Steps 4 and 5. These are concerned with the evaluation of the effectiveness of the current absence control programme, and with the design of a revised absence control programme.

Table 14.11 Absence cause priority listing produced by a management team

Number	Cause	Votes	Absence impact
10	Employee age	5	Major
1	Job boring	3	High
19	Accidents	3	High

Step 4   ALIEDIM: Evaluate the current absence control methods

Let us put the absences causes identified to one side temporarily, and concentrate instead on evaluating the effectiveness of the absence techniques and methods currently used by your organization to manage the absence problem.

In Table 13.1 at the end of Chapter 13, we presented a checklist of absence control methods used by companies. You were invited to identify which of these were currently used in your unit, section, department or company. That same list of the absence control methods (originally developed by Scott and Markham[4]) is reproduced in Table 14.12.

If you *have* already identified your company's absence control methods at the end of Chapter 3 then

- Refer back to Table 13.1 in Chapter 13, and transcribe your ticks on to Table 14.12 entering them under the column headed 'Used in this organization'.

- In the space at the end of Table 14.12, transcribe the additional approaches that you added to the end of Table 13.1

If you *have not* identified your company's absence control approaches, then do that now.

- Turn to Table 14.12

- Read each description of the absence control method in turn.

- Under the heading, 'Used in this organization', tick any that are used by your company.

- In the space at the end of Table 14.12, add any absence control methods that are used by your organization but which are not included in the list.

From now on, focus *only* on those absence control approaches that you have *ticked*. Consider each in turn, and rate it in terms of how effective you judge it to be on the following 1–4 scale:

Rating	Assessment
1	Not effective at all
2	Marginally ineffective (benefits just below cost).
3	Marginally effective (benefits barely worth the costs).
4	Definitely effective, successful

Table 14.12 Revised version of Scott and Markham's list of absence control methods

	Absence control method	Type	Used in this organization (✓)	Rating of effectiveness (1–4)
1	A consistently applied attendance policy.	P –		
2	Dismissal based on excessive absence.	P –		
3	Progressive discipline for excessive absenteeism.	P –		
4	Identification and discipline of employees abusing attendance policies.	P –		
5	At least monthly analyses of daily attendance information.	P –		
6	Daily attendance records maintained by personnel department.	P –		
7	Employees required to telephone in to give notice of absence.	P –		
8	A clearly written and communicated company attendance policy.	P –		
9	Daily attendance records maintained by supervisors.	P –		
10	Allow employees to build a 'paid absence' bank to be cashed in at a later date, or added to next year's holiday entitlement.	P +		
11	Employee interviewed after an absence.	P – +		
12	Flexible work schedules	W		
13	Inclusion of absenteeism rate on employee job performance appraisal	P – +		
14	Perfect/good attendance banquet and award ceremony	P +		
15	Formal work safety training programme.	W		
16	Screening applicants' past attendance records before making a selection decision.	P – +		
17	Supervisory training in attendance control.	W		
18	Inclusion of work unit absenteeism on supervisor's performance appraisal.	P – +		
19	Wiping clean a problem employee's record by subsequent good attendance.	P +		
20	Improving safety on the job.	W		

Table 14.12 (*Continued*)

	Absence control method	Type	Used in this organization (✓)	Rating of effectiveness (1–4)
21	Public recognition of employee's good attendance (e.g. in-house bulletin board, newsletters).	P +		
22	Job enrichment/job enlargement or rotation implemented to reduce absenteeism.	W		
23	A component on attendance in a formal employee orientation programme for newly appointed employees.	W		
24	Requiring a doctor's written excuse for illness/accidents.	P –		
25	Spot visits (or phone calls) to check up at employee's residence by doctor, nurse, or other company employee.	P –		
26	Operation of day care for employee's department.	W		
27	Substance abuse programme (alcohol, drugs).	W		
28	The absenteeism control programme has been negotiated in the union agreement.	W		
29	Employee bonus (monetary) for perfect attendance.	P +		
30	Education programme in health, diet, home safety.	W		
31	Attendance lottery or poker system (random reward).	P +		
32	Peer pressure encouraged by requiring work colleagues to fill in for absent employee.	W		
33	Chart biorhythms for accident-prone day.	W		
34	Letter to spouse indicating lost earnings of employee due to absence.	P –		
35	Combination of the complementary techniques (those described above plus others) which are part of a long-term, company-wide, productivity improvement strategy which has absence control implications.	O		
36	Other (insert here)	—		
37	Other	—		
38	Other	—		
39	Other	—		

Having completed a review of your current absence control programme it is now necessary to rate its overall effectiveness. Use Table 14.13 for this.

Table 14.13   How effective is your absence control programme?

In the light of your detailed assessment of your current absence control programme, how highly would you rate it? Indicate, by ticking the relevant box, which of the following five statements best describes the effectiveness of your present absence control programme.

1   In operation, this absence control programme has resulted in the achievement of an absence rate to match that of the 'excellent' organizations. Very effective, no change required, but monitoring is needed to ensure that it continues to deal satisfactorily with individual problem areas or pockets of absence.

2   The absence control programme is viewed within the organization as good. Nevertheless, a moderate improvement can be made to it to increase productivity, particularly if a sectional analysis is conducted to ensure that the policy is equally effective in all parts of the organization.

3   The absence control programme in operation is producing a tolerable absence level. However, if the programme were improved, a major productivity opportunity could be grasped, as viewed against the benchmark of 'excellent' organizations.

4   The level of absence indicates that the existing absence control programme is not working well. A serious absence problem persists in the organization. An outstanding productivity opportunity could be taken if suitable policy changes could be implemented.

5   This level of absence is totally unacceptable, and if sustained, could undermine the future viability of the company. The absence control programme is wholly ineffective. Absence in the organization, and its control, needs to be rethought from scratch. Radical rather than incremental changes are urgently required.

It is only readers who ticked box number 1 that might not require to amend their absence management programmes. The fact that you have progressed this far through the book suggests that your current absence control programme can stand improvement. In carrying out the review, you should bear two points in mind:

(a)   The techniques/approaches already used but considered ineffective, will influence choices when the programme is amended or redesigned.

(b)   Any amendment/redesign should not, 'throw the baby out with the bath water'. It may be that the absence control technique itself is perfectly satisfactory, but the method of its implementation may be faulty. Alternatively, a currently used technique may be exactly what is required, even though at the moment it does not work effectively because, for example, it requires to be supported by the introduction of

other (currently missing) elements, in order to make up
absence control programme.

Step 5 ALIEDIM: Design the absence control programme

The fifth step in the ALIEDIM approach is to design the absence control
programme for your organization. This section aims to help you to select
from the absence control methods that are available, the most suitable
elements, so as to enable you to design a programme that meets the needs of
your particular unit, section, department or company. We have already
argued that different organizations will have different needs. Hence, the
approach chosen will depend on circumstances.

Steps 1 to 4 have placed you in a good position to make the necessary
informed decisions. The magnitude of the absence problem has been
assessed; the problem absence group, unit, section, class or type of employee
has been identified; the most likely causes of absence have been determined;
and the effectiveness of your current absence control techniques has been
evaluated. Once you have reached this chapter, the writers assume that you
will feel that a new or adapted approach to absence control is needed. While
there are many different ways of reaching this decision, the one we propose
reflects our own values and beliefs. In brief, we argue for the need to achieve
the standards of the best companies, and to reject levels of attainment based
on either past efforts or some notion of an industrial sector 'average'.
Organizations which aim only to achieve an average performance in
important areas of productivity, will have little chance of sustaining a
competitive edge over time.

In Part three, we grouped the existing absence control policies into three
major families or types. These were labelled person-focused, work-focused
and organization-focused. It is useful to recap on the fundamental differences between the three. *People-focused* absence control techniques seek to
improve attendance directly. They focus upon the people involved, and seek
to modify employees' attendance behaviour. Thus, people-focused techniques do not address themselves to any of the underlying causes of absence
at work, nor do they necessarily seek to understand them. What is important
is that the desired change in the *attendance behaviour* of the individual is
achieved. The three main categories of people techniques are:

Negative incentive: control systems, discipline, punishment.

Positive incentive: based on positive (reward) incentives to attend.

Mixed consequence: containing a combination of positive incentives
                       ('the carrot') and negative consequences ('the
                       stick').

Work-focused techniques include strategies which seek to influence individual attendance behaviour indirectly by making changes or adaptions in the *nature of the work* that the employees carry out, or in the environment in which they do the work. Three examples of work-focused techniques are:

Job enrichment: including group-work design

Employee policy: changes that permit flexible attendance

Work environment: changes in the physical conditions in which work is carried out.

Organizationally-focused techniques involve the use of a *co-ordinated programme of activities*. A number of techniques come to be used either in parallel or sequentially. This strategy is based on the belief that absence from work is the result of the interaction of a number of factors related to the individual, the organization, and the environment.

In her book, *The Change Masters*, Rosabeth Moss Kanter[5], identified a number of characteristics of in-company projects (such as new absence control programmes) which assisted their acceptance within the organization. It is useful to select some of these and related programme features, and seek to incorporate them into an absence programme design. In this way, the chances of producing an acceptable absence control programme are enhanced. The six features one might mention include the following:

(a) Divisibility
Can the absence control programme be implemented in phases or steps?

(b) Complementing and using resources already available
Does the programme build upon the resources that have been committed already (e.g. existing computer facilities for monitoring absence)?

(c) Time-scale
Absence control approaches differ in the time needed to implement them and the time needed to see a pay-off from them, if they are successful. Does the proposed design fit into the required time-scales?

(d) Cost of implementation
Approaches differ in their relative costs of implementation. Management has to ask what the costs are likely to be (including both direct and indirect cost elements). Can it justify this level of expenditure on a cost—benefit comparison basis?

(e) Capability fit
Is the organization capable of implementing the approach? For example, some work-focused techniques cannot be tried because they necessitate a major restructuring of technology which involves significant capital costs.

(f) Culture fit
Does the programme *feel right* for the organization? Does the technique fit
in with the organization's culture? For example, a company whose philosophy emphasizes employee trust and self-control cannot realistically introduce an attendance bonus system without compromising its fundamental
values.

These dimensions represent important considerations when decisions have
to be made about the design of an absence control programme. Each
company will have its own additional criteria which will need to be met.
These can be added as additional items on the checklist.

We have consistently argued in this book against a one-shot quick-fix
solution to the absence problem. Instead, we propose the idea of a
systematically designed programme of measures to meet the different aspects
of an organization's absence problem. The identification of different absence
problem groups in a single organization indicates the need for a combination
of different but mutually consistent and self-reinforcing control measures.
One reason for this is the fact that in all organizations, the problem of
absence affects only a *minority* of employees. This is a point that we have
made several times throughout the book. The better a programme is targeted
at the problem absence group, the more successful it is likely to be.

Perhaps the failure of many past programmes can be attributed to the fact
that too often a company's 'absence problem' has been seen as exactly that –
a unidimensional, homogeneous difficulty, amenable to solution by a similarly single, undifferentiated technique. It may be more helpful to consider
an organization's problem as comprising a number of different mini-absence
problems, each with its own particular cause or causes. From this perspective, the solution consists of a unique combination of different control
elements which collectively make up an organization's absence control
programme.

Earlier in this chapter, we recapped on the range of different absence
control techniques – people-focused, work-focused, and organization-
focused. Designing an absence control programme to meet the specific needs
of a firm can, in our view, be thought of as baking a cake (Figure 14.2). One
takes ingredients from a number of different jars, and ensures that the tastes
will not conflict, but will complement each other.

This is perhaps the key paragraph in this entire book. If we were to
recommend the quick-fix solution to absence control, then this is where
we would write it. Instead, we refer you back to your analyses of your
company's situation, in terms of,

Assessing its absence problem   (Step 1)

Locating your absence problem   (Step 2)

Identifying and prioritizing the absence causes   (Step 3)

Evaluating the current absence control approach   (Step 4)

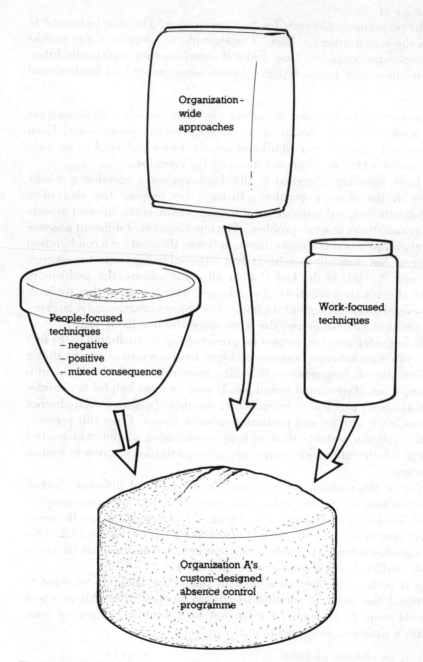

Figure 14.2　Recipe for a company absence control programme

Reviewing the absence programme design

If all the information is available to the managers, from Steps 1 to 4, then they, working alone, or better with other members of the management team, including the personnel manager, should be able to put together the elements of a suitable absence control programme that meets their organization's unique needs. All the different types of absence control techniques and their characteristics were described in Part three. It is from these elements that the final, company-specific design will be developed.

STOP
At this point you should review the information presented, and produce, with others, the absence control programme for your unit, section, department, or company.
    The remainder of this chapter assumes that such a programme design has been drafted.

When the draft of an absence control programme has been completed, it should be checked against the criteria that were presented earlier. This assessment framework is presented in Table 14.14 and represents a checklist for reviewing a draft absence control programme.

Table 14.14 Checklist for reviewing an absence control programme

Focusing on the draft programme that you have just designed,

1 Review each of the 6 dimensions presented below.

2 In Column 1, write in any other dimensions that have been omitted, but which are important in your organization/department/unit.

3 For each of the dimensions in turn, decide if it is important to you. Insert yes or no in Column 2.

4 If the answer is yes, consider how the suggested programme relates to this required dimension. Does the programme adequately match the requirement, or will certain elements need to be modified to enhance the chances of producing an acceptable absence control programme?

(1) Dimension	(2) Important (Y-N)	(3) Programme assessment
(a) divisible?		
(b) complementary?		
(c) time scale OK?		
(d) implementation cost OK?		
(e) capability fit?		
(f) culture fit?		
* other (insert) ...		
* other (insert) ...		

The amendments prompted by this review should now be incorporated into a final absence control programme document. It is this version of the programme which will be implemented in Step 6 of the ALIEDIM framework.

Step 6   Implement the absence control programme

Once the absence control programme has been designed and revised, the sixth step in the ALIEDIM approach is concerned with its implementation. This broad heading includes communicating information about the programme to those affected by it, winning acceptance for it, organizing the required training and, not least, overcoming resistance to the change.

In planning the various aspects of implementation, senior management can usefully consider two target groups which it has to influence. The first of these consists of all those staff who are charged with implementing the new absence control programme. We shall call these the *implementers*. The second group includes those employees for whom the new programme is primarily designed. These we shall refer to as the *consumers*.

Commonsense thoughts and research findings about implementation

What are the key issues about implementation that management needs to keep in mind? Past experiences of both successful and unsuccessful attempts at change offer us a few rules of thumb. Above all, perhaps, there is a need to be aware that one is dealing with a package of different measures, and hence implementation will have to be customized to the particular circumstances of the organization. In addition,

- Ensure that your communication about the changes is clear from the start, and continues to be effective throughout the process of implementation.

- Establish an adequate level of involvement amongst the relevant individuals and groups.

- Such involvement will need to take account of the relative *maturity* of different groups and individuals. By maturity, we mean their relative willingness and ability to contribute to, and support, the changes.

- Depending on their maturity level for each of the tasks in the package, choose the appropriate method of implementing each change in that group. The available range in matching task maturity is *delegation* (high maturity), *coaching, selling* or *telling* (low maturity).

- Consciously promote the *benefits* of the proposed changes through effective communication channels, for example, by using presentations to small groups.

- Remember that you cannot do everything at once.

- Since you are dealing with a package of changes, break down the implementation into stages or manageable chunks.

- Assign responsibilities for these different chunks to individuals and groups.

- Plan to achieve some early successes by going for the easier goals first.

- Do this by sequencing the implementation in such a way that items with the best chance of early payback (for example, those that do not involve major costs, which are not contentious, or which stand alone) are implemented first.

- Ensure from the outset, that there is top management commitment.

- Establish accountability so as to ensure that the change is not promoted as a personnel initiative, but that it is clearly seen as operating management's responsibility, and that management has ownership of it.

- Tie the implementation of changes, as far as possible, into existing company strategies, mechanisms and/or responsibilities. For example, in the case of any required changes in pay rates, ensure that you go through the proper channels so as to promote employee acceptance.

- Recognize the pressures on the implementers, and be aware that they too have their concerns which have to be addressed.

The research literature supports, and adds to these rules of thumb. Dunphy[6] studied a number of different change programme implementations, and produced the following checklist of the characteristics of successful organizational change programmes:

1 Clear objectives
2 Realistic and limited in scope, planned and simple
3 Informed awareness
4 Selection of appropriate intervention strategies
5 Good timing
6 Genuine participation
7 Support from key power groups
8 Using external power structure and experience
9 Open assessment beforehand
10 Majority support for perceived benefits
11 Competent staff support to offer temporary resources
12 Integration of new methods into routine operations

13   Transfer and diffusion of successful operations
14   Continuing review and modification
15   Adequate rewards for implementers and for those affected.

Gaining support and commitment

A major feature of implementing any new absence control programme is the
need to gain the support and commitment of those who will be carrying it out
– the implementers. These staff may, whether consciously or unconsciously,
sympathize with the absentees. Some of our own interviewees stated how
boring they considered the jobs of many workers to be, and did not express
surprise that they absented themselves. They may have considered such
behaviour to be quite natural. Other supervisors may be reluctant to expend
the extra effort that a new absence programme might involve. They may be
asked to follow up on absentees more closely, or counsel them more
frequently. Still other managers may not believe that anything can be done
about absence. They consider it a fact of life, and may be reluctant to devote
extra time to a goal which they believe is unattainable.

The personal theories of managers to which we referred at the start of the
book can also affect the success or failure of absence control programme
implementation. A supervisor may prefer a negative consequence (punishment) method because he finds it easier to understand and easier to
implement, and because it also reinforces his or her own status, power and
authority. The supervisor may therefore be hostile to a correctly diagnosed,
and carefully designed work-focused change programme which might
undermine his or her position by, for example, establishing self-regulating
work groups which are given more autonomy and responsibility.

The consumers, in their turn, might also offer resistance to the new
absence control programme. Indeed both implementers and consumers are
likely to show similar responses when resisting a change, such as a new
absence control programme. They may show: *resentment* at the manner in
which the change is introduced (perhaps without warning, consultation or
participation of those affected); *frustration* at the perceived loss of valued
aspects of the current programme; *anxiety* at the perceived threats that the
new programme might pose; *dissatisfaction* at the reorganization which will
affect their working lives; *fear* of not being able to meet the new challenge
that the change might pose. Finally, perhaps, *insecurity* might be a problem,
caused by the loss of order and certainty that accompanied the familiar past
practices on absence.

Causes of resistance to new absence control programmes

Let us now briefly consider any new absence control programme as an
instance of organizational change. Any change has both positive and

negative aspects for those involved in it. It means experimentation and the creation of something new. It may be resisted because it involves both confrontation with the unknown, and the loss of the familiar. For this reason, resistance to a change in absence control, can have a number of causes. These have been labelled parochial self-interest, misunderstanding and lack of trust, contradictory assessment, and low tolerance of change[7]. Let us examine each of these briefly.

Parochial self-interest

People protect the status quo with which they are content, and in which they see a number of advantages. Many will have a vested interest in perpetuating the existing absence control plan, and its outcome. The example of a supervisor preferring a punishment-centred individual approach that enhances his or her status to a work-focused one which reduces it, has already been mentioned. Employees, in their turn, may have worked out ways of getting round the rules of the existing absence control plan. The change may be personally inconvenient for different people for different reasons. It may disturb arrangements that may have taken time and effort to establish. Perceived as well as actual threats to the interests and values of individuals will therefore generate resistance to the establishment of a new absence control programme.

Misunderstanding and lack of trust

People resist a change when they do not understand what the change involves, the reasons for it, or its likely consequences. If managers do not trust employees, then they may withhold or distort information about the impending absence policy changes. Incomplete and incorrect information creates uncertainties and inaccurate rumours. This increases employees' perceptions of threat, increases their defensiveness, and reduces still further any effective communication about the changes.

Thus, for example, a proposal by management to introduce work changes, may be viewed by employees as a devious way of getting more work out of them without paying for it. Additionally, it may create the fear that, in the future, fewer people will be required. The converse is also true. If the employees do not trust management, then the legal compliance (acceptability) which has to underlie any absence control programme will be missing. Thus, *the way in which the change is introduced* can be resisted rather than the change itself.

Contradictory assessments

People in an organization evaluate the costs and benefits of change in different ways. In the end, it is human values that determine whether the new absence control policy will be promoted, and whether it will succeed or fail. Individuals differ in their perceptions of what a particular change will mean for them and their firm as a whole. Perceptions are most likely to differ when information about the change is inadequate, or where all the right people do not have the relevant information. Thus, in introducing a tough new policy to curb casual absenteeism, management may believe that it will gain the support of the good attenders. However, these people may have a different perception, and may feel that it is *they* who are being punished.

Low tolerance of change

Individuals differ in their ability to cope with change and to deal with uncertainty. Changes that require people to think and behave in different ways (as absence programmes often do), can challenge an individual's self-concept. Self-doubt and self-questioning are raised as employees consider whether they personally will be able to handle the change. Some people have a very low tolerance of ambiguity and uncertainty. The anxiety and apprehension that they suffer can lead them to oppose changes that they know to be beneficial.

The elimination of clocking on and off is a good example, since many companies are introducing this as part of their harmonization policies. From management's viewpoint, the elimination is perceived to be a positive thing, and as something to be offered as a reward for good attendance. However, some hourly-paid employees may, initially at least, take a negative view of this type of change, and see it as an insidious form of management control. Traditionally, hourly-paid groups have a strong collective identity, and for some of their members the thought of becoming *staff* may threaten the security that the membership of a group provides. Individual treatment can be perceived as a way of weakening the group's power base, by letting management gradually pick off people one by one (divide and rule).

Effective implementation of a new absence control programme

If senior management recognizes the causes of resistance to change, and if it is able to identify the likely responses that are typically identified with such resistance, then it can plan to manage the successful implementation of any new absence control programme. How can management overcome the resistance to its changes, and effect a successful implementation of the new policy? A number of specific methods have been identified by researchers[8].

Studies show that successful change depends on the redistribution of power in the organization. Managements which impose changes unilaterally or autocratically upon others, without their participation, are usually responsible for ineffective or less effective changes. In their series of booklets on the implementation of technical change, David Boddy and David

Buchanan[9] offer a number of ideas which are equally relevant to implementing a new or redesigned absence control programme. Many build upon and extend the points made earlier in this section. They discuss these under a number of headings, but the most relevant ones for us are *people*, *system* and *power*.

Where people are concerned, they recommend *marketing the change*, rather than just selling it. Find out, they say, what benefits can be offered, and how these can meet the needs of different people. *Publicize the benefits*. Do not keep them hidden, but document them, and make that information widely known. Third, take care to allay fears where possible.

Under the system heading, these authors recommend *involving the consumers* where practicable, in order to allow them to develop a sense of ownership of the new absence system. Second, if feasible, *pilot the programme*. This goes back to Kanter's point. Try to learn lessons from a pilot scheme before putting the full one into operation. Third, *check that it works*. Double-check that the redesigned programme will actually do the job. The writers note that employees may be quite right to resist a bad system that is unfair.

Finally, under the heading of power, Boddy and Buchanan refer to being *alert to losers*. By this they mean paying attention to those whose authority might be eroded (for example, the supervisors) and also ensuring that good attenders are not penalized. Second, *identifying leaders* is important. That is, identifying opinion leaders in the group, and securing their acceptance and support. Finally, *managing power changes* is necessary. Check whether or not changes in autonomy and decision-making really are needed, and not just accidental. It is useful to elaborate at least three of the points that Boddy and Buchanan make.

(a) Think about the individuals and groups likely to be affected

It is useful when considering a change of this sort, to view it from an organization-wide perspective. Indeed many companies will be implementing changes designed to give them a competitive edge in the market-place. Thus, improved productivity will be the goal, and reduced absenteeism will represent the means.

At the start of the chapter we distinguished between the programme implementers and consumers. Both will need to be persuaded of the benefits of the proposed changes. A number of strategies can be used and the process can be likened to a sales situation. First, management must earn the confidence of the customer groups by showing concern for their needs. It does this by asking questions, listening to the answers, and helping to solve the problems raised.

Second, it must sell the benefits of the new absence control programme, and not its attributes. An attribute is something which concerns the seller, while a benefit is something that concerns the customer. The benefits will vary from customer to customer. The benefits perceived by the supervisor implementing the programme will be different from those perceived by the shopfloor employee who will be affected by it.

Third, management can turn a programme attribute into a benefit by using the phrase, *that means*, supported by the word, *because*. Fourth, one benefit will usually sell the idea of a new control programme, if you have used the right one. Finally, management should ask questions to find out what implementers' and consumers' wants are, and decide which benefit to present.

To increase its effectiveness at influencing these groups, management needs to answer the question, *what's in it for them?* People are often stirred into action by the knowledge that they will be better off choosing one behaviour or programme, and not another. Thus, for each group or individual, management has to establish what the benefits of the new proposal are. Here it is important to avoid assuming that one's own reasons for wanting something are necessarily shared by others.

(b) The likely reactions and sources of resistance

By anticipating the reaction of different groups of people, one can do something about it beforehand. Thus, those who are resisting the change can be involved in its planning and implementation. Such *co-optation*, as it is called, or collaboration, can act to reduce opposition and encourage commitment. It can reduce the fear that individuals have about the impact the change will have on them. It also uses their skills and knowledge. Of course, this strategy can only work if participants have the knowledge and ability to contribute effectively, and are willing to do so.

It may be necessary to reach a mutually agreed compromise by trading and exchange. The exact rules and procedures of the new absence control programme may be adjusted to meet the interests and concerns of potential resistors. Management may need to negotiate rather than impose change where there are individuals or groups who are going to be affected, and who have enough power to resist. Management may choose to put forward proposals which appeal to the specific interests of key groups involved in the change, such as the implementing supervisors.

(c) The shifts in influence and authority that are involved

Management needs to be sensitive to the shifts in influence and authority that a new absence control programme is likely to involve. Many years ago, when Chaim Schreiber took over the management of the Hotpoint factory in Wales, he established a sick-pay committee. The committee covers only hourly-paid workers, and meets weekly to decide whether or not sick pay will be given. At the present time this consists of two management and two hourly-paid representatives, and is chaired by the production manager.

While the representatives of the hourly-paid workers are nominated by the trade unions, they are not shop stewards. At Baxi Heating the 130 workers in the maintenance and production areas are covered by six sick-pay committees.

Far from giving away authority and control, the strategy of establishing joint management–employee or management–union sick-pay committees has been used by companies who fear that the introduction of harmonized sick-pay schemes might lead to higher sickness absence levels amongst manual workers who abuse the improved sick-pay entitlement. The overall effect has been to increase management control. Initially, at Baxi Heating, there was some reluctance amongst the workers to elect representatives to sit on these committees. It should be noted that unions and employees may resist becoming involved in 'policing' the attendance of fellow workers. However, trade unions will frequently support such schemes in return for a substantially improved sick-pay scheme.

Conclusion

How an absence control programme is implemented is as important as getting the problem diagnosis and the programme design correct. The research literature is full of cases where the appropriate solution failed solely because of faulty implementation. Having hopefully implemented the programme effectively, all that now remains is to establish a system to monitor its effectiveness. This represents the seventh and final step of the ALIEDIM approach.

Step 7 Monitoring the effectiveness of the absence control programme

Once the new absence control programme has been implemented, it is important to monitor it, so as to ensure that it is having the desired effect. Moreover, it is also critical to identify quickly any unanticipated negative consequences that may be produced. Such evaluation has to be carried out on a broad perspective. Measurements should be taken of the factors which really do affect the company's competitive performance. Hence, management will wish to use a number of different criteria against which to measure the performance of their absence control programme. What happens to the absence rate itself, with reference to the absence problem groups or classes of employees is an important, but by no means the only, measure of performance. There are other indicators that might be used. For example,

— the response of employees to the new programme

— changes in morale amongst the workforce

— improvements in the quantity and quality of the product/service provided

— percentage of orders completed on schedule

— reductions in payroll related costs

Such monitoring can be considered as a *process* which consists of a number of phases. These are:

● setting performance criteria for evaluation

● measuring actual performance against the criteria specified

● comparing actual performance with target performance on each criterion

● deciding if corrective action needs to be taken

● ensuring corrective action is taken

● continuing to measure performance.

The process of monitoring is summarized in Figure 14.3. This process of monitoring is intended to ensure that the absence control programme is achieving its objective, and that any necessary corrective actions are taken. Having spent so much time analysing and implementing an absence programme, management may feel reluctant to devote still more time to monitoring it. However, it is essential to do so, and there are many benefits to be gained.

The preparatory work of assessment, evaluation and planning of the new absence control programme should be supported by effective monitoring to ensure that the primary objective of reducing the absence rate has been achieved. The new programme may involve added expense, and it is important to obtain value for money. By having clear absence targets, the section, unit or entire company can be guided consistently towards them. Monitoring permits corrections to be carried out on a systematic basis, rather than through argument and conflict. Let us comment on each phase of the monitoring procedure as it pertains to an absence control programme.

(a) Setting performance criteria for evaluation

The performance criteria set for the new absence control programme will depend on the particular section, unit, department, class or grade of employee being considered. There is also a need to decide on a time frame. By when, will the objective be achieved – next month, six months hence, next year?

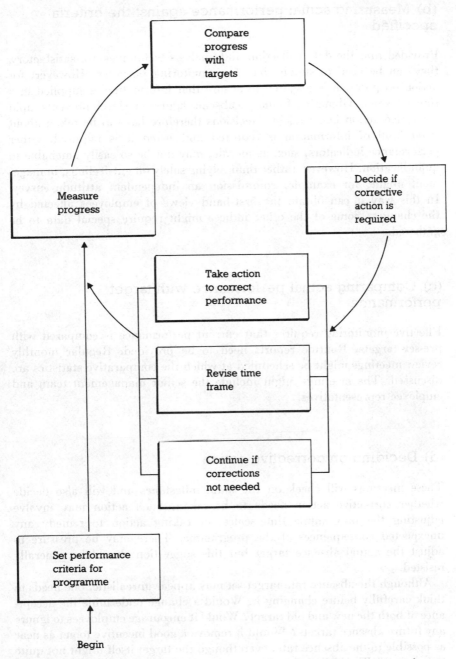

Figure 14.3 Monitoring the effectiveness of an absence control programme

(b) Measuring actual performance against the criteria specified

Provided that the data collection and analysis techniques are satisfactory, they can be used to supply data for monitoring purposes. However, for action purposes, it is essential to ensure that information is supplied in a timely fashion. Obtaining January's absence figures in March prevents rapid corrective action being taken. Decisions therefore have to be taken about *what* kind of information is required and *when* it is required. Other performance indicators, such as morale, may not be so easily amenable to quantification. However, rather than relying solely on gut-feelings, management might, for example, commission an independent attitude survey. In this way it can obtain the first-hand views of employees affected by the changes. Some of the other indices might require special data to be gathered.

(c) Comparing actual performance with target performance

Effective monitoring requires that current performance is compared with pre-set targets. Routine reports need to be provided. Regular monthly review meetings might be scheduled at which the comparative statistics are discussed. The meetings might include the senior management team and employee representatives.

(d) Deciding on corrective action

These meetings will check on the main milestones and will also decide whether corrective action needs to be taken. Such action may involve adjusting the programme time-scales, or taking action to remedy any unexpected consequences of the programme. There may be pressure to adjust the actual absence target but this suggestion should be generally resisted.

Although the absence rate target set may appear unrealistic, one needs to think carefully before changing it. Would a change undermine the acceptance of both the new and old target? Would it encourage employees to ignore any future absence targets? Would it remove a good incentive to get as near as possible to the absence rate, even though the target itself might not quite be reached? Would it make those who really exerted themselves feel that it was a waste of effort? It is important to select internal and external benchmarks carefully, so as to ensure that an amendment of the target absence rate does not become necessary.

(e) Ensuring corrective action is taken

Whatever corrective action is deemed to be necessary, one must ensure that it is taken. For example, an attendance bonus payment scheme may have been introduced which paid a bonus at the end of every three months. If the period is reduced to, say, one month, someone has to communicate this decision to the employees affected, and to the records and salaries departments which monitor the absence figures and arrange the bonus payments. The efficient implementation of the mundane details of any absence control programme can be as essential to its success, as getting the overall structure correct.

(f) Continuing to measure performance

The corrective adjustment may or may not be sufficient. Continued monitoring will be required to check that it is in fact having the desired effect. This will be part of the continuing process of collecting employee absence data and analysing it on a regular basis. The corrective action that can be taken, depends upon the measurement and information feedback system that has been set up.

This model has been used to illustrate how absence levels can be monitored, and the appropriate corrective action taken when necessary. However, this same model can also be used, very effectively, to monitor the progress and performance of any of the sub-elements of the absence control programme. For example, where the programme includes such features as training courses, overtime management, improving equipment reliability, and so on. Standards for these items can be set, measured and amended in line with the suggested monitoring processes.

Conclusion

In this chapter we have presented, in detail, the seven steps that make up the ALIEDIM approach to absence control. By following each of our steps, we believe that you will be able to arrive at an absence programme design that is uniquely suitable for your circumstances. In the next chapter we describe how the steps of the ALIEDIM approach were applied to address an absence problem faced by Arlanda Electronics.

Chapter 15

Applying the ALIEDIM approach: a case study

Introduction

The aim of this final chapter is to describe how one company has attempted to deal with its absence problem in the systematic manner that we propose. We believe that such an approach will increase substantially the chances of finding a workable solution to the absence problem. The Arlanda case study is not offered as an example of a success story, in the style of many other management books. Instead, it illustrates that overcoming the absence problem requires thought, time and patience. Arlanda's management has recognized that there are no easy, quick-fix solutions, and is devoting resources to tackling the problem. Our purpose then, in using this case study, is to illustrate the potential worth of dealing with absenteeism in an informed and systematic manner. The various steps of our approach, the ALIEDIM process, were defined and illustrated in the previous chapter.

This chapter will provide some general background on the company, and show the need for absence reduction as part of a productivity improvement programme. The incidence of absenteeism will be considered in some detail, and will be followed by an assessment of the resultant costs and operational impact. Company approaches to the monitoring and control of absence will then be evaluated. We shall show that, where understanding is lacking, managers reach for *personalized theories* which are based on wide-ranging, and often contradictory, assessments of human behaviour. The application of the ALIEDIM approach to absence control at Arlanda Electronics will be described in detail.

Company background

Arlanda Electronics is a real company whose identity has been disguised. The absence data presented is taken directly from the company's own records. The factory is located in a relatively depressed part of the United Kingdom, and when it first opened, manufacturing was restricted to producing a range of components for the company's domestic consumer products. Over the years however, a considerable expansion and diversification has occurred, and the main manufacturing activities now comprise diskette manufacture, circuit-board assembly, and screen monitor production. In addition, the company has recently expanded into the assembly of electronic testing equipment on a subcontracting basis.

The workforce consists of about 1350 employees, who can be classified according to work area, manufacturing system and shift pattern. This information is shown in Table 15.1.

The majority of the workforce lives within five miles of the plant. Arlanda Electronics is one of the few remaining major private sector employers in the area which, during the last decade, has become an unemployment blackspot. Unemployment is running at 20%. Historically, Arlanda has regarded itself as a progressive, caring organization. The company is non-unionized, but workers are represented by an elected employees' committee. Pay rates, working conditions, and employment practices are outstanding. Considerable progress has been made towards harmonization, and although hourly-paid workers still clock on, they enjoy most of the benefits traditionally associated with staff status. These include common

Table 15.1 Arlanda Electronics: manufacturing facility overview

	Factory Unit 1		Factory Unit 2		
	Diskette Division	Circuit-board Division	Screen Monitor Division	Test Equipment Division	Services and Administration Division
(a) *Manufacturing system*	Mass Production Capital intensive	Mass Production Capital intensive	Mass Production Assembly-line/labour intensive	Mass Production Assembly-line/labour intensive	— —
(b) *Work pattern* Direct	3-shift rotating	Day/4-hr twilight	Day	4 × 4-hr part-time	—
Indirect	3-shift/ day	Day/4-hr twilight	Day/shift	Day/shift	Mainly day
(c) *Employees* Direct	135	20	330	150	—
Sex	Male	Female	Female	Female	
Indirect	180	5	240	25	260
Sex	M/F	M/F	M/F	M/F	M/F
	315	25	570	175	260

pension rights, cafeteria facilities, and payment terms for sickness and authorized absence. These aspects reflect the 'Arlanda Belief System' passed down through the organization by its founder. The belief system emphasizes two inseparable ideals. These are excellent products, and a worthwhile working life for members.

In the early 1980s, the company's products were extremely profitable. However, since about 1984 profits and unit sales have been eroded by increased competition both in the home electronics field and in the business computer sector. To remain competitive, the company has had to introduce a number of improvement programmes aimed particularly at operating efficiencies, manning levels, and cost reductions. Clearly, absence levels represent a key variable in the determination of productivity. The company has, for many years, struggled to control absenteeism which seemed to be particularly high in certain areas of the plant. Overall absence levels were viewed increasingly as unacceptable and inconsistent with future company objectives. Arlanda had an absentee problem. However, every problem can also be seen as an opportunity, and in this case, it represented a major opportunity to increase productivity. For this reason, management focused its attention on the absenteeism.

Managers were aware that something was wrong, and felt that reducing absence could contribute positively to the required productivity drive. Towards the end of 1986, the company decided to address its absence problem squarely, by developing a formal absence control policy, of which, we shall examine the results and consequences later in the chapter. At this stage, it is useful to consider the information available to management, and the managerial perceptions of the absence problem in 1986. We can do this by asking six questions,

- How was absence defined, recorded and monitored in 1986?

- How great was the absence problem?

- Where did most of the absence occur?

- What was the cost and impact of absence?

- How was absence controlled in 1986?

- What were held to be the main causes of absence at the time?

Definition, recording and monitoring of absence in Arlanda Electronics

Absence at Arlanda referred to, and included, sickness absence, authorized absence, and all forms of unauthorized absence. It did not include certain types of permissible absence such as holidays, educational and training courses, public duties, such as jury service, and maternity leave. This categorization was reasonably consistent with the recommended practice of, for example, the Arbitration and Conciliation Advisory Service (ACAS). The most common measure of absence is the *lost time rate*, which was used by the company to determine the overall severity of its absence problem. This rate shows the percentage of time lost through absence in relation to the total time available for work, viz.

$$\frac{\text{Total absence in period (days + part days)}}{\text{Possible total time available (days)}} \times 100\%$$

Absence data was collected by the company at the individual employee level by means of a clocking system for hourly-paid personnel, and by manual records for salaried staff. This information was fed into a computerized personnel database that enabled management to monitor total absence versus available work-days at individual, departmental, and divisional level through the use of a comprehensive package of absence reports. Statistics could be compared over a period, and were classified according to whether they related to certified sickness, self-certified sickness, authorized absence, or unauthorized absence. Such a detailed classification and analysis ostensibly formed part of an absence information and control system. However, formal personnel policies on absence tended to concentrate mainly on the procedural and administrative aspects related to the notification, recording and payment of different types of absence.

How great was the absence problem?

The company's lost-time rates for the three years 1984–6 are summarized in Table 15.2, which shows that over 80% of absence was ostensibly attributable to sickness. This finding is consistent with other studies. The table

Table 15.2 Arlanda Electronics: Absence analysis by type of absence (percentage of days' absence versus available working days)

Absence type	1984	1985	1986
Certified sickness	3.3	2.6	2.6
Self-certified sickness	1.8	2.4	2.2
Authorized absence	0.9	0.8	0.9
Unauthorized absence	0.3	0.2	0.2
Average	6.3	6.0	5.9
Paid absence	6.0	5.7	5.7

also shows that Arlanda's overall absence rate had remained fairly stable over the 1984–6 period at around 6%. This compared favourably with the 8% rate which was the UK national average for firms in the industry group 'Other manufacturing' *(General Household Survey, 1984)*. Nevertheless, management was conscious that its absence rate would have to be reduced considerably from this 6% figure, if the necessary productivity gains were to be achieved.

Where did most absence occur?

As the data was probed more deeply, an uneven picture of absence rates was revealed across the divisions. This is shown in Table 15.3.

This analysis clearly highlighted to managers the major differences that existed in absence rates. The first difference to be noticed was between

Table 15.3 Arlanda Electronics: Absence analysis by division (percentage of days' absence versus available working days)

	1984 %	1985 %	1986 %	Three-year average %	Average days lost per man year %
All employees					
Total company	6.3	6.0	5.9	6.1	14
Monitor Division	7.6	7.6	7.4	7.5	17
Diskette/Circuit-board Divisions	5.3	4.4	5.6	5.1	12
Test Equipment Division	—	—	3.5	3.5	8
Administration	4.3	4.0	4.1	4.1	9
All hourly					
Total company	7.6	7.5	7.2	7.4	17
Monitor Division	8.8	9.1	8.8	8.9	20
Diskette/Circuit-board Divisions	5.8	5.1	6.4	5.8	13
Test Equipment Division	—	—	3.6	3.6	8
Administration	6.2	5.9	5.6	5.9	13
All salaried					
Total company	3.6	2.9	3.5	3.3	7
Monitor Division	3.5	2.8	3.5	3.3	7
Diskette/Circuit-board Division	3.6	2.2	3.4	3.1	7
Test Equipment Division	—	—	0.9	0.9	2
Administration	3.7	3.4	3.6	3.6	8

hourly-paid and salaried employees. The relative proportions which are shown below are typical and not unusual. An absence policy to reduce the absence of hourly-paid staff to the level of salaried staff would represent a reasonable productivity improvement target for Arlanda.

	Absence	*Average days lost*
Hourly-paid	7.4%	17
Salaried	3.3%	7

A second finding from the table was the significant difference in average absenteeism amongst the four divisions. For example, the absence rate of hourly paid monitor staff (8.9%/20 days) compares very unfavourably with that of hourly workers in the Test Equipment Division (3.5%/8 days). This latter group of hourly-paid staff in fact, had virtually the same absence rate as the salaried staff.

An examination of the departmental records revealed a third finding. This was that the absence rate of hourly-paid (direct) employees, was about 2% higher than that of the hourly-paid (indirect) employees. A direct worker is one who is involved in the production process at first hand. These results proved to be extremely difficult for management to interpret at company level. This was particularly so when individual departments or specific groups of workers regularly attained absence levels that were inconsistent with those of their peers.

Cost and impact of absence

What effect did absence have on the company? Table 15.2 showed that nearly all the absence was either certified sickness, self-certified sickness or authorized absence. For this reason, almost all of it was paid for by the company. Arlanda commissioned its accounts department to calculate the cost of absence for 1986. Basing the calculations on an analysis of the absence data and employee pay rate information, the cost of absence was computed by the accountant. This is shown in Table 15.4. Although no

Table 15.4 Arlanda Electronics: Absence payment and fringe costs, 1986

	£
Certified sickness	240 000
Self-certified sickness	160 000
Other absences	50 000
	450 000
Less: NHI benefit offset	−60 000
Net absence payments	400 000

further figures were calculated, the accountant did draw management's attention to a number of indirect costs which were also caused by absence and which he felt were significant. For example, the manufacturing divisions of the company operated to tight production targets which had to be met 'at all costs'.

In order to safeguard output in the face of significant employee absence, the company's operating plans included two budgeted on-costs. First, there were the *labour-intensive assembly areas*. Surplus personnel were carried in line with budgeted absence levels. At the time of writing, this represented a surplus labour pool of about 40 people, who, if the absence rate was zero, would not have been required. Second, there were the *capital-intensive areas and support groups*. Additional overtime allowances, including premia, were budgeted in line with historical absence levels in each department. Once again, this would not have been necessary had the absence rate been lower.

In assessing the indirect impact of absence, the company noted three main effects. These were that managers and supervisors experienced difficulties in balancing manning; there were adverse effects on product quality, and demotivating effects on other employees. Discussions with supervisors and managers also revealed a loss of group cohesion and a fall in morale. Both of these arose from the practice of spontaneously moving employees around the different manufacturing areas in response to temporary labour shortages. It was felt that this practice itself exacerbated the absence problem. Absence cover, either through overtime or redeployment, also had a detrimental effect on operating efficiencies. The factory relied heavily on traditional work-study techniques, and experience had shown that established standards of performance were not being achieved in absence cover situations. In the Diskette Production Division, equipment utilization and run-times suffered, while in the Screen Monitor Division, optimal labour performance became unachievable as key skills went absent.

How was absence being controlled in 1986?

On the surface, company policy did make provision for absence control by defining the appropriate disciplinary procedures. For example, it stated that employees might be discharged for unsatisfactory performance. This was held to include frequent absenteeism and bad timekeeping. In addition, disciplinary measures, including dismissal, might be appropriate if employees were absent without proper justification, or if they made false statements in connection with an application for sick pay. The disciplinary procedures were designed to comply with the Employment Protection Act (Consolidated) 1980, which required that employees should be given every opportunity to correct unsatisfactory performance prior to discharge. Provision was therefore made for the progressive passage of absenting employees through counselling, verbal warning, written warning, final written warning, and ultimately dismissal, when improvements were not forth-coming.

Closer scrutiny of these procedures, and the nature of the absence itself, gave rise to a number of practical difficulties. Typically, senior management would react from time to time to unacceptably high absence statistics by insisting that management and supervisors should improve performance by enforcing the disciplinary code more strongly. Efforts to counsel employees therefore generally occurred at first-line supervisory level, with the personnel department providing co-ordination and advice.

However, there was no clear definition inside the company of what constituted unsatisfactory performance. Thus, supervisors who, in other areas of activity were encouraged to exercise discretion, were often unsure of their ground. As a result, considerable inconsistency arose in the application of the policy, and many employees felt unfairly treated. This problem was made more difficult because supervisors tended to concentrate their efforts on deterring those whom they considered to be malingerers and those who 'played the system'. The fact that the bulk of the absence problem was presented to the company as legitimate sickness made their policing role difficult, and led to most absence going unquestioned.

The managers and supervisors in the company felt that although the information systems and control procedures were informative and super-ficially adequate, they failed to provide an appropriate framework for managing absence. This view was borne out by a study of the trends. Despite a number of management purges on absentees, absence levels had not been reduced, and the disciplinary procedures had had little impact. At the last count, only four employees were on a final written warning, and virtually no one had been dismissed for unsatisfactory attendance for a number of years.

Arlanda's management, along with many others, was aware that medical certificates were being issued virtually on demand. Since 1982, all UK employees have been able to complete self-certification forms without a doctor's signature for up to seven days. Commentators generally agree that it is virtually impossible to establish the real facts in many cases of reported sickness absence. In this situation, there was an urgent need to reduce this kind of absence, yet the company had no clear policy to guide such attempts.

What were the main causes of absence held to be at the time?

The failure to solve the absence problem at Arlanda derived to a large extent from a failure to understand the real causes of absence. In the absence of knowledge of these, there was no shortage of personal theories amongst company managers and supervisors. Every Arlanda manager had a set of views and concepts relating to all the problems faced at work, including absence. The important point about personal axioms is that they begin with a set of assumptions, and then they go on to describe or prescribe a set of actions possible under the assumed conditions. Finally they purport to predict and explain the causal linkages determining the set of results.

At Arlanda, all managers had their own particular perspective of the absence problem. Depending on whom you asked, you would be told that employees abused the system in areas where supervision was weak; that when jobs were repetitive and boring, absence was bound to be high; that salaried staff had a different code of behaviour from shopfloor workers; that many women had conflicting domestic responsibilities and in most cases their job would take second place; and that if you wanted to improve attendance, you had to reward the good attenders.

These statements represent personal theories that guided action. For example, the statement that employees will abuse the system when supervision is poor implies a set of beliefs about employees' attitudes towards work, and their predispositions towards company goals. Given these assumptions, the axiom indicates what will happen (employees will take excessive time off) if management does not behave in a given manner (if it does not exercise control and supervise closely).

The real significance of these sets of beliefs lies in the influence that they exert on management decisions and actions. Clearly the choice of 'solutions' (absence control techniques) which managers design, depends upon their implicit theories about the problem under consideration. An individual manager's personal theories may be inconsistent with one another. The situation becomes more complex as inconsistencies arise between the theories of different managers and different supervisors. It is hardly surprising therefore that in such a situation, the company had difficulty both in assembling a cohesive view of the absence problem and its causes, and in deciding upon an appropriate approach to control it. In such a climate there was a strong temptation to reach for a quick-fix solution for which there was no shortage of such prepackaged advice on offer.

Of all the personal theories about absence that were put forward at the time, one in particular received a great deal of support from the members of the management team. This was the view that the main cause of the problem was the disciplinary procedure itself. It was held that the existing procedure was unfair, poorly understood, and inconsistently applied. In the opinion of the employees, the absence policy encouraged supervisors to speculate freely about the honesty of individual workers. Inevitably, as disciplinary measures were taken, the procedure became unworkable due to the resistance of the employees, which was based on their perceptions of its weaknesses. Moreover, the supervisors were unable to produce hard evidence to support their beliefs when they were confronted by denials from employees.

Thus, in 1986, management thought that the absence problem was caused by a poor disciplinary system. This view was important for at least two reasons. First, it led managers to try to solve the problem by devising an alternative disciplinary system without the limitations of the procedure they already had. Second, and perhaps most important, management's attitude towards this issue meant that no attention was paid at all to the crucial question of *why* certain sections of the workforce had consistently high rates of absence, while other areas of the factory had excellent attendance. Thus, the true causes of the absence were never considered.

Absence control plan selected

Arlanda's management perceived employee absence to be a disciplinary problem. In response, they adopted a no-fault absence plan, which was introduced in January 1987. The principle underlying this approach is that every employee is paid to be present at work. Under the no-fault plan, employees are considered to be either at work or absent. Each type of absence carries a predetermined penalty, with the exception of a few clearly defined 'non-chargeable absences'. Absences are called 'occurrences', and an occurrence can be for any length of time. It may be one, two, three, four or more days. The strategy is geared to management's costliest and most troublesome absence problem – the chronic offender. This is the employee who incurs many single day absences. Under the no-fault plan, employees who are frequently absent, quickly collect multiple occurrences and are subject to disciplinary action. On the other hand, the employee who is occasionally away for three or four days is considered to be genuinely ill. In theory at least, the no-fault policy tries to place heavier penalties upon the persistent absentee, without penalizing the person with a real illness.

Under the no-fault plan, *all* occurrences, regardless of their reason are chargeable for purposes of disciplinary action. These include short-term illness, illness of family members, transportation problems, and emergencies at home. There are a few, very narrowly defined non-chargeable occurrences. These include funerals, jury service, official union business, hospital confinement and work-incurred injury. The plan absolves the employee from having to justify an absence, and management does not have to determine whether an employee's absence is justified or not. The need for justifications is eliminated. In essence, an employee is either at work or not. The burden of responsibility for good attendance is placed squarely on the shoulders of the employee.

No-fault plans can reward employees by incorporating a provision for one occurrence to be removed by a calendar month of perfect attendance. At the same time, a no-fault plan punishes employees. Absence records are maintained for a consecutive 12-month period beginning with the employee's first absence occurrence. All the disciplinary action taken by the company is related to the number of occurrences accumulated during the previous 12-month period. The disciplinary procedure is administered according to the number of occurrences or 'points' that the employee has accumulated. The policy usually incorporates a progressive disciplinary procedure that involves greater penalties as points accumulate, with dismissal as the final disciplinary step. Management determines the number of points that will trigger the different disciplinary actions.

Arlanda's management saw 6 benefits in introducing this scheme. It offered them *consistency* in that it dealt with absolute values, while relying on accurate data. It possessed *objectivity* in that the system could not prejudge an issue, and it was therefore profoundly honest. Third, it had a *reporting* advantage in that it gave supervisors time to deal with the problem rather than involving them in establishing the facts of the absence, and interpreting them. It placed *responsibility* on the individual to attend, and was *flexible* by having narrowly-defined, 'non-chargeable' occurrences. Finally, it was *discipline-focused* which allowed for a counselling and consultation process to take place that might ultimately lead to a disciplinary action if all else failed.

Arlanda's no-fault absence plan produced an *absence profile* or index for each person. The plan was really a statistically based control system which could create 'hit lists' of high absence employees based on scores that were a function of the frequency of absence and duration of absence (rate) over a rolling 12-month period. An example of a profile is shown in Table 15.5.

Employees were graded into the top 10%, 7%, 3% and 1%. A series of warnings were given, depending upon the stage that the individual had reached in the disciplinary procedure. The monitoring system was computer-driven, and utilized the attendance recording system that was required for payroll costing to establish an individual absence database. The computer identified the people with the highest (10%) absence index over a 12-month period. These would be automatically counselled. The system was adopted on a company-wide basis. Figure 15.1 shows a flowchart of the absence monitoring procedure that accompanied the introduction of the no-fault plan. Its purpose was to set an acceptable standard, to monitor results, provide feedback through reports, and to counsel employees into improved attendance.

Arlanda's employees saw the implementation of the new absence control plan as a typical management response, and as a confirmation of their view that management was not to be trusted. Employees feared that those who

Table 15.5 Example of Arlanda's employee absence profile

Employee	(a) Number of absence occurrences (frequency)	(b) Number of days off (duration)	(a) × (b) Absence index
A	5	20	100
B	7	12	84
C	3	15	45
D	1	25	25

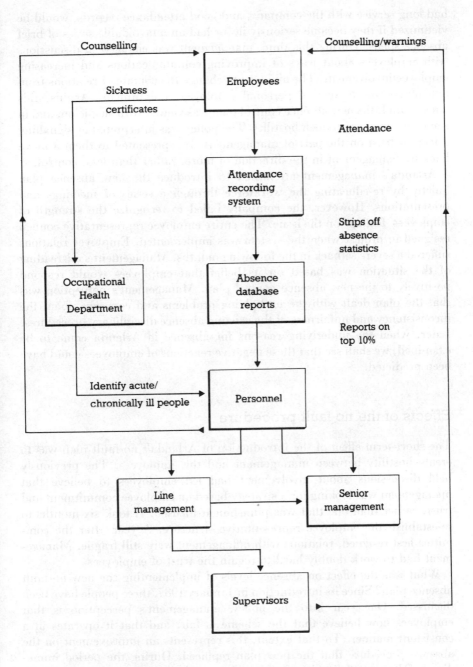

Figure 15.1 Flowchart of Arlanda's no-fault absence control plan

had long service with the company, and good attendance records, would be victimized if they became seriously ill, or had an unavoidable series of brief absence spells. During this time, management was engaged in discussions with employees about ways of improving communications and increasing employee involvement. The aim was to change the climate of relations from one of control to one of personal employee commitment. Against this background, the new absence control plan was viewed with suspicion, and in some instances, with open hostility. The policy was interpreted as signalling a lack of trust on the part of management. It represented to them a move back by management in the direction of more, rather than less, control.

Arlanda's management attempted to introduce the new absence plan quietly by re-educating the workforce through a series of meetings and presentations. However, the company failed to recognize the strength of employees' feelings on the issue. The entire employee representative council resigned in protest when the system was implemented. Employee relations suffered a severe setback in the following months. Management's misreading of the situation was based on its belief that employees would respond positively to the new absence control plan. Management's perception was that the plan dealt with the underlying problems and concerns about the inconsistency and unfairness of the existing absence disciplinary procedures. Later, when the underlying reasons for absence in Arlanda come to be examined, we shall see that these negative reactions of employees could have been predicted.

Effects of the no-fault procedure

The short-term effect of the introduction of Arlanda's no-fault plan was to create hostility between management and the employees. The previously held discussions about involvement had led employees to believe that management was looking for a strategy based on employee commitment and trust, rather than one that was punishment-focused. It took six months to re-establish the employee representative structure. A year after the committee first resigned, relations with management were still fragile. Management had to work doubly hard to regain the trust of employees.

What was the effect on absence levels of implementing the new no-fault absence plan? Since its introduction in January 1987, three people have been dismissed. One year into the policy, management's perception is that employees now believe that the scheme is fair, and that it operates in a consistent manner. To that extent, this represents an improvement on the absence procedure that the new plan replaced. During the period immediately following the implementation of the no-fault plan there did appear to be a marked improvement in attendance. However, it is possible to question this cause-and-effect relationship because, during the period under consideration, a number of temporary employees were recruited, and past records showed that the absence rates of this class of worker have been consistently lower than those of permanent or longer-term workers.

Arlanda's management team now generally recognizes that in the second half of 1987 the underlying absence figures showed a drift back up to pre-1987 levels. In some sections of the company, where absence was particularly high, there has still been a moderate improvement. However, management's view is that in overall company terms, the no-fault absence policy has not had the major effect expected, and has not really altered the underlying absence behaviour. The comparative statistics are shown in Table 15.6.

Table 15.6 Arlanda's absence rates 1984-7

| | Absence rate (%) | | |
| | | 1987 | |
Division	Three-year average 1984-6	Full year	Last 3 months
All employees	6.1	4.7	5.2
Monitor Division	7.5	5.5	6.4
Diskette/Circuit-board Division	5.1	4.8	5.2
Test Equipment Division	3.5	3.0	3.0
Administration	4.1	3.3	3.6

At the start of 1988, we were invited by Arlanda's management to look at the company's absence situation to pinpoint the possible causes of absence, and to make recommendations for improvements. The case of Arlanda Electronics provided an excellent opportunity to illustrate the various steps of the ALIEDIM Seven-Step Approach and to demonstrate the potential effectiveness of this systematic plan in controlling absence.

We applied the ALIEDIM Seven-Step Approach to deal with Arlanda's absence problem. The steps were detailed in Chapter 14 and we shall now describe each of them in relation to Arlanda Electronics. In the first five we shall describe what actually was done. For the remaining two, we shall present our recommendations for the implementation and monitoring of the absence control programme.

Step 1   Arlanda Electronics: assess the absence problem

Earlier in the chapter, we explained that Arlanda's management already felt that employee absence was excessive. Thus, there was no need to persuade it to take the problem seriously. It was not necessary to establish whether or not a significant absence problem existed. Attention could therefore be paid immediately to the *size* of the productivity improvement opportunity afforded by absenteeism.

Activity A: external comparisons

By using the external benchmarks recommended and by inserting Arlanda's actual absence rate, the management recognized that a *medium* productivity opportunity existed. This is shown in Table 15.7. The figure of 5%–6% was an average for the whole of the company. In our discussion of Step 1 in Chapter 14, we stressed that an apparently satisfactory overall situation may disguise an underlying problem at the section, department, or unit level. It was felt that the same review could be conducted for specific sections of Arlanda's operations. Using the same independent external absence benchmarks, the review might reveal areas of the company where *large* productivity opportunities existed. It will be shown later, that this was in fact the case.

Table 15.7 Comparison of Arlanda's absence figure with external benchmarks

External absence benchmark	Arlanda's absence figure	Productivity improvement opportunity
3% 3-4%		Small
5-8%	5%-6% over four years	Medium
9-10% 10%		Large

Activity B: internal comparisons

We now turned to consider the internal benchmarks. This requires the provision of regular comparative figures. Usually, these figures compare the performance of one unit or section of a factory or company with that of similar units or sections. The absence data from Arlanda indicated that absenteeism was not equally distributed throughout the different sections and divisions of the company. Indeed, it was possible to use the absence figures to create a league table with three rankings of absence (low, medium and high). There were the sections in each division which had low absence rates and where, therefore, the scope for relative improvement was small. At the other extreme, there were those sections whose absence figures were dramatically high, and where there was ample scope for improvement. The comparative internal comparisons are shown in Table 15.8.

If similar internal comparative rankings were conducted at lower levels in the company, for example by department, or by the type of employee, then

Table 15.8 Ranking of Arlanda's divisions based on an internal comparison of their absence rates

Section ranking	Scope for relative improvement—by division
1 Test Equipment Division	Small
2 Administration	
3 Diskette/Circuit-board Division	Medium
4 Screen Monitor Division	High

particular areas where there was a large scope for relative improvement would certainly be identified. The subsequent analysis will show this.

Activity C: cost of absence

We mentioned earlier that the magnitude of an absence problem will be judged by the true cost of absenteeism to the company and the operational impact that it has. The initial cost of absence calculation, conducted in 1986, was based upon the direct, short-term, and easily quantifiable costs such as sickness payments. This gave a figure of £400 000. See Table 15.4.

We asked Arlanda's accountant to conduct a second, and this time more thorough, calculation. Using the 1986 data once again, we asked him to identify the indirect, longer-term, and less easily assessed costs. To help him in this task, he was supplied with the ALIEDIM *Calculating the true costs of absence checklist* which was presented in the previous chapter. The figures that he produced, using this checklist, are shown in Table 15.9.

This more detailed analysis revealed that at £775 000, the true cost of absence to Arlanda, was almost double the direct cost estimate that had been provided by the company's accountant earlier. Having obtained these more realistic figures, management now had the opportunity to make comparisons, and assess the productivity opportunity that reduced absence offered.

Comparisons for Arlanda:

- absence cost as a percentage of annual turnover = 1.0%
- absence cost as a percentage of annual profit (before tax) = 10.5%
- absence cost as a percentage of total annual operating costs = 1.1%
- absence cost as a percentage of added value = 3.0%

Table 15.9 Arlanda Electronics: Calculating the true costs of absence

		£ (annual)
1	*Direct costs of absence*	
1.1	Sick pay	350 000
1.2	Continued payment of fringe benefits during absence	50 000
1.3	Overtime payments for those filling in for absentees	100 000
1.4	Overtime payments arising from absence for employees farther down the line	20 000
1.5	Excess cost of temporary staff employed (i.e. employment agency premium)	Not relevant to Arlanda
1.6	Overstaffing to cover for absence *Weekly wage plus employment cost × number of extra staff × 52*	40 operators, but in this case it would duplicate the true cost to include the payroll of these workers as the penalty to the company is already covered in items 1.1 and 1.2 above. This may not be the case for other organizations.
2	*Indirect costs*	£ (annual)
2.1	Cost of recruiting and training extra staff *Cost per person × number of persons* <u>*40 persons × £500 per person*</u>	20 000
2.2	Cost of management/supervisory time devoted to dealing with absence-related issues, e.g. revising schedules, disciplining, record-keeping, counselling *Hours devoted per week × hourly rate × 52* <u>*200 hours × £6 × 52*</u>	60 000
2.3	Reduced productivity from work being done by less experienced/more tired employees, from returning workers operating at lower point in learning curve *Excess hours per annum required to achieve standard output × hourly pay rate* <u>*10 000 hours × £4 per hour*</u>	40 000

Table 15.9 (*Continued*)

2 Indirect costs	£ (annual)
2.4 Lower product quality of work due to replacement of staff	
Cost of rejects, i.e. cost of scrap materials	20 000
and	
cost of rework, i.e. materials and labour costs to put things right	20 000
and	
cost of extra premiums to maintain saleable volume, e.g. extra overtime to make up the volume	20 000
2.5 Cost of disruptions/section shutdown due to absenteeism	
Estimate of profit forgone by lost production or financial penalty incurred due to late delivery, cost of feeding other parts of the company.	Not applicable to Arlanda
2.6 Extra costs incurred to meet slipped deadlines, e.g. freighting by air instead of sea	Not applicable to Arlanda
2.7 Loss of customers due to failure to meet deadline or to inferior product quality (last financial year)	
Profit loss from customers who did not reorder as expected (when this can be related to absence)	Not applicable to Arlanda
2.8 Low morale amongst other employees caused by lax attendance of certain employees (lateness, turnover, failure to work at measured standard performance).	
Very difficult to measure, but if Arlanda assumed that the impact was a 1% productivity loss, then the penalty would be:	50 000
2.9 Imagine that your company did not have an absence problem, i.e. that it was less than 1%. What equipment would no longer be necessary, how many absence-monitoring staff could be dispensed with or reallocated to other work? Estimate the cost savings involved in equipment purchase or hire, and wages and employment costs for staff, i.e. what are the excess costs incurred against the best attainable.	
Again difficult to estimate, but for Arlanda a guesstimate would be:	25 000
2.10 Insert any other calculations relevant to your organization or section.	None identified
Annual cost of absence GRAND TOTAL	£775 000

Finally, Arlanda's management used these more realistic figures to determine the potential gains that could be achieved if absence were to be reduced in the factory.

- Anticipated profit (before tax) improvement for a 1% improvement in absence   = £130 000

- Anticipated profit (before tax) improvement by meeting the targeted external benchmark   = £400 000

Having conducted the analysis, management judged the factory productivity opportunity to be:

SMALL ☐

MEDIUM ☐

LARGE ☑

Thus, while the company's absence rate was better than the industry sector average (6% versus 8%), the calculations demonstrated that while the absence problem itself may have been *medium* in size, the productivity improvement opportunity that its reduction offered to Arlanda was *large*.

Step 2   Arlanda Electronics: locate the absence problem

Arlanda's absence data was held in a powerful, computerized personnel database adjacent to the history files of individual employees. After discussion with the data processing staff, it became apparent that it would be possible to conduct a more detailed statistical analysis of the absence data and that this analysis could examine the association of a number of variables. By correlating absence data with the personnel history files, a number of analyses were conducted, and absence was analysed by:

(a)   division
(b)   work classification
(c)   pay classification
(d)   age
(e)   sex
(f)   shift pattern
(g)   employment category
(h)   job category
(i)   marital status
(j)   length of service

Arlanda's absence rate of 6% was below the national average rate of 8% for

Table 15.10   Arlanda Electronics: Absence by division

Division	Sample size	Days lost (%)	Average number of absence spells
Monitor	569	7.4	2.8
Diskette	314	5.6	3.0
Test Equipment	175	3.5	1.9
Circuit-board	26	5.5	1.5
Administration	258	4.1	2.1

companies in the *other manufacturing* category of the *General Household Survey (1984)*. However, it has been shown that absence represented an annual cost to the company of approximately £0.75 million, and caused it numerous operational difficulties. In addition, it was found that the incidence of absence was spread unevenly. There was a higher absence rate amongst hourly-paid workers (especially those in the Screen Monitor Division), and a particularly low absence figure amongst salaried staff and those employed in the Test Equipment Division.

The above report, generated by a simple computer program, illustrates what can be done by this method and shows the format used by Arlanda to analyse company absence by key variables. Any thorough analysis of absence should take account of both *the rate of lost time*, and also *the frequency rate* (number of spells of absence). This has been done. All the analyses were based on one year's results to December 1986, and this particular sample showed the total absence of 1342 employees analysed by division (Table 15.10).

Besides producing company-wide analyses such as this, a program was written to interrogate the subsets of information. For example, the following example shows a summary of direct labour only (636 employees) analysed by shift pattern (Table 15.11).

In all, some sixteen summary reports were extracted in this way from the computer database, and these are all shown in Table 15.12. These analyses

Table 15.11   Arlanda Electronics: Absence type of labour/ shift pattern

| Category: Direct labour | | Ref: Report 12 | |
| Variable: Shift pattern | | | |
Shift pattern	Sample size	Days lost (%)	Average number of absence spells
Day	263	10.5	3.2
Part-time	262	3.7	1.7
Shift	111	6.4	3.6
Total	636	7.1	3.6

Table 15.12 Arlanda Electronics: Absence analysis by 16 variables - summarized form

	Classification	Group	Number	%age Days Absence (Jan–Dec 1986)	Average Spells Absence
1	All employees by division	Test equipment	175		
		Administration	258		
		Diskette	314		
		Circuit-boards	26		
		Monitor	569		
			1342		
2	All employees by work class	Indirect	706		
		Direct	636		
3	All employees by pay class	Monthly	218		
		Weekly	180		
		Hourly	944		
4	All employees by age	16 – 24	137		
		25 – 34	350		
		35 – 44	488		
		45 – 54	294		
		55 +	73		
5	All employees by sex	Male	638		
		Female	704		
6	All employees by shift pattern	Part-time	319		
		Shift	385		
		Day	638		
7	All employees by employment cat.	Temporary	200		
		Permanent	1142		
8	All employees by job category	Sal. – Mgmt.	33		
		Sal. – Supv'n.	49		
		Sal. – Admin./Tech.	159		
		Sal. – Clerical	157		
		Hrly. – Skilled	78		
		Hrly. – Manual	866		
9	All employees by marital status	Married	1083		
		Single/widowed	259		
10	All employees by length of service	1 – 5	286		
		6 – 10	759		
		11 +	297		
11	Direct labour by division	Sub-contracting	150		
		Screen	21		
		Diskette	135		
		Monitor	330		
			636		
12	Direct labour by shift pattern	Part-time	262		
		Shift	111		
		Day	263		
13	Direct labour by employment cat.	Temporary	150		
		Permanent	486		
14	Indirect labour by division	Sub-contracting	25		
		Screen	5		
		Administration	258		
		Diskette	179		
		Monitor	239		
			706		
15	Indirect labour by pay class	Monthly	218		
		Weekly	180		
		Hourly	308		
16	Indirect labour by sex	Male	480		
		Female	226		

%age Days Absence scale: 1 2 3 4 5 6 7 8 9 10
Average Spells Absence scale: 1 2 3 4

provided a rich database to be considered by Arlanda's management. In addition, several of the classifications related closely to the factors discussed in the literature review of absence causes presented in Part two. These were age, shift pattern, and job type.

A number of striking patterns emerged from this analysis. The job classification analysis (Classification 8) illustrated the progressive increase in the absence rate percentage as the status of the 'job family' was reduced. From a low of about 1% for the top job family of *management*, absence rose to almost 7% for the lowest job family, that of *hourly-paid manual workers*.

Classification 5 related to the sex of the workers, and is also significant. It showed a higher level of absence amongst female workers (7.0%) than amongst male workers (3.7%). In attempting to pinpoint areas which could serve as the basis for further analysis, attention should be paid both to the *time lost* rate and to the *frequency* rate. This data can be analysed usefully in many ways, and at many different levels. We proceeded to identify the most significant absence areas, in line with the ALIEDIM approach presented in Chapter 14, and considered the absence problem in terms of both lost time and frequency.

Was it a *lost time rate* problem?

Classification 2 (absence by work class) showed that the absence rate was higher for direct workers (7.1%) than for indirect employees (4%). Classifications 11, 12 and 13 examined direct labour performance in more detail by considering them by division, shift pattern, and employment category. The data showed that not all the direct labour groupings had high absence. From this information it was possible to produce a profile of the poor attender (when measured by the lost time rate). It was found that this person was a *direct* worker employed on a *permanent* basis, and working *dayshift* in the *Monitor Division* of the company. The absence rate for this profiled employee was almost 10%.

Was it a *frequency rate* problem?

Classification 1 (absence by division) showed that when the absence frequency measure was used, the location of the worst level of absence changed. It was the Diskette Division that had the highest absence frequency over the year. This observation was considered in conjunction with Classifications 11, 12 and 13. It was found that the profile of the frequent absentee, as measured on a frequency rate basis was a *direct* worker employed on a *permanent* basis and working *rotating shifts* in the *Diskette Division*. This grouping was found to have an average of 3.6 spells of absences per annum, as compared with the factory average of 2.6 absences per employee per annum.

By using the available absence data, the writers were able to locate the company's absence problem. The analysis revealed that there were two major groupings of high absence in the company. If these were addressed, then the overall level of absence could be lowered significantly. The two groups were,

Group A *Direct* workers employed on a *permanent* basis, and working *dayshift* on the *Screen Monitor Division* (lost time problem).

Group B *Direct* workers employed on a *permanent* basis and working *rotating shifts* in the *Diskette Division* (frequency problem).

The benefit of locating the absence groups so accurately, was that when it came to producing an absence control programme, management could target these groups accurately, instead of having to apply a blunderbuss solution to the problem.

Step 3   Arlanda Electronics: identify and prioritize the absence causes

Having located the absence problem in the employee subgroups, the writers now had to identify the causes of absence. In doing this, they were greatly assisted by the availability of the results of an employee attitude survey that had been commissioned by management in 1984 following some organizational changes. The survey itself had been conducted amongst the workforce by an outside firm of consultants. Answers were obtained directly from employees on their attitudes to work, supervision, pay and other relevant aspects of their job. Information from this survey was used to identify and prioritize the possible causes of absence. Each absence group was considered in turn.

Group A

Group A were the direct workers employed on a permanent basis, and working dayshift on the Screen Monitor Division. They comprised hourly-paid, female employees employed in a mass production assembly line environment. An initial examination by management, suggested that the major influences on attendance might be

— personal characteristics (e.g. sex)
— employee values (women less committed to job?)
— reduced ability to attend (family responsibilities)
— nature of work situation.

The implication that absence might be associated with the sex of the employee was supported by the finding that indirect female absence was also higher than indirect male absence (see Table 15.12, Classification 16). However, it should be noted that *indirect* female absence was less than 6%.

In fact, a separate analysis showed that *salaried* female workers, excluding hourly-paid indirects, had an absence level below 4%. These findings suggested that *the nature of the work situation* could be an important influence on the absence problem as well.

The findings of the attitude survey mentioned earlier, revealed that, in the case of the absence problem of workers in Group A, there was significant dissatisfaction amongst the female direct labour force in the Screen Monitor Division. In particular, concerns were voiced about

- The monotony of the work

- The frustration caused by production interruptions, equipment breakdowns, and defective materials

- The work rates that were required. Specifically, these were perceived as being unreasonably high; they were felt to have been introduced without sufficient consultation, and, it was thought that their introduction had been accompanied by inadequate training.

- The frequency of unplanned job moves between work areas, in response to sudden scheduling changes and absence cover needs

- The lack of good communications and the perceived inability to influence management on matters of policy.

These concerns resulted in low satisfaction with the job situation and could have had a consequent negative effect on the general level of *attendance motivation* of the employees. In this situation, the ultimate decision to attend would largely depend on the influence of the various *pressures to attend* on the workers. However, it has already been shown that Arlanda's absence control systems were inadequate. Most employees could expect to receive full pay for non-attendance. When these aspects were taken into account in conjunction with the aforementioned impediments to organizational commitment, a situation could be clearly identified in which an unacceptably high level of absence was likely to develop. Supporting evidence for this conclusion was provided by the fact that *temporary* direct workers employed in the Screen Monitor and Test Equipment Divisions who were not paid when absent, had an average absence level of less than 2% (see Table 15.12, Classification 13).

Group B

We now turn our attention to the absence problem of Group B, which was identified as being the direct workers employed on a permanent basis and working rotating shifts in the Diskette Division. This group consisted of permanent male workers engaged in the mass production, capital-intensive manufacturing environment. The statistical analysis identified that, while the group's absence rate was below that for all the factory 'directs', this class of employee did have a particularly high incidence of absence spells (see Table 15.12, Classification 6). These shift employees worked in highly cohesive groups and their relatively satisfactory overall absence rate was consistent with research findings for shift workers.

In order to find the possible causes for the high spells of absence, attention was again initially focused on the employee attitude survey results. Although the survey findings indicated a number of concerns about the job situation amongst Diskette workers, these concerns were far less pronounced than the views expressed by the Monitor direct workforce which were quoted earlier. The Diskette shift workers, however, appeared to be much more concerned with certain aspects of the reward system. In particular, they mentioned that,

- From their point of view, they received inadequate rates of pay in relation to their skills, and,

- Premia payments to compensate for shift work were viewed as inadequate,

- The earning potential of direct Diskette workers had been unfavourably affected by cut-backs on overtime working in recent years. This was seen as an unfair productivity gain implemented by management at the expense of employees.

These preliminary findings obtained from the attitude survey suggested that it might be appropriate to concentrate on the area of *pressure to attend* and, in particular, to examine the incentive/reward system, taking account of the operational procedures for covering employee absence. The Diskette Division, unlike the Monitor Division, did not carry surplus people to provide absence cover. Instead, cover was achieved by asking other employees to work overtime, often in the form of 'double shifts' at very short notice.

This agreement was very lucrative for the employees concerned. Each additional eight-hour shift attracted up to twenty hours earnings when overtime premia, 'loss of sleep' allowances, and 'unsocial hours' payments were aggregated. In this situation, it may be hypothesized that, as management had attempted to achieve cost savings by reducing overtime levels, a number of workers had become 'absence system players', arranging overtime and absence to their mutual collective advantage. The introduction of Statutory Sick-Pay Regulations in 1983 with the attendant provision for 'self-certification' would have assisted this practice. It is significant that Arlanda's company doctor reported a 60% increase in the number of sickness spells in the Diskette Division between 1980 and 1984.

Taking into account the initial considerations about the possible causes of absence in Groups A and B, a formal review of the causes of absence was conducted using the ALIEDIM Absence Cause Analysis Checklist (Table

14.5). The results of this analysis carried out by Arlanda's managers are shown in Table 15.15 and Table 15.17.

Stage 1

On the ALIEDIM Absence Cause Analysis Checklist provided, each manager entered the name of the two absence problem groups to be considered. These were,

Group A   Monitor directs (permanent, dayshift)
Group B   Diskette directs (permanent, rotating shifts)

Stage 2

Next, working alone, each manager completed an individual analysis without reference to that of colleagues. They considered each problem group in turn (first Group A, and then Group B).

- For each cause listed, they decided if it was relevant to the group being analysed.

- They ticked those causes that they considered relevant.

- For the ticked causes they noted briefly the evidence for their individual views in the space provided adjacent to the cause description.

- They added additional causes that they felt were relevant to Arlanda, and again included their evidence.

At the conclusion of Step 2, all the members of Arlanda's management team had their own completed checklists. An example of one of these completed checklists is shown in Table 15.13.

Stage 3

Each manager in Arlanda's senior management team completed his or her individual absence cause analysis sheet. These were filled in first for Group A, and then for Group B. Having identified the potential causes of high absence in these two groups, the management team moved on to Stage 3 which was concerned with agreeing and prioritizing the absence causes identified, in terms of their importance to the problem.

Of the two types of prioritizing analyses available (ranking and comparison), the Arlanda management team considered the latter approach to be the more appropriate. The mechanics of this were described in the previous chapter.

Table 15.13   Arlanda Electronics: completed absence cause analysis checklist

Absence cause	Group A evidence	Group B evidence
Job situation		
1 The job is boring and lacks challenge.	✓ Attitude survey	
2 The job causes the individual stress.	✓ Attitude survey	
3 Frequent job moves disrupt employee work patterns.	✓ Attitude survey	
4 The organization of shifts and the hours of work contribute to absence.		✓ Statistics suggest that shift workers have more absence spells.
5 The quality of supervision contributes to the level of absence.		✓ Supervisors promoted on the basis of technical not interpersonal skills
6 The physical work environment demotivates employees.		
7 The work-group size is too big to allow individuals to identify with the group.	✓ Attitude survey	
Employee values and job expectations		
8 Employees have incompatible values and job expectations.		
Personal characteristics		
9 The length of time employees have been with the company seems to influence their absence rate.		
10 The age of the employee seems to determine the likelihood of absence.		
11 People with certain types of personalities seem to be off more frequently.		✓ There do appear to be certain employees who are inclined to take frequent days off.
12 The sex of the employee affects the frequency of absence.	✓ Absence statistics (may be misleading)	
Satisfaction with the job situation		
13 Dissatisfaction with the job situation seems to affect absence levels.	✓ Attitude survey	

Table 15.13   (*Continued*)

Absence cause	Group A evidence	Group B evidence
Pressure to attend		
14 People are absent less when the financial pressures on them are greater.	✓ Temporary workers absent less (not paid when absent)	✓ Absence drops when heavy overtime available to meet seasonal sales demand.
15 The company's incentive/reward system contributes to the absence problem.		✓ Attitude survey related to 'lost' earnings and the particularly high premia available when working overtime to cover for absent colleagues
16 The sick-pay/NHI benefits that employees get do not encourage them to come to work.	✓ Temporary workers absent less frequently (not paid when absent)	
17 The work-group norms either do not operate, or else they discourage regular attendance.	✓ Provision of absence cover means that employees are not 'missed' when absent	× Opposite effect observed – due to highly cohesive nature of work groups
18 The personal work ethic of the employees does not demand that they give of their best.		
Ability to attend		
19 Genuine illness and accidents at work are a regular cause of absence.		✓ On constant three-shift working, employees are less likely to come in when feeling 'poorly'
20 Many employees come from far away, and local transport problems put many off from coming in sometimes.		

(*Continued*)

Table 15.13 (Continued)

Absence cause	Group A evidence	Group B evidence
21 The family responsibilities of employees often take precedence over work attendance.		
Other		
22 Certain days of the week have exceptionally high absence levels.	✓ Statistics support this	
23 Certain employees have a history of poor attendance.		
24 Self-certification has resulted in employees taking extra days off.	✓ Possible but not conclusive	
25 Other ... (please insert) 'poor communications and negative view of management style'.	✓ Attitude survey	✓ Attitude survey

Comparison ranking

Group A   Monitor directs

Using a flipchart, the managers read out their individual judgements and these were charted. The chart was simplified by listing the 12 causes identified:

Group A (Monitor directs) absence causes

1   Job boring
2   Job stress
3   Disruptive work moves
7   Work-group size
12   Employee sex
13   Job satisfaction
14   Financial pressure
16   Sick pay/NHI
17   Work-group norms
23   Individual employee attendance history
24   Self-certification
25   Poor communications/management style

In total, 12 separate possible causes were offered by the managers. This is a particularly large number, but perhaps it provides a good indicator of why

Arlanda's management had experienced such difficulty in the past in understanding absence causes. Next, the *evidence* for each of the absence causes listed was provided by the managers who had ticked them. This ensured that all group members could judge the evidence available.

The numbers of the 12 absence causes were listed on a chart both horizontally and vertically so that each cause could be compared with every other one, in order to identify the most likely causes for absence in Group A. This was done by the managers working as a team, and the conclusions reached are shown in Table 15.14.

From the table, it is immediately apparent that certain causes were generally accepted as being very important. Cause 13 – job satisfaction, received a maximum score of 11 from the management team. In contrast, other causes were rated very low. For example, self-certification received only two votes, while sex was allocated none. The point about sex is particularly noteworthy, given the fact that Group A consisted of women. This is because self-certification and sex were two factors that tended to figure prominently in Arlanda's managers' hunches and personal theories about absence when these were discussed with them prior to this exercise. Yet, when this systematic group analysis was conducted, and their assumptions were challenged by their being required to supply evidence, a very different picture of the likely causes of absence emerged.

In summary, the main absence causes for the Monitor directs, in rank order of importance, are shown in Table 15.15.

The main cause of absence amongst the Monitor directs was held to be the

Table 15.14 Arlanda Electronics: Absence Group A: cross-comparison of absence causes

Absence cause	1	2	3	7	12	13	14	16	17	23	24	25	Total
1	X	1	1	1	1	13	14	16	1	1	1	1	8
2	1	X	2	2	2	13	14	16	2	2	2	2	7
3	1	2	X	7	12	13	14	16	3	23	3	25	2
7	1	2	7	X	7	13	14	16	7	7	7	25	5
12	1	2	12	7	X	13	14	16	17	23	12	25	2
13	13	13	13	13	13	X	13	13	13	13	13	13	11
14	14	14	14	14	14	13	X	16	14	14	14	25	8
16	16	16	16	16	16	13	16	X	16	16	16	25	9
17	1	2	3	7	17	13	14	16	X	17	17	25	3
23	1	2	23	7	23	13	14	16	17	X	23	23	4
24	1	2	3	7	12	13	14	16	17	23	X	25	0
25	1	2	25	25	25	13	25	25	25	23	25	X	7
Total	8	7	2	5	2	11	8	9	3	4	0	7	64

Table 15.15 Arlanda Electronics - absence causes ranking (rate problem) in Group A (Monitor directs)

Absence number	Cause	Score	Estimated absence impact
13	Job satisfaction	11	Major
16	Sick-pay/NHI	9	
14	Financial pressures	8	High
1	Job boring	8	
2	Job stress	7	High
25	Poor communications/management style	7	
7	Work-group size	5	Moderate
		55 (of 64)	

lack of a satisfying job. It was felt that the jobs were both boring and stressful and that employees did not perceive themselves to be the members of a work group or team. This was compounded by the lack of any strong financial pressure to return to work, because of the sickness payments received from the company and the state support provided to those deemed to be absent due to illness. Finally, inadequacies were identified in communications and in the management style used.

Even at this stage it was worth while testing and retesting the evidence. For example, one of the strong conclusions that could be drawn from the analysis was that the company's generous sick-pay scheme, and the lack of financial pressure on employees to attend were important factors in the decision of permanent workers in this category to be absent. This conclusion was substantiated by statistical evidence which showed that temporary workers who were not paid when absent exhibited very low absence rates.

However, when this conclusion was probed more deeply, a more comprehensive picture of the real pressures and influences in operation emerged with regard to the attendance behaviour of the temporary employees. In an area of high unemployment, the main ambition of workers employed on a temporary basis was to secure a permanent position. Such permanent positions were offered from time to time as vacancies arose, and were offered to those temporary employees who had a satisfactory performance record. The most important single consideration in the appointment decision, was the candidate's attendance record. Thus, while financial pressures may have been an important factor in the low absence rate amongst these temporary employees, it is likely that the threat of losing their temporary employment, and the incentive of possibly securing a permanent job, were the chief motivations for good attendance amongst this group of workers.

Group B: Diskette directs

Next, the management team considered the second absence problem group. This was Group B, the Diskette directs. Exactly the same procedure was followed. Each of the managers read out individually the absence causes that they had entered for this group of employees, together with their evidence. On this occasion, seven causes were identified, and were listed on the flipchart:

Group B (Diskette directs) absence causes

4   shift working
5   quality of supervision
11 personality type
14 financial problems
15 incentive/reward system
19 genuine illness
25 poor communication/management style

Again, a comparison analysis was carried out upon these causes, and the results are shown in Table 15.16.

This table shows that, once again, certain causes were widely accepted as being particularly important with regard to the absence frequency problem amongst the Diskette directs. For example, the incentive/reward system (Cause 15), and the quality of supervision (Cause 5), were highlighted in the points allocated. As in the case of the Monitor directs, other factors that had previously been held to be significant, were now deemed to be of lower importance, through the ranking procedure. For example, poor communication (Cause 25) and genuine illness (Cause 19), which were commonly proposed as the main causes of absence amongst these workers, received

Table 15.16 Arlanda Electronics: Absence Group B: cross-comparison of absence causes

Absence cause	4	5	11	14	15	19	25	Total
4	X	5	4	14	15	4	4	3
5	5	X	5	14	15	5	5	4
11	4	5	X	14	15	19	11	1
14	14	14	14	X	15	14	14	5
15	15	15	15	15	X	15	15	6
19	4	5	19	14	15	X	19	2
25	4	5	11	14	15	19	X	0
Total	3	4	1	5	6	2	0	21

Table 15.17　Arlanda Electronics - absence causes ranking (frequency problem) in Group B (Diskette directs)

Absence number	Cause	Score	Estimated absence impact
15	incentive/reward system	6	major
14	financial pressure	5	
5	quality of supervision	4	high
4	shift working	3	
19	genuine illness	2	moderate
		20 (of 21)	

none and two votes respectively. The main absence causes amongst the Diskette directs, in range order of importance, are shown in Table 15.17.

The analysis of the absence causes for the Monitor directs (Table 15.15) and for the Diskette directs (Table 15.17) can be related to the Steers and Rhodes process model of employee attendance which is shown in Figure 15.2. It illustrates the pertinent absence causal variables that operate amongst each of these two absence problem groups. As importantly, it highlights those variables that do *not* appear to be having an influence.

In the case of the Monitor directs, the dominant issue was that of *job satisfaction*. Most of the absence causes were tracked down to Box 1, that concerned with the job situation. A second, important issue, was the *pressure to attend*. Of equal significance was the realization that, amongst this group of workers, there was no evidence that their values and expectations (Box 2), their personal characteristics (Box 3) or their ability to attend (Box 7), played any major part in their attendance decision. Thus, at least for the moment, these three could be ignored by management, and attention paid to developing an absence programme which addressed the two issues of job situation (Box 1) and pressure to attend (Box 5).

In the case of the Diskette directs, the situation was a little different. Here the *pressure to attend* (Box 5) was identified to be the major cause. *Job situation* (Box 1) was also held to have a high impact, in terms of the quality of the supervision, and a moderate one, with respect to the effects of shift working. Genuine illness, an aspect of the *ability to attend* (Box 7), rated a lower status. Thus, in the case of the Diskette directs, management's absence programme would need to be geared primarily to addressing absence causes related to the pressures to attend, and then, to some extent, to specific aspects of the work situation. The eventual absence programme developed by management, for the Diskette directs would therefore differ from that of the Monitor directs. Different types of absence problems require different solutions.

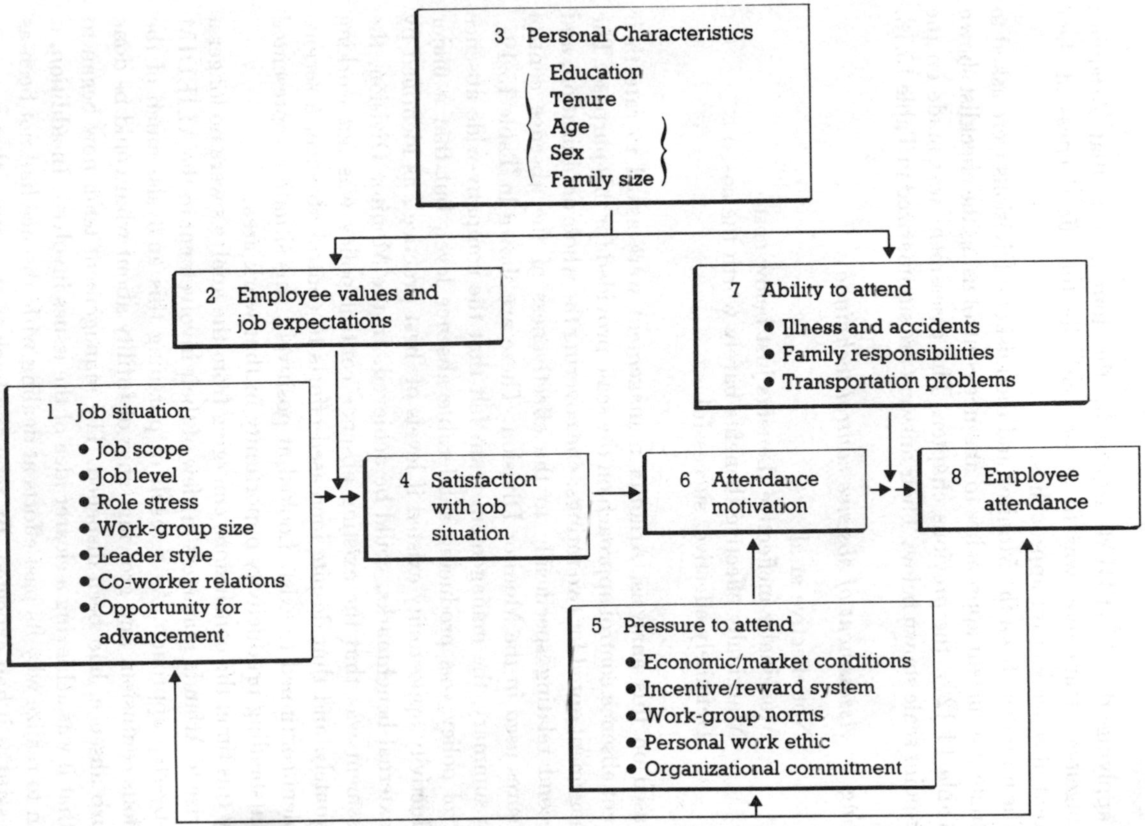

Figure 15.2 Major influences on employee attendance: the Steers and Rhodes process model

3 Personal Characteristics

Education
Tenure
Age
Sex
Family size

7 Ability to attend

● Illness and accidents
● Family responsibilities
● Transportation problems

8 Employee attendance

6 Attendance motivation

5 Pressure to attend

● Economic/market conditions
● Incentive/reward system
● Work-group norms
● Personal work ethic
● Organizational commitment

4 Satisfaction with job situation

2 Employee values and job expectations

1 Job situation

● Job scope
● Job level
● Role stress
● Work-group size
● Leader style
● Co-worker relations
● Opportunity for advancement

Step 4   Arlanda Electronics: evaluate the current absence control methods

In applying the ALIEDIM approach, the fourth step that Arlanda's management team took was to assess critically the effectiveness of their current absence control approaches.

The managers from the Monitor and the Diskette Divisions were asked to evaluate the current approaches to absence control using the checklist shown in Table 14.12 of the previous chapter. The assessment was made on the four-point scale shown below. Their answers are summarized in Table 15.18.

Rating	Assessment of absence control technique
1	Not effective at all
2	Marginally ineffective (benefits just below cost)
3	Marginally effective (benefits barely worth the costs)
4	Definitely effective, successful

Based on this analysis, Arlanda management were asked to rate their current absence control approach on the scale provided for this purpose. The management opted for two ratings: one covering the whole organization, and a second relating specifically to the effectiveness of the absence control measures used in the Monitor Division. These are shown in Table 15.19.

In summary, the management team felt that the company-wide absence control policy was producing a tolerable absence level, but that a major productivity opportunity existed if levels of 'best practice', as identified by the external benchmarks, could be achieved. In the Monitor Division, the assessment was that the existing absence control policy was not working adequately, and that despite increased efforts to control absence, a serious problem continued to exist. Looked at positively, this situation represented an outstanding productivity opportunity in that work area.

By this time, the conclusions emerging from the analysis were no longer a surprise to Arlanda managers in view of their involvement in the ALIEDIM step-by-step approach. As a result of pursuing this analysis, much of the previous confusion, and growing sense of futility about what could be done to curb absence, had been dispelled. The management team now began to feel that it was achieving a clearer idea of the issues involved. In addition, it began to realize why its past efforts at dealing with absence had not been as successful as it had expected. By referring back to the causes that management had identified for each of the problem groups, it became apparent to managers that their existing absence control techniques did not properly address the underlying causes and issues of absence.

For example, in the Monitor Division, where absence was at least partly job-related, it became clear that the disciplinary procedures that took no account of the already high pressures and stresses on the individual

Table 15.18 Arlanda Electronics: Review of current absence control methods

	Control method	Type	Used in this organization (✓)	Rating of effectiveness (1-4)
1	A consistently applied attendance policy.	P –	✓	3
2	Dismissal based on excessive absence.	P –	✓	3
3	Progressive discipline for excessive absenteeism.	P –	✓	3
4	Identification and discipline of employees abusing attendance policies.	P –	✓	3
5	At least monthly analyses of daily attendance information.	P –	✓	3
6	Daily attendance records maintained by personnel department.	P –	✓	
7	Employees required to telephone in to give notice of absence.	P –		
8	A clearly written and communicated company attendance policy.	P –	✓	3
9	Daily attendance records maintained by supervisors.	P –		
10	Allow employees to build a 'paid absence' bank to be cashed in at a later date, or added to next year's holiday entitlement.	P +		
11	Employee interviewed after an absence.	P – +		
12	Flexible work schedules	W		
13	Inclusion of absenteeism rate on employee job performance appraisal	P – +		
14	Perfect/good attendance banquet and award ceremony.	P +		
15	Formal work safety training programme.	W	✓	3
16	Screening applicants' past attendance records before making a selection decision.	P – +		
17	Supervisory training in attendance control.	W	✓	2
18	Inclusion of work unit absenteeism on supervisor's performance appraisal.	P – +		
19	Wiping clean a problem employee's record by subsequently good attendance.	P +	✓	3
20	Improving safety on the job.	W	✓	4

(Continued)

Table 15.18 *(Continued)*

Control method	Type	Used in this organization (✓)	Rating of effectiveness (1-4)
21 Public recognition of employee's good attendance (e.g. in-house bulletin board, news-letters).	P +		
22 Job enrichment/job enlargement or rotation implemented to reduce absenteeism.	W		
23 A component on attendance in a formal employee orientation programme for newly appointed employees.	W		
24 Require doctor's written excuse for illness/accidents.	P −		
25 Spot visits (or phone calls) to check up at employee's residence by doctor, nurse, or other company employee.	P −		
26 Operation of day care for employee's department.	W		
27 Substance abuse programme (alcohol, drugs).	W		
28 The absenteeism control programme has been negotiated in the union agreement.	W		
29 Employee bonus (monetary) for perfect attendance.	P +		
30 Education programme in health, diet, home safety.	W	✓	4
31 Attendance lottery or poker system (random reward).	P +		
32 Peer pressure encouraged by requiring work colleagues to fill in for absent employee.	W		
33 Chart biorhythms for accident-prone day.	W		
34 Letter to spouse indicating lost earnings of employee due to absence.	P −		
35 Combination of the complementary techniques (those described above plus others) which are part of a long-term, company-wide, productivity improvement strategy which has absence control implications.	O		
36 *Other (insert here)*			
Non-payment for absence for temporary staff	P −	✓	4
37 Other			
Early dismissal for absence for temporary staff	P −	✓	4

Table 15.19 Arlanda Electronics: Arlanda management's rating of the effectiveness of its current absence control programme

---

1 In operation this technique has resulted in the achievement of an absence rate to match the level achieved by 'excellent' organizations. Very effective, no change required, but monitoring needed to ensure that it continues to deal satisfactorily with individual problem areas or pockets of absence.

2 The absence control policy is viewed within the organization as being good. Nevertheless, a moderate improvement can be made to it to increase productivity, particularly if a sectional analysis is conducted to ensure that the policy is equally effective in all parts of the organization.

3 The absence policy in operation is producing a tolerable absence level. However, if improvements were to be made to it, a major productivity opportunity could be grasped, compared to the benchmark of excellent organizations. | Overall company |

4 The level of absence indicates that the existing absence control policy is not working well. There is still a serious absence problem in the organization. It represents an outstanding productivity opportunity if suitable policy changes can be implemented. | Monitor Division |

5 This level of absence is totally unacceptable, and if sustained, could undermine the future viability of the company. The absence control policy is wholly ineffective. Absence in the organization, and its control, need to be rethought from scratch. Radical rather than incremental changes are urgently required.

---

employees, were unlikely to make any fundamental impact upon absence behaviour. Arlanda's managers also came to recognize that such a control policy could aggravate an already strained and difficult situation, and could indeed create other problems which, on the surface, might seem to be unrelated. For example, it could cause a lowering of the level of trust between employees and management, and might reinforce the view that supervisors were both uncaring and insensitive in dealing with employees. Additionally, it could create a widespread unwillingness amongst the workforce to participate in any discussions related to change, even where such changes, in management's view, were clearly to the employees' benefit.

In the Diskette Division, management saw that the factory-wide absence control policy, which sought to identify high absenteeism, was badly designed to satisfy the specific needs of particular divisions of the company, and the sections within them. The way in which the system operated meant that the high absence rate in the Monitor Division masked the absences of the employees in the Diskette Division. The latter tended to have frequent short absences. These rarely became apparent in the critical zone of the factory-wide disciplinary absence procedure. Because of the way the computer tracked the absentees and flagged the high absentees to their managers, the Diskette directs were slipping through the net.

Finally, management recognized that current absence control policies took no account of the special influences of pay, supervision and shift-working which, following the ALIEDIM analysis, came to be seen as significant issues in the Diskette Division. All in all, management recognized that fundamental changes needed to be made to Arlanda's absence control programme.

Step 5   Arlanda Electronics: design the absence control programme

The design, or more usually the redesign, of any company's absence control programme has to take account of the absence causes and existing control procedures. In the case of Arlanda, the preceding diagnosis identified two quite different absence problems. These differed in terms of both their *form* (rate versus frequency), and their underlying *causes*. In considering what it should do, management needed to take cognizance of the existence and effectiveness of its current absence control methods.

However, in designing a new absence control package, it is important to remember a point that was made earlier. This is that there are many areas in the organization that *do not have an absence problem*. Moreover, even within an identified area of concern, there are many employees who have an excellent attendance record. Arlanda's data processing department was asked to write a computer program that would provide forced distributions of employees' absences, both by rate (total days taken off) and by frequency (number of spells of absence) for the year 1986. The results of the analysis are shown in Table 15.20.

This table clearly shows that serious absence was a problem limited to a small *minority* of the workforce, and that the majority of employees were excellent attenders. This revelation indicated to Arlanda's managers that a rifle strategy (aimed accurately at the small number of bad attenders) should be preferred to a blunderbuss approach (which struck at everybody, irrespective of their attendance record).

Considering the tables in depth, management could see that 53.6% of the workforce had an absence rate of 3% or less. Moreover, 21.6% had had no absence whatsoever in 1986. Similarly, 54.4% of employees were absent only once or twice during that year. The fact that absence was viewed as a problem by Arlanda management could therefore be attributed to the disproportionately high absence of a minority of the workforce, and it was at this group of employees that the new, rifle-type control programme, was targeted.

In designing and implementing such a programme, management recognized that it was essential that the possible reactions of the good attenders (who constituted the majority of the workforce) should be borne in mind if dysfunctional consequences were to be avoided. Management already knew

Table 15.20(a)   Arlanda Electronics: Distribution of total
workforce by absence rate, 1986

Absence rate (%)	Distribution of employees	% of workforce	Cumulative (%)
0	291	21.6	21.6
1	152	11.3	32.9
2	139	10.3	43.2
3	140	10.4	53.6
4	137	10.2	63.8
5	88	6.5	70.3
6	59	4.4	74.7
7- 8	130	9.6	84.3
10-12	65	4.8	89.1
13-15	39	2.9	92.0
16-18	25	1.8	93.8
19-21	16	1.1	94.9
22-25	10	0.7	95.6
26-50	40	2.9	98.5
51-75	7	0.5	99.0
76-99	0	0.0	99.0
100	4	0.3	99.3
Total	1342	100.0	100.0

Mean rate: 5.9%

Table 15.20(b) Arlanda Electronics: Distribution of total workforce by absence
frequency, 1986

Absence frequency per annum (No.)	Distribution of employees	% of workforce	Cumulative (%)
0	291	21.6	21.6
1	229	17.0	38.6
2	212	15.8	54.4
3	210	15.6	70.0
4	148	11.0	81.0
5	98	7.3	88.3
6	61	4.5	92.8
7	44	3.2	96.0
8	25	1.8	97.8
9	13	0.9	98.7
10 and over	11	0.8	99.5
Total	1342	100.0	100.0

Mean frequency: 2.6 spells

that good attenders were unhappy about the effects of the no-fault absence control policy. It was reasonable to surmise that in designing (and particularly in implementing) the original absence strategy, insufficient account had been taken of the views of this majority group of employees. The serious consequences of this oversight have already been described. Against this historical background, management cautiously proceeded to put together the elements which would make up the redesigned absence control programme.

Designing the new absence programmes

In seeking to revamp the existing absence control programme, Arlanda's management team reflected on the magnitude of the absence problem in the company. It paid particular attention to the fact that the problem was located primarily amongst 2 groups of employees. Through a detailed and extensive consideration of the absence causes for each group in turn, it believed that it now had a clearer understanding of the causes of the two different types of absence patterns. Finally, it recognized that its current absence control procedures were not having the desired impact on the problem. From this basis, it proceeded to plan its new control programme. The so-called rifle-strategy to control absence required a new technique to be designed to deal with each of the key absentee groups.

Absence control programme for Monitor directs

The computer analysis revealed that Arlanda's absence problem was concentrated in the Monitor Division. Measured on a *lost time rate* basis, the Monitor Division's figure of 7.4%, was clearly above that of both the Diskette Division (5.6%) and the Circuit-board Division (5.5%). Moreover, by the *frequency rate* measure (spells of absence), the Monitor Division's figure was 2.8, which was only slightly below the worst (3.0) that had been achieved by the Diskette Division. Further analysis by work class, shift pattern and employment category, revealed that, when measured on a *lost time* basis, the worst attender was a direct worker, employed on a permanent basis, and working on a permanent basis in the Monitor Division. The absence rate for this profiled employee was almost 10%. The people involved were hourly-paid, female workers who were employed in a mass-production, assembly-line environment.

An identification of the possible causes of absence, based on computer data and the results of an employee opinion survey, yielded no fewer than twelve possible causes. Following an extensive cross-comparison analysis of absence causes by Arlanda's management, problems in the work situation and lack of job satisfaction amongst the Monitor directs, were assessed to constitute the main cause of absence. A second cause, rated as high, was the effect of sick pay and the lack of financial pressure on employees to return to work. A third causal grouping, also rated high, related to the work situation. This had to do with the job's being perceived as boring and stressful, and employees considering that communication was inadequate and the management style inappropriate. The fact that employees did not see themselves as members of a small group to which they had an obligation, was considered to exert a moderate influence on absence.

On reviewing the adequacy of the existing absence control programme, Arlanda's management considered that its impact on the employees in its Monitor Division was less than on the company overall. Drawing on management's knowledge of people, work and the organizationally-focused approaches described in Part three, it proceeded to put together the elements of a plan to deal with absence amongst the Monitor directs. The following decisions were made.

People-focused elements

- *Retaining the no-fault plan in a modified form*
  Feedback showed that the no-fault plan had produced a consistency in dealing with absentees. Moreover, it had achieved some degree of acceptance amongst employees. The expected punitive effects that employees had expected, had not materialized. However, the concerns that employees had about the plan would be addressed by strengthening the safeguards, for example, for employees with a good track record, or with a chronic illness (i.e. on-going), or with an acute condition (i.e. major, one-off illness or injury).

- *Introducing positive reinforcements*
  Do this so as to match the negative aspects, thereby creating a *mixed consequence* system. However, this would not be done by means of an attendance bonus since this would breach one of the company's major principles. Instead, good attenders would no longer have to clock in, and they could participate in a flexitime scheme. At the time, Arlanda was also reviewing the introduction of an employee profit-sharing scheme, and good attendance would represent a personal qualification to participate in such a scheme.

- *Introducing visible comparisons*
  This involved comparing actual absence performance against the set targets, perhaps compiling league tables to compare the absence performance of different departments. These performances could be widely publicized on charts and noticeboards displayed in public areas. Management would also keep stressing the costs and consequences of absence to the workforce, while recognizing excellent individual attendances through non-financial means.

Work-focused elements

When drawing upon the range of work-focused techniques, Arlanda's managers incorporated the following elements in their absence control strategy directed at Monitor directs.

- *Reducing employee stress*
  — Provide stress management counselling.

  — Where practicable and financially feasible, look for opportunities to make equipment changes so as to eliminate the most stressful tasks.

  — Improve maintenance programmes to reduce equipment failure. Where justifiable, have spare equipment. Research had shown that operators of well-maintained equipment were absent less often.

  — Improve production planning. This was not always possible, but at the very least, employees should be given as much advance warning of changes as possible, have the reasons for the scheduled changes explained to them, and be allowed the maximum of participation when determining how the new requirements might be satisfied.

  — Review work-rate standards, recognizing that industrial engineering could treat people as machine appendages.

- *Improving job challenge*
  — Introduce planned job rotation, job enlargement and job enrichment. The technology in use with the Monitor directs did provide scope for such changes.

Organizationally-focused elements

The preceding package of changes began to form a whole organizational programme for the Monitor Division. Arlanda's management believed that, over time, these changes could be consolidated into an organizational programme if they were supplemented by:

- Investment in training to increase personal skills. Most importantly, training should not be seen as a cost.

- The progressive reduction of budgeted absence cover to either a bare minimum or to a point where it was totally eliminated. In the past, absentees had not been 'missed' as extra people were available to cover for them.

- The encouragement and development of employees to operate in self-supporting work groups.

- An increase in the employee's personal identification with his or her job and work team, thereby ending the perception of being one of a large impersonal mass.

- Moving away from fragmented, repetitive jobs with little scope for personal expression, and towards autonomous work-groups, involvement of workers in work redesign so as to improve performance, and engender a personal responsibility for quality and the review of progress.

- A continuing emphasis on personal responsibility and accountability.

- Implementing changes in management and supervisory style, so as to complement and encourage meaningful employee participation and involvement.

- The conscious creation of an improved company climate of mutual trust, through genuine honesty, improved communications and openness.

- An emphasis on job security in situations when employees co-operate in change programmes.

Absence control programme for Diskette directs

Having considered the absence programme for the Monitor directs, Arlanda's management turned to focus upon the Diskette directs. Let us recap on the analyses that had been conducted by Arlanda's managers to bring them to this point. The computer analysis had revealed that, when calculated on a lost time rate the Diskette Division's figure of 5.6% was on par with that of the Circuit-board Division (5.5%), and below that of the 7.4% of the Monitor Division. However, when a frequency rate measure was used (number of spells of absence), the Diskette Division with its average figure of 3.0 spells, exceeded the Monitor Division's average figure of 2.8 spells, and both were well in front of the figures for the Test Equipment Division (average 1.9 spells) and for the Circuit-board Division (average 1.5 spells).

Further data analysis, this time by work class, shift pattern and employment category, identified the frequent absentee (as measured on a frequency rate), to be a direct worker, employed on a permanent basis, and working rotating shifts in the Diskette Division. The workers with this profile were found to have an average of 3.6 spells of absence per annum, as compared with the factory average of 2.6 spells of absence per employee per annum. This group consisted of permanent male employees who worked in a mass-production, capital-intensive, manufacturing environment.

The causes of absence amongst these Diskette directs were identified by the management. Judgements were made on the basis of statistical data and on the results of an employee attitude survey. A total of seven causes were identified, and these were subsequently subjected to a cross-comparison. As a result, the company's current incentive and reward system, plus the lack of financial pressure on employees when they were absent, were judged to be the two major causes of absence amongst workers in the Diskette directs. Also rated highly was the poor quality of supervision. Finally, shift working and genuine illness were held to exert a moderate influence upon attendance behaviour amongst this group.

Since the causes of absence were deemed to be different from those of the Monitor directs, Arlanda's management acted to design a second, customized, absence control programme to deal with unique features of this particular problem. It did so while recognizing that absence here was an important, although not massive problem, and thus what was required was a measured response aimed at balancing the effort expended with the benefits to be gained. Once again, therefore, it drew upon the available people, work and organizationally-focused approaches to produce a relevant absence control programme.

People-focused elements

The elements applied to the Monitor directs would be applicable here too. Specifically:

- The modified no-fault plan
- Positive reinforcements to produce a mixed consequence system.

In the case of the no-fault plan, it was decided to modify the analysis and the presentation of the data in order to make it a more effective component of the absence control programme for the Diskette Division. As originally devised, the no-fault plan treated all the divisions of the factory as one total population. From this standpoint, it highlighted the poorest attenders in the factory on the basis of their combined absence duration and absence frequency. Progressive warnings were then issued to employees, depending on whether their names appeared in the top 1%, 4%, 7% or 10% of the absence profile.

However, a further review of the employees in these categories revealed that a large majority of the employees receiving warnings worked in the Monitor Division. This was, in many ways, a genuine reflection of high absence within that division, especially amongst the direct labour group. It was also the case however, that the Monitor Division had the largest number of employees. The *combined effect* of the high absence and the high population of the Monitor Division, acted to hide other problem groups whose absences, although not as high, were nevertheless serious within their own context. The Diskette direct labour group, was one such clear example.

One option that was available to deal with this data collection anomaly would have been to extend the overall catchment level of the high absentees to the top 15% or even 20% of the workforce. This would have increased the chances of highlighting a broader cross-section of employees who were serious absentees. This idea was rejected by Arlanda's management since it was felt that it would dilute the overall effectiveness of the no-fault absence plan.

Instead, it was decided to separate the Diskette and Monitor workers for the purposes of the calculation and operation of the no-fault plan. This policy was compatible with the policy of decentralization, divisional autonomy, and making people responsible for their own work performance. Moreover, the changes would allow management to focus on the frequent absentees in the Diskette Division, those who regularly took one or two days off. By requiring supervisory and managerial staff to question every absence, it would convey the message that the company viewed any spell of absence seriously.

Work-focused elements

Four main elements were selected from the range of techniques and strategies under this heading. These concerned:

- matching people to shift working,

- reviewing the pay structure,

- managing overtime and manning more effectively, and

- training supervisors.

Matching people to shift working
Under this heading three ideas were recommended. These were,

— Offering day-working to those employees not wanting to do shifts, especially older workers who had been on shifts for many years, and employees with minor recurring health problems.

— Recognizing the financial constraints involved in coming off shifts by protecting pensions levels, and cushioning lost shift earnings over a period of time. In money terms such a strategy would not cost the company a great deal of money, and it was consistent with its basic values and philosophy.

— In selecting replacement shift workers, taking careful account of their past attendance records and interviewing them to establish, as far as possible, whether they would be suited to shift working.

Reviewing the pay structure
Arlanda Electronics regularly conducted pay surveys to monitor the competitiveness of its compensation levels. Recent survey results revealed a

fundamental contradiction in its pay structure. They indicated that, on the one hand, the company's basic shift allowances were lower than those of the better companies in the area. On the other, it showed that Arlanda gave unusually generous allowances for double shift working, making this a very attractive work pattern for shift employees. Management therefore suggested that the pay structure should be revised by improving basic shift allowances, while at the same time, reducing the financial benefits that could be obtained for double shift working.

It was recognized that this would not be an easy change to sell either to the employees involved (who valued the special payments), or to the Diskette Division supervisors (who believed that high premia were essential to induce shift workers to work double shifts on absence cover). The irony of this latter point was not lost on the Diskette Division's management while, on the former point, the company legitimately argued that sixteen hours of non-stop working was an unacceptable work pattern that would no longer be sanctioned, except at times of the direst emergency.

Managing overtime and manning effectively
The third decision taken related to the management of overtime in the division and the review of sectional manning levels so as to ensure that a proper balance of resources existed. A number of decisions were made here:

— It was agreed to establish and implement overtime allocation procedures which would prevent employees with significant absence records, benefiting from the available overtime.

— A review was commissioned of sectional manning levels. It was accepted that, in some sections of the division, employee numbers might have been cut back too far. At the time, some sections had to work excessive amounts of overtime, while others had no opportunity to do overtime (other than to meet absence cover requirements).

— Management recognized that, traditionally, employees expect and have depended upon overtime earnings to supplement their gross income. It may not be unreasonable to include a moderate level of planned overtime in the financial budget and work arrangements, but it is necessary to ensure that what is available is allocated fairly across all the sections. Managed effectively, an element of overtime can be shown to be cost-effective in many situations.

— Overtime is the traditional way in which employees increase their earnings. 'Playing the system' as regards overtime is common in organizations. While overtime may be useful for workers, it is not necessarily helpful for the company. There are better ways of allowing employees to earn more, for example by paying more for the possession of increased skills. This facilitates more flexible working arrangements, and offers benefits to the individual and the company in equal measure. Another possibility, with similar benefits both to the company and to the employees, could be the *annual hours* concept. However, Arlanda's management recognized that these were longer-term ideas for which the company climate was not yet prepared.

Training supervisors

The fourth and final element in the control approach to be applied to the Diskette directs, was the introduction of a training programme for supervisors. A number of key issues were seen as relevant:

— The people-aspects of the proposed absence control programme.

— The importance of the supervisory role and its responsibilities.

— The need for supervisors to take a pro-active approach to absence, and not just wait for the system to flag the high absentees. Each absence occurrence had to be treated seriously.

— Making the absence rate of each supervisor's section a personal performance measure on their appraisal.

— Stressing the importance of good attendance behaviour modelling, and employee counselling.

Reviewing the draft absence control programme

Having completed drafts of the revised absence control programmes for the Monitor directs and for the Diskette directs, Arlanda managers checked each one against the criteria that were described in Table 14.14 of the previous chapter.

Focusing on the draft programme that they had designed, the managers reviewed each of the six dimensions of divisibility, complementarity, timescale, implementation cost, capability fit and culture fit. They added other dimensions which were not on the checklist, but which were important to the company. These were *management/supervisory ability* and *employees' willingness*. These were defined by the following questions:

Management/supervisory ability

Given the experience, training, past practices and personal views or theories of the managers and supervisors responsible for implementing these programmes, would they have the necessary skills, abilities and motivation to implement the suggested range of organizational and technical changes?

Employees' willingness

Given the industrial relations history of the company, and the current attitude of the workforce, would employees be willing to support these change programmes and participate in their detailed design? Would they participate in the implementation of many of the initiatives which would affect both the working environment and their relationships?

Arlanda's managers read through the list shown in Table 14.14, and decided, for each of the eight dimensions that it now contained (the original six plus the two they added), whether these were important for the success of the proposed absence control programme. Where the dimension was felt to be important, the management team considered how the planned changes related to the required dimensions. In some instances, they suggested areas requiring caution, and pointed to aspects of the proposed programme that might require amendment to enhance the chances of ultimately producing an acceptable absence control programme. These assessments and suggestions are shown in Table 15.21.

To many readers, this description of Arlanda's approach to absence control may appear laboured. It may remind some of the story of the man who asked another the time, and was given a detailed description of how a watch worked. There is no doubt that this company's programme is

Table 15.21 Arlanda Electronics: Checklist for reviewing absence control programme

(1) Dimension	(2) Important (Y-N)	(3) Programme assessment
(a) Divisible?	Yes	The different elements of the programme lend themselves very well to a phased introduction.
(b) Complementary?	Yes	Proposals make good use of the existing computer system for monitoring absence. Some additional resources will need to be allocated in the Monitor Division to achieve equipment changes and improve the maintenance programmes.
(c) Time-scale OK?	Yes	Proposals can be implemented over a period. Early improvements in attendance are a priority, but this should be feasible provided that the essential supporting elements are themselves introduced in phases once the necessary preparations have been made.
(d) Implementation cost OK?	Yes	The elements of the programme that address themselves purely to absence will result in a modest financial outlay which will be recouped many times over, if the expected absence reductions are realized. Other related aspects of the programme such as equipment changes, training programmes, work redesign, management and

Table 15.21 (*Continued*)

(1) Dimension	(2) Important (Y-N)	(3) Programme assessment
		supervisory development, and employment security commitments, will undoubtedly involve considerable resources and costs. However, these proposals are totally consistent with the company's general change and productivity strategies.
(e) Capability fit?	Yes	Most elements of the programme can be implemented within the present organizational situation. However, the suggestions that relate to autonomous team working and job redesign, will require significant capital changes in the manufacturing processes. However, while such changes are consistent with the company's longer-term strategy, Arlanda's management has decided to consider these aspects separately so that the required investments could be assessed on their merit on a return on investment (ROI) basis.
(f) Culture fit?	Yes	This aspect has been a continuing consideration throughout the process of design of the programme. Hence, only those changes that were consistent with the values of Arlanda, have been incorporated into the final proposals.
● Other (insert) ... Management/ supervisory ability?	Yes	The programme has been recognized as an important challenge to both managers and supervisors. Hence, they will need help in acquiring the necessary skills with which to carry it out. This in turn implies the provision of extra resources while they do their day-to-day work. Project teams will be set up to manage the different elements of the programme. Unless a sense of ownership of the absence programme is created amongst supervisors, it will struggle. It is proposed that control of absence should be included on their performance appraisal.
● Other (insert) ... Employees' willingness?	Yes	Since this is a difficult task, it will be necessary to sell the benefits of the absence programme and not its attributes. Many of its aspects will indeed benefit the workforce. Since resistance to change is anticipated, the method of implementation will be critical. Start with the simple, non-controversial aspects, and generate common awareness.

ambitious, and that certain elements of it have to be regarded as long-term goals.

Considering first the short term, and limiting oneself solely to the question of absence, one can consider the issue as one of how much effort should be expended in relation to the benefit. The benefit on offer is an operating cost reduction of £775 000 per annum, which is Arlanda's true cost of absence. Management has to decide how much it is prepared to spend now in terms of new procedures, training, management time, and so on, in order to gain these benefits.

From a longer-term point of view, the changes need to be seen as part of Arlanda's thrust to achieve a competitive edge through improved perform-ance. From this perspective, they represent minimum requirements. They are the price of the ticket to ride on the excellence train into the future. The question that readers have to ask is: what price is my own organization prepared to pay to remain competitive?

Step 6   Arlanda Electronics: Implement the absence control programme

Having designed and revised the new absence control programmes, Arlanda's managers are now at the stage of planning their implementation, and intend to do this task themselves. By using their own internal resources, they will be able to develop a sense of ownership of the programme's different elements.

Before proceeding, however, the company did ask for the advice of the authors. Their absence control programme represents an example of an organizational change. As such, the principles that apply to the successful introduction of any organizational change are relevant here. These were detailed in the previous chapter, and include the need to communicate effectively, involve individuals, secure early successes and so on. The planning associated with the implementation of Arlanda's absence control programme took account of the considerations raised by its management, which were detailed in Table 15.21. It is useful to focus on the specifics of Arlanda's situation, while being aware of general principles of change implementation. In particular, it was agreed that the implementation of the absence control programme at Arlanda, would be aided by the following features.

The mode of implementation had to support the company's objectives and culture. From the review, it was clear that the process of implementation would be a phased one, rather than a 'big bang' occurring on a single day. In certain areas, progress towards implementation would depend on additional but relatively small resources being made available. At a later stage, more substantial financial outlays would be required. Successful implementation would therefore require the wholehearted support of the supervisors. The benefits would need to be first sold to them. They would then support the proposed programme. To achieve this, the supervisors needed to see how the changes would benefit them. Additionally they needed to develop new skills, as well as a sense of ownership of the change. Resistance to change amongst the workforce was anticipated, so it was planned to implement the non-controversial aspects of the programme first. Working with Arlanda's management, the authors identified a number of important aspects of the implementation strategy:

- The absence control programme should, wherever possible, tie in with what was already available in the company, and use change mechanisms which had already been shown to work. For example, Arlanda's management had found that, in the past, when communicating major changes, small group briefings supported by question-and-answer sessions, visual aids and good explanatory notes, had been well received by the workforce.

- Arlanda decided that a top-down, cascading implementation approach would be used. It would begin with the managers, filter down to the supervisors, and then finally work its way down to shopfloor employees, with small group briefings at the final stage.

- The method of implementation was considered critical. The planned strategy was to identify key individuals at the different levels and seek to persuade them first. In this way, a sympathetic and supportive core group could be built up which would help to carry the programme forward towards implementation.

- It was decided to try to achieve early successes, and use these, by publicizing them, to generate interest and momentum throughout the workforce.

- Arlanda had, for a number of years, been running an extensive in-company management and supervisory development programme of a general nature. This used external consultants and the business department of a local university. It was agreed to customize the next phase of this on-going training, and link it in with the specific objectives of the absence control programme.

  With regard to the absence control elements of the plan, course members would be trained in the specifics of the operation of the absence programme, and in the behavioural aspects of counselling and handling absentees effectively. In addition, many of the other programme elements such as work redesign, improved communication, and managerial style changes, would require both a new awareness and new skills amongst many managers and supervisors. As an approach, it was agreed that Action Learning would be an effective method, and a logical extension of the established development plan.

- The company was working hard to re-establish both the credibility and status of the employee representative system. This had collapsed when the original no-fault absence plan had been implemented. Where appropriate, proposals would be channelled through this mechanism, so as to ensure the legitimacy of the changes, and to facilitate employee involvement.

  The new representative structure had a number of subcommittees which could be involved meaningfully in the review and implementation of several aspects of the new programme. For example, the Policy Subcommittee would be very interested in helping to rework the details of the no-fault plan. The Finance Subcommittee, meanwhile, would certainly be involved, at an early stage, in any proposals concerned with the compensation package (profit-sharing, premia payments).

- Arlanda was shortly to embark on a programme of *industrial citizenship* which would involve all its employees. This was part of the company's overall employee development strategy. The plan would focus on explaining to them the nature of the business (the strategies, financial position, prospects, threats, challenges), the concept of stakeholders, and the question of employees' rights and responsibilities.

- It was agreed that this citizenship programme would be used as one of the major vehicles for developing, in employees, the recognition of the need for a change in the company's current absence control approach. Stress would be placed upon individual responsibility, and the importance of each employee's behaviour. The company would acknowledge that it could help by providing better job satisfaction and by reducing stress. The industrial citizenship programme would also provide an excellent opportunity to communicate the main aspects of the new programme, sell its benefits, and deal with employee concerns.

- Since there was an existing team-briefing mechanism (operated monthly throughout the factory), Arlanda's management proposed to use this, in order to update employees on the progress and status of the different aspects of the implementation of the absence control programme. It was also to be used to obtain employee feedback on areas of concern. The authors agreed to this in principle, but warned that the effectiveness of the team-briefing system should first be checked, before it was used as a major communication channel.

  Past experience of team briefing in different companies had shown that, if it was to be successful, both managers and supervisors had to be trained properly in its use. Over and above the skills element, there was an attitudinal issue. Since information is power, some studies of the use of team briefing have shown that information passed on in team-briefing sessions was being filtered and distorted. In Arlanda's case, there had been instances of supervisors not taking responsibility for the message that they were passing on ('I've been asked to tell you about the importance of X, but I don't personally believe in it').

● Arlanda was also in the process of training its supervisors in performance appraisal. Moreover, it was moving towards a pay-for-performance system, which would operate right down to first-line, supervisory level. Having assigned responsibilities for the implementation of different aspects of the absence control programme to appropriate managers and supervisors, the authors suggested that it would be possible to make the achievement of these tasks both a performance criterion and a pay factor for these individuals.

● The use of joint working parties and project leaders would be promoted as a vehicle for achieving change. Management would involve the employees' representatives (Arlanda had no union), while not by-passing the supervisory levels of management. Getting the balance right would be important here.

A conscious decision was taken to involve as many employees as possible in working parties and similar arrangements, rather than solely working through employees' representatives. As an influencing strategy, co-optation had been successfully used in the past, and would be applied in the future. This involved identifying and sucking into the decision-making process a wide range of employees including those who might be hostile to the changes, who would be typically labelled 'trouble-makers', and normally excluded from any working party.

Experience had shown that involving them, and challenging them to offer suggestions, was an effective way of overcoming their resistance. Recently, management had been concerned that its attempts to communicate the annual business and financial results to the workforce had been ineffective. It decided to form a working party to redesign this annual presentation of information, and co-opted a number of employees to incorporate their views. One particularly critical employee (who had made a point of not supporting any joint management-workforce initiatives in the past), became engaged in conversation on this subject with a manager. After this employee had expressed, at great length, his views on what was wrong with the present presentations, the manager surprised him by agreeing fully with his opinions. He then stated that this was exactly the sort of input that had been lacking in the past, and managed to persuade him to join a working party which was redesigning the presentation. Subsequently, this employee became one of the biggest contributors to the newly-designed employee presentation, which turned out to be a resounding success with the workforce.

● On a longer-term basis, the company was embarking on a work redesign programme throughout the factory. This initiative had been activated by the opinion survey, and absence data obtained from the Monitor directs had confirmed the need for such a change. Pilot work on this aspect was to begin shortly in this division, and it would be based upon techniques and approaches which had proved to be successful in a number of other companies.

● It was consciously decided to try to achieve early successes, and, by publicizing them, to use these to generate interest and momentum throughout the workforce.

● To get the thing started, and to keep up the momentum, it was seen as important to subdivide the programme, assign responsibilities to individuals, develop timetables and agree actions. Making people personally responsible for specific actions, while getting them to operate within the context of a team, was the preferred approach.

● Finally, as was mentioned earlier, adequate resources had to be provided. These were of two types. First, financial investment was required. Second, if line management people were to be asked to take on the extra responsibility of managing the implementation of a major programme, then additional (dedicated) programme staff would be required in some areas. It was felt that these could be provided by reassigning and redeploying the people who had been released from the previous productivity programmes. This reallocation of employees, based on productivity gains, was consistent with Arlanda's policy of job-security assurances.

Step 7   Arlanda Electronics: monitor the effectiveness of the absence control programme

While planning the implementation phase, Arlanda's management also gave thought to the process of monitoring the absence control programme, once it had been implemented. It also sought the advice of the writers on this issue.

An old adage says that, 'you cannot control what you can't measure'. Monitoring the effects of absence control would be part of Arlanda's general approach to the collection and analysis of employee absence data. It would be based on the modified no-fault absence control system described earlier. However, as will have been shown, the monitoring of the effects of the absence control programme, involves more than merely checking on the absence rate and absence frequency of groups of employees. It also includes management's checking that it is doing what it planned to do, and fulfilling its commitment to employees. The monitoring will also include obtaining the responses of the workforce to the changes implemented both directly (through team-briefing sessions where it will make its views known), and indirectly (as measured by indicators such as self-certification levels, participation in the profit sharing scheme, and in the numbers of employees no longer required to clock in and off).

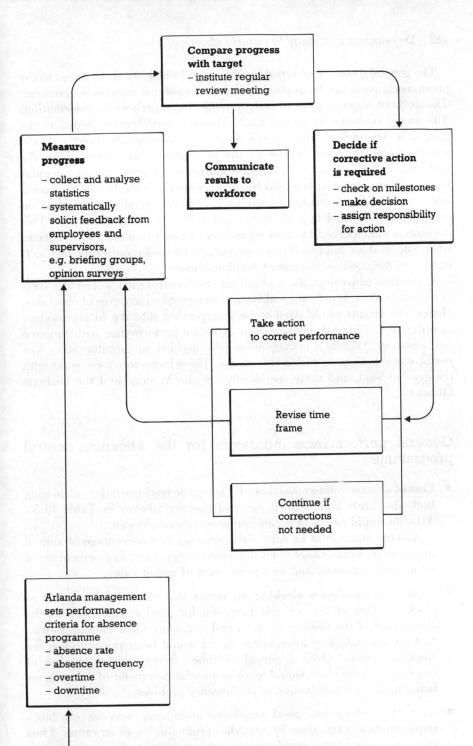

Figure 15.3 Arlanda Electronics: monitoring the effectiveness of an absence control programme

The general model of monitoring and control which was introduced in the previous chapter, can be applied to Arlanda's absence control programme. The no-fault absence plan already produced comprehensive information. The model is shown in Figure 15.2. The only modification added to the model, is Arlanda's management's desire to communicate directly *to the workforce* the on-going results of the programme, as measured by the performance indicators. Such information would be provided on a regular basis. The absence results would be incorporated into the business metrics, and would be displayed on boards on the shopfloor, along with data on quality, output, efficiency, delivery, and other business measures. This decision is underpinned by the management's belief that such information, when supplied to employees, can encourage the self-monitoring and self-control of their own performance and behaviour.

At the time of writing, the no-fault absence control plan lacked any sorts of targets or aims. It only showed the absence problem in terms of absolutes. Hence, the targets would need to be incorporated into the future reports, in order to facilitate the comparison of actual performance with targeted performance. Arlanda's management also decided to monitor other key performance indicators within this model. These indicators were set at both the general level, and more specifically, for the Monitor and the Diskette Divisions.

General performance indicators for the absence control programme

● Cost of absence-related overtime. By using the framework for calculating both the direct and indirect costs of absence (shown in Table 14.5), Arlanda would establish a continuous monitoring system.

   Absence cost would be expressed variously as a percentage of annual turnover, as a percentage of annual profit (before tax); as a percentage of total operating costs, and as a percentage of added value.

● Number of employees clocking in, versus those no longer required to clock on. One of the rewards proposed for good attendance was the elimination of the need to clock in and out. Only those employees who had an unsatisfactory attendance record would be required to use the clocking system. Over a period of time, therefore, the number of employees on the clock would serve as a useful barometer of the progress being made in the reduction of the absence problem.

● As with clocking on, good employee attendance was an eligibility requirement to participate in Arlanda's profit-sharing programme. Thus the percentage of the workforce who become eligible for profit-sharing (the participation rate), could be used as a measure of the success of the absence control programme. However, care would have to be taken in using this statistic, since eligibility for profit-sharing was also dependent on service and other disciplinary criteria.

- The rate of uptake of stress management counselling by employees. Job stress had been rated as a high cause of absence amongst the Monitor directs. Management had instituted a stress management programme which was available to all employees. It would be useful to monitor what percentage of the workforce were availing themselves of this service. While any direct correlation between stress counselling and absence rate reduction was unlikely, management would expect to see a high degree of interest in the stress management facility, if stress was in fact as important as management believed it to be.

- Check the level of self-certification. It had been argued that absence was basically an individual attitudinal problem, and that it was the outcome of the interaction of the motivation to attend and the ability to attend. The company doctor had already produced statistics showing a rise in self-certification in recent years. Self-certification levels should continue to be monitored closely, and the company would expect to see reductions in this area as the absence control programme took effect. It may not be overstating the case to suggest that the future level of self-certification could serve as an on-going referendum on the changes being implemented, by those employees who, in the past, have 'voted with their feet'.

- As part of the on-going absence monitoring process, absence levels would, in future, be reviewed at section level for each group of employees reporting to an individual supervisor. The absence level of each supervisor's section would now be included in his or her performance appraisal. In consequence, supervisors would have more personal accountability for the attendance of the people reporting to them than in the past. This feature of absence programme monitoring would provide an additional stimulus for improvement, since it is well known that people pay particular attention to those performance elements on which they are measured and rewarded.

Monitor Division: specific performance indicators

Specifically in relation to the Monitor Division, Arlanda's management identified a need for a set of performance indicators that would be relevant to this group of employees.

- Once the company begins to implement its improvement programmes in the areas of reduced equipment downtime and better production schedule forecasting, it will also develop monitoring tools to measure whether improvements in these areas are occurring over time. Arlanda's engineers already record downtime extensively for technical diagnostic purposes, and it would be easy to extract some simple summary data from these engineering databases, in order to monitor overall trends in equipment downtime. This data would be made available to employees to show that progress was being made in response to a concern specifically raised by them with respect to schedule changes. All such data already exists in the production planning department, and once again it would be simple to commission some summary reports to track the reliability of production forecasts, sudden changes, and shopfloor disruption.

- Job rotation programmes. Even though some degree of job rotation should take place all the time, an analysis of the employees' skills register revealed that some employees were never given a job change, while others seemed to be moved around at random. Hence, it was agreed that, as part of the absence control programme, job rotation would be monitored so as to ensure that it happened properly. This, in turn, would require supervisors and foremen to develop the necessary skills. This aspect was mentioned earlier with respect to the management and supervisory development programme.

- Employee training. It was agreed that the training of employees was one of the core elements of the entire absence control programme. For this reason, the company had to monitor itself to check that it was meeting its own commitments. The Nissan motor-car company in Tyne and Wear has been reported as spending more than $4000 a year per employee on training. In its first year of operation which ended in June 1987, its productivity rose by 10%. ICL, the British computer company, has committed itself to a prespecified number of training days per employee per year. Moreover, it has invited employees to complain to their managers if they did not receive their quota of training.

Diskette Division: performance indicators

By using the data from the analysis of absence causes in the Diskette Division, Arlanda's management was able to establish the following performance indicators for that division:

- Measure the *frequency* absence rate more closely. The problem had been found to be people taking many short spells of time off.

- Monitor the age profile and health patterns of the shift workers in this division. The plan was to encourage the older workers, and those with health problems, to come off the shifts. It was necessary to ensure that this was in fact happening, and that over time, a different distribution of shift employees was established.

- Monitor overtime levels in general, but also the pattern and individual distribution of overtime. The intention was to reduce overtime in the long term. In the short term, however, the aim was to ensure that overtime was more fairly distributed, and that unacceptable overtime work patterns were prevented both at the section and at the individual level.

The process of monitoring had to be underpinned by top management's commitment. As the saying goes, 'that which is measured gets done'. For this reason, it was essential that progress on the absence programme should be a performance measure for managers and supervisors in their appraisal.

As well as collecting numerical data, it was also planned to monitor what one manager called, 'soft data'. The way to obtain feedback on the soft data was to apply Peters and Waterman's principle of MBWA – Management By Walking About. The kind of information they sought included supervisors' attitudes, assessments of employee morale, and employee involvement in, and support for, plant activities such as waste-reduction campaigns, safety competitions, first-aid training, and similar ones which, in the past, had sometimes received a disappointing response.

Much of the monitoring data required to track progress on the various absence-related programmes would undoubtedly be quantifiable, and would relate directly to many of the items outlined earlier. However, first-hand feedback was just as important in indicating the progress being made in the change process. Compared with hard statistics, such information may also offer a much clearer picture of what was in fact going on, and where modifications might be necessary.

In addition, it was decided to keep attuned to any changes in Arlanda's supervisors' and managers' personal theories about the management of the company and the workforce. Over time, it was hoped that simplistic and narrow views would give way to, and be ultimately replaced by, a broader and richer appreciation of the many issues involved. The goal was to move to a position where the performance of the company in general, and the solution of the absence problem in particular, were perceived to be the joint responsibility of all of Arlanda's employees – shopfloor workers, foremen, supervisors, technical staff and middle and senior management.

Conclusion

In this book, we have not offered you any universal panaceas to solve your organization's absence problem. We believe that each company's situation, with respect to absence, will be different. Instead, we have presented the ALIEDIM approach which will allow you to address your unique absence problem in a systematic manner. In conclusion, we should like to quote Jay Lorsch, an eminent American academic and management consultant. He wrote that,

'Situational theories of behaviour are harder to apply than universal ones, but they work more often … Managers need to recognize that the easy way doesn't work and to act as intelligent consumers in rejecting theories that aren't relevant, in being more diagnostic, and in keeping their staffs educated in the tools available.'

References

Chapter 1

1 Incomes Data Services (1988), *Absence Control*, Study 403, London
2 Rhodes, S. and Steers, R. (1981), 'A systematic approach to diagnosing employee absenteeism', *Employee Relations*, Vol. 3, No. 2, pp. 17–22
3 Confederation of British Industry (1987), *Absence from Work: A Survey of Non-attendance and Sickness Absence*, London
4 Taylor, P. J. (1974), 'Sickness absence: facts and misconceptions', *Journal of the Royal College of Physicians*, London, Vol. 8, No. 4, pp. 315–34
5 Incomes Data Services (1984), *Controlling Absence*, Study 321, London
6 Klein, B. (1983) 'Missed work and lost hours', *Monthly Labour Review*, May
7 Confederation of British Industry (1987), *Labour Force Sample Survey of the European Communities (1983)* quoted in *Absence from Work: Survey of Non-attendance and Sickness Absence*, London, p. 5
8 Bureau of National Affairs Inc. (1985), *Quarterly Report on Job Absence and Turnover*, Washington, D.C.
9 Central Statistical Office (1984) *Annual Abstract of Statistics* 1984
10 *General Household Survey* (1984), HMSO, London
11 *Survey of Absence Rates and Attendance Bonuses* (1985), New Series 3, The Industrial Society
12 The Industrial Society (1987), *Study of Absence Rates and Control Policies*, New Series No. 8, Industrial Society Press
13 CBI (1987). See reference 3.
14 Underwood, L. (1987), 'Absent in body and spirit', *The Director*, Vol. 40, No. 11, pp. 61–2
15 CBI (1987). See reference 3.
16 National Economic Development Council (1971), *The Control of Absenteeism: A Checklist for Action by Management*, HMSO, London
17 *General Household Survey* (1984). See reference 10.
18 Taylor, P. J. (1982), *Absenteeism – Causes and Control*, Industrial Society, London
19 Advisory and Conciliation Arbitration Service (1983), *Absence: Advisory Booklet Number 5*, ACAS, London
20 Matthewman, J. (1985), *Controlling Absenteeism*, Institute of Personnel Management, London

21   Barlow, D. H. (1982), *An Employer's Guide to Absenteeism and Sick Pay*, Kogan Page, London
22   Matthewman (1985). See reference 20.
23   Finniston, M. (1978), Foreword to Behrend, H. *How to Monitor Absence From Work, From Head Count to Computer*, Institute of Personnel Management, London

Chapter 2

1   CBI (1987). See Chapter 1, reference 3.
2   The Industrial Society (1987). See Chapter 1, reference 12.
3   Rees, R. (1979), 'Getting people to work – a step by step approach', *Works Management*, January, pp. 86–95
4   Miles, R. E. (1975), *Theories of Management: Implications for Organizational Behaviour and Development*, McGraw-Hill, New York
5   Miles (1975). See reference 4.
6   Shepherd, R. A. (1976), 'Research under review', *Personnel Management*, September, pp. 28–31

Chapter 3

1   Taylor (1982). See Chapter 1, reference 18.
2   Taylor, P. J. (1982), *Absenteeism: Causes and Control*, The Industrial Society, 4th edition
3   The Industrial Society (1985), *Survey of Absence Rates and Attendance Bonuses*, London
4   The Industrial Society (1987). See Chapter 1, reference 12.
5   The Industrial Society (1987). See Chapter 1, reference 12.
6   The Industrial Society (1987). See Chapter 1, reference 12.
7   Thorpe, R. (1982), 'Productivity measurement' in Bowey, A. M. and Lupton, T. (eds), *Handbook of Salary and Wage Systems*, Gower, Aldershot
8   Wild, R. (1980), *Production and Operations Management: Principles and Techniques*, Holt, Rinehart and Winston, New York
9   Thorpe, R. (1984) in 'Productivity' in Bentley, T. (ed.), *Management Services Handbook*, Holt Saunders, London
10   Lawler, E. E. (1971), *Pay and Organizational Effectiveness*, McGraw-Hill, New York
11   Underwood (1987). See Chapter 1 reference 14.
12   See, for example:

Muchinsky, P. (1977) 'Employee absenteeism: a review of the literature', *Journal of Vocational Behaviour*, Vol. 10, pp. 329–37

Chadwick-Jones, J. K., Brown, C. A. and Nicholson, N. and Shepard, C. (1971), 'Absence measures: their reliability and stability in an industrial setting', *Personnel Psychology*, Vol. 24, pp. 463–70

Hammer, T. H. and Landau, J. (1981), 'Methodological issues in the use of absence data', *Journal of Applied Psychology*, Vol. 66, pp. 574–80

Smulders, P. G. N. (1980), 'Comments on employee absence/attendance as a dependent variable in organizational research', *Journal of Applied Psychology*, Vol. 65, pp. 368–71

Gibson, R. O. (1966), 'Towards a conceptualization of absence behaviour of personnel in organizations', *Administrative Science Quarterly*, Vol. 11, pp. 107–33

13   McCurdy, J. and Bowey, A. M. (1982), *Absenteeism* Working Paper No. 8202, University of Strathclyde Business School, Glasgow

Chapter 4

1   Kesby, J. (1987), 'Skiving worse than strikes', *Daily Telegraph*, 31 May

2   Confederation of British Industry (1987), *Absence From Work: A Survey of Non-Attendance and Sickness Absence*, London

3   Jones, R. M. (1971), *Absenteeism: Manpower Papers No. 4*, HMSO, London

4   McCurdy, J. and Bowey, A. M. (1982), *Absenteeism*, Working Paper 8202, University of Strathclyde Business School, Glasgow

5   Taylor, P. J. (1968), 'Personality factors associated with sickness absence, A study of 194 men with contrasting sickness absence experience in a refinery population', *British Journal of Industrial Medicine*, Vol. 25, pp. 106–8

6   Nicholson, N. (1977), 'Absence behaviour and attendance motivation – a conceptual synthesis', *Journal of Management Studies*, Vol. 14, pp. 231–52

7   Taylor, P. J. (1967), 'Shift and day work: comparison of sickness absence, lateness, and other absence behaviour at an oil refinery from 1962 to 1965', *British Journal of Industrial Medicine*, Vol. 24, pp. 93–102

8   Martin, J. (1971) 'Some aspects of absence in a light engineering factory', *Occupational Psychology*, Vol. 45, No. 2, pp. 77–89

9   Pocock, S. J. (1973), 'Relationship between sickness absence and length of service', *British Journal of Industrial Medicine*, Vol. 30, pp. 54–70

10   Behrend, H. (1974), 'A new approach in the analysis of absences from work', *Industrial Relations Journal*, Vol. 5, No. 4, pp. 4–21

11   Nicholson, N., Brown, C. A. and Chadwick-Jones, J. K. (1976), 'Absence from work and job satisfaction', *Journal of Applied Psychology*, Vol. 61, pp. 728–37

12   Jackson, S. E. (1983), 'Participation in decision making as a strategy for reducing job-related strain', *Journal of Applied Psychology*, Vol. 68, No. 1, pp. 3–19

13   Taylor, P. J. (1982), *Absenteeism – Causes and Control*, The Industrial Society, London

14   Steers, R. M. and Rhodes, S. R. (1978), 'Major influences on employee attendance: a process model', *Journal of Applied Psychology*, Vol. 63, No. 4, pp. 391–407

Chapter 5

1   Nicholson *et al.* (1976). See Chapter 4, reference 11.

2   Taylor (1968). See Chapter 4, reference 5.

3   Cheloha, R. S. and Farr, J. L. (1980), 'Absenteeism, job involvement, and job

satisfaction in an organizational setting', *Journal of Applied Psychology*, Vol. 65, No. 4, pp. 467–73

4   Katz, R. L. and Kahn, R. H. (1966), *The Social Psychology of Organizations*, Wiley, New York

5   Locke, E. A. (1976), 'The nature and causes of job satisfaction' in Dunette (ed.) *Handbook of Industrial and Social Psychology*, Rand McNally, Chicago, pp. 1293–349

6   Porter, L. W. and Steers, R. M. (1973), 'Organizational work and personal factors in employee turnover and absenteeism', *Psychological Review*, Vol. 80, pp. 151–76

7   Muchinsky, P. M. (1977) 'Employee absenteeism: a review of the literature', *Journal of Vocational Behaviour*, Vol. 10, pp. 316–40

8   Steers and Rhodes (1978). See Chapter 4, reference 14.

9   Breugh, J. A. (1981), 'Predicting absenteeism from prior absenteeism and work attitudes', *Journal of Applied Psychology*, Vol. 66, No. 5, pp. 555–60

10   Cheloha and Farr (1980). See reference 3.

11   Dittrich, J. E. and Carrell, M. R. (1979), 'Organizational equity, perceptions, employee job satisfaction, and departmental absence and turnover rates', *Organizational Behaviour and Human Performance*, Vol. 24, pp. 29–40

12   Ilgen, D. R. and Hollenback, J. H. (1977), 'The role of job satisfaction in absence behaviour', *Organizational Behaviour and Human Performance*, Vol. 19, pp. 141–61

13   Johns, G. (1978), 'Attitudinal and non-attitudinal predictors of two forms of absence from work', *Organizational Behaviour and Human Performance*, Vol. 22, pp. 431–44

14   Watson, C. J. (1981), 'An evaluation and some aspects of the Steers and Rhodes model of employee attendance', *Journal of Applied Psychology*, Vol. 66, pp. 385–89

15   CBI (1987). See Chapter 4, reference 2.

16   Ivancevich, J. M. and Matteson, M. T. (1980), *Stress and Work: A Managerial Perspective*, Scott Foresman, Glenview

17   Seyle, H. (1956), *The Stress of Life*, McGraw-Hill, New York

18   Cooper, C. L. (1987), 'Stress in the workplace: recent research evidence', Presidential Address to Inaugural Conference, British Academy of Management, University of Warwick, September

19   Kelly, M. and Cooper, C. L. (1981), 'Stress among blue collar workers', *Employee Relations*, Vol. 3, pp. 6–9

20   Kasl, S. V. (1973), 'Mental health and the work environment', *Journal of Occupational Medicine*, Vol. 15, No. 6, pp. 509–18

21   Cooper, C. L. and Smith, M. J. (1985), *Job Stress and Blue Collar Work*, Wiley, Chichester

22   Cobb, S. and Rose, R. H. (1973), 'Hypertension, peptic ulcer and diabetes in air traffic controllers', *Journal of the Australian Medical Association*, No. 224, pp. 489–92

23   Margolis, B. L., Kroes, W. H. and Quinn, R. P. (1974), 'Job stress – an unlisted occupational hazard', *Journal of Occupational Medicine*, Vol. 16, No. 10, pp. 659–61

24   Gupta, N. and Beehr, T. A. (1979), 'Job stress and employee behaviours', *Organization Behaviour and Human Performance*, Vol. 23, pp. 373–87

25   Cooper, C. L., Davidson, M. J. and Robinson, P. (1982), 'Stress in the police service', *Journal of Occupational Medicine*, Vol. 24, pp. 30–6

26   Cox, T. (1980), 'Repetitive work' in *Current Concerns in Occupational Stress*, Cooper, C. L. and Payne, R. (eds), Wiley, Chichester

27   Davidson, M. J. and Veno, A. (1980), 'Stress and the policeman' in Cooper, C. L. and Marshall, J. (eds) *White Collar and Professional Stress*, Wiley, Chichester

28   Cooper, C. L. and Marshall, J. (1976), 'Occupational sources of stress: a review of the literature relating to coronary heart disease and mental ill-health', *Journal of Occupational Psychology*, Vol. 49, pp. 11–28

29   Margolis *et al.* (1974). See reference 23.

30   Gupta and Beehr (1979). See reference 24.

31   Breaugh, J. A. (1980), 'A comparative investigation of three measures of role ambiguity', *Journal of Applied Psychology*, Vol. 65, pp. 584–9

32   Gray-Toft, P. A. and Anderson, J. G. (1985), 'Organizational stress in the hospital: development of a model for diagnosis and prediction', *Health Services Research*, Vol. 19, pp. 753–73

33   Brooke, P. B. (1986), 'Beyond Steers and Rhodes' model of employee attendance', *Academy of Management Review*, Vol. 11, No. 2. pp. 345–61

34   French, J. and Caplan, R. (1972), 'Organizational stress and individual strain' in Marrow, A. J. (ed.) *The Failure of Success*, AMACOM, New York

35   Shirom, A., Eden, D., Silberwasser, S. and Kellerman, J. J. (1973), 'Job stresses and risk factors in coronary heart disease among occupational categories in Kibbutzim', *Social Science and Medicine*, Vol. 7, No. 11, pp. 875–92

36   Karasek, R. A. (1979), 'Job demands, job decision latitude and mental strain: implications for job redesign', *Administrative Science Quarterly*, Vol. 25, June, pp. 285–309

37   Cooper, C. L. and Davidson, M. J. (1982), *High Pressure: Working Lives of Women Managers*, Fontana, London

38   Davidson, M. J. and Cooper, C. L. (1984), *Stress and the Woman Manager*, Blackwell, Oxford

39   Payne, R. (1980), *Organizational Stress and Social Support*, Wiley, London

40   French and Caplan (1972). See reference 34.

41   French, J., Caplan, R. and Van Harrison, R. (1982), *The Mechanisms of Job Stress and Strains*, Wiley, New York

42   Margolis *et al.* (1974). See reference 23.

43   Cooper, C. L. (1981), *The Stress Check*, Prentice-Hall, Englewood Cliffs, NJ

44   Hedges, J. N. (1973), 'Absence from work – a look at some national data', *Monthly Labour Review*, July, pp. 24–30

45   Illsley, J. A. (1988), 'Informal groups and their role in the organization', Glasgow Business School, Glasgow

46   Almond, J. M. (1975), 'The management of absenteeism', *The Production Engineer*, December, pp. 649–54

47   Taylor, P. J. (1974), 'Sickness absence: facts and misconceptions', *Journal of the Royal College of Physicians*, Vol. 8, No. 4, pp. 315–34

48   Walker, J. and de la Mere, G. (1971), 'Absence from work in relation to length and distribution of shift hours', *British Journal of Industrial Medicine*, Vol. 28, pp. 36–44

49   Taylor (1974). See reference 47.

50   Taylor (1982). See Chapter 4, reference 13.

51   Argyll, M., Gardiner, G. and Cioffi, F. (1958), 'Supervisory methods related to productivity, absenteeism and labour turnover', *Human Relations*, Vol. 11, No. 1, pp. 23–40

52   Ross, I. C. and Zander, A. (1957), 'Need-satisfaction and employee turnover', *Personnel Psychology*, Vol. 10, pp. 327–38

53   Oberman, S. E. and Rainer, G. P. (1983), 'Effective control of absenteeism', *Health Care Supervisor*, Vol. 1, No. 3, pp. 17–30

54   Morgan, L. G. and Herman, J. B. (1976), 'Perceived Consequences of Absenteeism', *Journal of Applied Psychology*, Vol. 61, pp. 738–42

55   Dalton, D. R. and Perry, J. L. (1981), 'Absenteeism and the collective bargaining agreement: an empirical test', *Academy of Management Journal*, Vol. 24, pp. 425–31

56   Seatter, W. C. (1961), 'More effective control of absenteeism', *Personnel*, Vol. 38, pp. 16–39

57   Rhodes, S. R. and Steers, R. M. (1981), 'Conventional vs. worker-owned organizations', *Human Relations*, Vol. 34, pp. 1013–35

58   Winkler, D. R. (1980), 'The effect of sick leave policy on teacher absenteeism', *Industrial and Labour Relations Review*, Vol. 33, pp. 232–40

59   Popp, P. O. and Belohlav, J. A. (1982), 'Absenteeism in a low status work environment', *Academy of Management Journal*, Vol. 25, pp. 677–83

60   Winkler (1980). See reference 58.

61   Taylor (1982). See Chapter 4, reference 13.

62   (1987), 'Memo to the boss: Help, we are being bored to death', *Daily Telegraph*, 5 August, p. 4

63   Herzberg, F., Mausner, B. and Snyderman, B. B. (1959), *The Motivation to Work*, Wiley, New York

64   Industrial Society (1985), *Survey of Attendance Rates and Attendance Bonuses*, New Series No. 3, Industrial Society Press, London

65   Industrial Society (1987) *Study of Absence Rates and Control Policies*, New Series No. 8, Industrial Society Press, London

66   CBI (1987). See Chapter 4, reference 2.

67   Bendell, E. R. D. (1965), *Nursing Times*, Vol. 61, p. 760

Chapter 6

1   Goldthorpe, J. H., Lockwood, D., Bechhofer, F. and Platt, J. (1968), *The Affluent Worker: Industrial Attitudes and Behaviour*, Cambridge University Press

2   Allen, P. T. (1982), 'Size of workforce, morale and absenteeism: a re-examination', *British Journal of Industrial Relations*, Vol. 20, No. 1, pp. 83–100

3   Morgan, L. G. and Herman, J. B. (1976), 'Perceived consequences of absence', *The Journal of Applied Psychology* Vol. 61, No. 3, pp. 738–42

4   Hill, J. M. and Trist, E. L. (1955), 'Changes in accidents and other absences with length of service', *Human Relations*, Vol. 8, pp. 121–52

5   Martin (1971). See Chapter 4, reference 8.

6   Almond (1975). See Chapter 5, reference 46.

7   Pocock (1973). See Chapter 4, reference 9.

8   Pocock (1973). See Chapter 4, reference 9.
9   Nicholson, N., Brown, C. A. and Chadwick-Jones, J. K. (1977), 'Absence from work and personnel characteristics', *Journal of Applied Psychology*, Vol. 62, No. 3, pp. 319–27
10   See:

Nicholson *et al.* (1977). See reference 9.

Nicholson, N. (1977), 'Absence behaviour and attendance motivation: a conceptual synthesis', *Journal of Management Studies*, Vol. 14, No. 3, pp. 231–52

Cooper, R. and Payne, R. L. (1965), 'Age and absence: a longitudinal study in three firms', *Occupational Psychology*, Vol. 39, pp. 31–5

Gertenfeld, A. (1969), 'Employee absenteeism: new insight', *Business Horizons*, Vol. 12, October, pp. 51–61

Shore, H. H. (1975), 'Absenteeism, Part 1: How to analyse cause and effects', *Supervisory Management*, September, pp. 9–16
11   Gibson, R. O. (1966), 'Towards a conceptualization of absence behaviour of personnel in organizations', *Administrative Science Quarterly*, Vol. 11, pp. 107–33
12   Horgan, J. F. (1981), 'Absenteeism', *Management World*, June, pp. 14–15
13   Central Statistical Office (1985), *Social Trends*, Labour Force Survey, Department of Employment, HMSO, London
14   Incomes Data Survey (1988), *Absence Control*, Study 403, London
15   Industrial Society (1987). See Chapter 5, reference 65.
16   See:

Kilbridge, M. D. (1966), 'Turnover and absences rates as indicators of employee dissatisfaction with repetitive work', *Industrial and Labour Relations Review*, Vol. 15, No. 1, pp. 21–32

Isambert-Jamati, V. (1962), 'Absenteeism among women workers in industry', *International Labour Review*, Vol. 85, pp. 248–61

Chadwick-Jones, J. K., Brown, C. W. and Nicholson, N. (1973), 'A-type and B-type absence: empirical trends for women employees', *Occupational Psychology*, Vol. 47, Nos 1–2, pp. 75–80

Flanagan, R. J., Strauss, G. and Ulman, L. (1974), 'Worker discontent and workplace behaviour', *Industrial Relations*, Vol. 13, pp. 101–23

Garrison, K. R. and Muchinsky, P. M. (1977), 'Attitudinal and biographical predictors of incidental absenteeism', *Journal of Vocational Behaviour*, Vol. 10, pp. 221–30

Johns, G. (1978), 'Attitudinal and non-attitudinal predictors of incidental absenteeism', *Organizational Behaviour and Human Performance*, Vol. 22, pp. 431–44
17   Hedges (1973). See Chapter 5, reference 44.
18   Incomes Data Survey (1984), *Controlling Absence*, Study 321, London
19   Paringer, L. (1983), 'Women and absenteeism – health or economics?', *American Economic Review*, Vol. 73, No. 2, pp. 123–7

20   Leigh, J. P. (1983), 'Sex differences in absenteeism', *Industrial Relations*, Vol. 22, No. 3, pp. 349–61

21   Gibson (1966). See reference 11.

22   Sinha, A. K. P. (1963), 'Manifest anxiety affecting industrial absenteeism', *Psychological Reports*, Vol. 13, p. 258

23   Stewart, H. (1965), 'The relationship between physical illness to the IPAT 16 Personality Factors Test', *Journal of Clinical Psychology*, Vol. 21, pp. 264–6

24   Taylor (1968). See Chapter 4, reference 5.

25   Thurlow, H. J. (1967), 'General susceptibility to illness: a selective review', *Canadian Medical Association Journal*, Vol. 97, pp. 1397–404

26   Porter, L. W. and Steers, R. M. (1973), 'Organizational, work and personnel factors in employee turnover and absenteeism', *Psychological Bulletin*, Vol. 80, No. 2, pp. 151–76

27   Heron, A. (1960), 'Aging and employment' in Schilling, R. S. F. (ed.), *Modern Trends in Occupational Health*, Butterworth, London

28   Neugarten, B. L. (1963), 'Personality and the aging process' in Williams, R. H., Tibbitts, C. and Donahue, W. (eds) *Process of Aging: Vol. 1*, Atherton Press, New York

29   Chown, S. M. (1962), 'Rigidity and age' in Tibbitts, C. and Donahue, W. (eds), *Social and Psychological Aspects of Aging*, Columbia University Press, New York

30   Nicholson *et al.* (1977). See reference 9.

31   Smith, P. C., Kendall, L. M. and Hulin, C. L. (1969) *The Measurement of Satisfaction in Work and Retirement*, Rand McNally, Chicago

32   See:

Hackett, R. D. and Guion, R. M. (1985), 'A re-evaluation of the absenteeism–job satisfaction relationship', *Organizational Behaviour and Human Decision Processes*, Vol. 35, pp. 340–81

Scott, K. D. and Taylor, G. S. (1985), 'An examination of conflicting findings on the relationship between job satisfaction and absenteeism: a meta analysis', *Academy of Management Journal*, Vol. 28, pp. 599–612

Vroom, N. (1977), *Work and Motivation*, Wiley, New York

Brayfield, A. H. and Crockett, W. H. (1955), 'Employee attitudes and employee performance', *Psychological Bulletin*, Vol. 52, pp. 396–424

Gibson, R. O. (1966), 'Towards a Conceptualization of Absence Behaviour of Personnel in Organizations', *Administrative Science Quarterly*, Vol. 11, No. 1, pp. 107–13

Illgen, D. R. and Hollenbeck, J. H. (1977), 'The role of job satisfaction in absence behaviour', *Organizational Behaviour and Human Performance*, Vol. 19, No. 1, pp. 148–61

Organ, D. (1977), 'A re-appraisal and re-interpretation of the satisfaction–causes–performance hypothesis', *Academy of Management Review*, Vol. 2, No. 1, pp. 46–53

33   Clegg, C. W. (1983), 'Psychology of employee lateness, absence and turnover: a methodological critique and empirical study', *Journal of Applied Psychology*, Vol. 68, No. 1, pp. 88–101

Chapter 7

1   Nicholson, Brown and Chadwick-Jones (1976). See Chapter 4, reference 11.

2   Behrend, H. (1953), 'Absence and labour turnover in a changing economic climate', *Occupational Psychology*, Vol. 27, No. 2, pp. 67–79

3   Crowther, J. (1957), 'Absence and turnover in the division of one company: 1950–5', *Occupational Psychology*, Vol. 31, No. 4, pp. 256–69

4   Industrial Society (1985). See Chapter 5, reference 64.

5   Industrial Society (1987). See Chapter 5, reference 65.

6   CBI (1987). See Chapter 4, reference 2.

7   Gowler, D. (1969), 'Determinants of the supply of labour to the firm', *Journal of Management Studies*, Vol. 6, pp. 73–95

8   Bernardin, H. J. (1977), 'The relationship of personality variables to organizational withdrawal', *Personnel Psychology*, Vol. 30, pp. 17–27

9   Matthewman, J. (1985), *Controlling Absenteeism*, Institute of Personnel Management, London

10 Taylor (1974). See Chapter 5, reference 47.

11 Doherty, N. A. (1979), 'National Insurance and absence from work', *The Economic Journal*, Vol. 89, pp. 50–65

12 Pocock (1973). See Chapter 4, reference 9.

13 Taylor (1982). See Chapter 4, reference 13.

14 Blau, G. J. and Boal, K. B. (1987), 'Conceptualizing how job involvement and organizational commitment affect turnover and absenteeism', *Academy of Management Review*, Vol. 12, No. 2, pp. 288–300

15 Edwards, P. (1979), 'Strikes and unorganized conflict', *British Journal of Industrial Relations*, Vol. 17, pp. 95–8

16 Shaw, M. E. (1976), *Group Dynamics*, McGraw-Hill, New York

17 Ilgen, D. R. and Hollenback, J. H. (1977), 'The role of job satisfaction in absence behaviour', *Organizational Behaviour and Human Performance*, Vol. 19, pp. 148–61

18 Porter, L. W. and Lawler, E. E. (1965), 'Properties of organization structure in relation to job attitudes and job behaviour', *Psychological Bulletin*, Vol. 64, pp. 23–51

19 Glaser, E. M. (1976), *Productivity Gains through Worklife Improvement*, The Psychological Corporation, New York

20 Turner, A. N. and Lawrence, P. R. (1965), *Industrial Jobs and the Worker*, Harvard University Press, Boston

21 Buchanan, B. (1974), 'Building organizational commitment: the socialization of managers in work organizations', *Administrative Science Quarterly*, Vol. 19, pp. 533–46

22 Morris, J. H. and Sherman, J. D. (1981),'Generalizability of an organizational commitment model', *Academy of Management Journal*, Vol. 24, pp. 512–26

23 Price, J. D. and Mueller, C. W. (1986), *Absenteeism and Turnover among Hospital Employees*, J.A.I. Press, New York

24 Mowday, R. T., Porter, L. W. and Steers, R. M. (1982), *Employee-organizational Linkages: The Psychology of Commitment, Absenteeism and Turnover*, Academic Press, New York

25 Steers, R. M. (1977), 'Antecedents and outcomes of organizational commitment', *Administrative Science Quarterly*, Vol. 22, pp. 46–56

26   Rhodes, S. and Steers, R. (1981), 'A systematic approach to diagnosing employee absenteeism', *Employee Relations*, Vol. 3, No. 2, pp. 17–22

27   Jamal, M. (1981), 'Shift work related to job attitudes, social participation and withdrawal behaviour: a study of nurses and industrial workers', *Personnel Psychology*, Vol. 34, pp. 535–47

28   Clegg, C. W. (1983), 'Psychology of employee lateness, absence and turnover', *Journal of Applied Psychology*, Vol. 68, pp. 88–101

29   Kanungo, R. (1982), *Work Alienation: An Integrative Approach*, Praeger, New York

30   Hall, D. T., Goodale, J. G. and Rabinowitz, S. and Morgan, M. A. (1978), 'Effects of top down departmental job change upon perceived employee behaviour and attitudes: a natural field experiment', *Journal of Applied Psychology*, Vol. 63, pp. 62–72

31   Rabinowitz, S. (1981), 'Towards a development model of job involvement', *International Review of Applied Psychology*, Vol. 30, pp. 62–72

32   Rabinowitz, S. and Hall, D. T. (1977), 'Organizational research on job involvement', *Psychological Bulletin*, Vol. 84, pp. 265–88

33   Ruh, R. A., White, J. K. and Wood, R. R. (1975), 'Job involvement, values, personal background, participation in decision making and job attitudes', *Academy of Management Journal*, Vol. 18, pp. 300–12

34   Saal, F. E. (1978), 'Job involvement: a multivariate approach', *Journal of Applied Psychology*, Vol. 63, pp. 53–61

35   Steers, R. M. and Rhodes, S. R. (1984), 'Knowledge and speculation about absenteeism' in Goodman, P. S. and Atkin, R. S. (eds) *Absenteeism*, pp. 229–75, Jossey Bass, San Francisco

36   Paringer (1983), See Chapter 6, reference 19.

37   Hedges, J. N. (1975) 'Unscheduled absence from work: an update', *Monthly Labour Review*, August, Number 98, pp. 36–39

38   Miner, J. B. and Brewer, J. F. (1976) 'The management of ineffective performance' in Dunette, M. D. (ed.), *Handbook of Industrial and Organizational Psychology*, Rand McNally, Chicago, pp. 995–1029

39   Yolles, S. F., Carone, P. A. and Krinsky, L. W. (1975), *Absenteeism in Industry*, Charles C. Thomas, Springfield, Illinois

40   Alcohol Concern (1987) *The Drinking Problem*, Alcohol Concern, London

41   Roman, P. M. and Trice, H. M. (1976), 'Alcohol abuse and work organization' in Kissen, B. and Begleiter, H. (eds), *Social Aspects of Alcoholism*, pp. 445–517, Plenum, New York

42   Asma, F. E., Hilker, R. R., Shevlin, J. J. and Golden, R. C. (1980), 'Twenty-five years of rehabilitation of employees with drink problems', *Journal of Occupational Medicine*, Vol. 22, No. 4, pp. 241–4

43   Kurtz, N. R., Googins, B. and Howard, H. C. (1984), 'Measuring the success of occupational alcoholism programmes', *Journal of Studies on Alcoholism*, Vol. 45, pp. 33–45

44   Trice, H. M. and Roman, P. M. (1978) *Spirits and Demons at Work*, ILR Paperback No. 11, New York State School of Industrial and Labour Relations, Cornell University, New York

45   Beaumont, P. B. and Hyman, J. (1987) 'The work performance indicators of problem drinking: some British evidence', *Journal of Occupational Behaviour*, Vol. 8, pp. 55–62

46 Almond (1975). See Chapter 5, reference 46.

47 IDS (1984). See Chapter 6 reference 18.

48 Taylor (1974). See Chapter 5, reference 47.

49 Taylor (1982). See Chapter 4, reference 13.

50 Winkler (1980). See Chapter 5, reference 58.

51 CBI (1987). See Chapter 4, reference 2.

52 Hedges (1975). See reference 37.

53 Krauz, M. and Freibach, N. (1983), 'Effects of flexible working time for employed women upon satisfaction, strain and absenteeism', *Journal of Occupational Psychology*, Vol. 56, pp. 155-9

54 McCroskey, J. (1982) 'Work and families: what is the employer's liability?', *Personnel Journal*, Vol. 61, No. 1, pp. 30-8

55 Martin (1971). See Chapter 4, reference 8.

56 McCurdy, J. and Bowey, A. M. (1982). See Chapter 4, reference 4.

57 Industrial Society (1987). See Chapter 5, reference 65.

58 Behrend, H. and Pocock, S. (1976). 'Absence and the individual: a six-year study in one organization', *International Labour Review*, Vol. 114, No. 3, pp. 311-27

59 Pocock (1973). See Chapter 4, reference 9.

60 Ivancevich, J. M. (1985), 'Predicting absence from prior absence and work attitudes', *Academy of Management Review*, Vol. 28, No. 1, pp. 219-28

61 Breugh (1981). See Chapter 5, reference 9.

62 Keller, R. T. (1983), 'Predicting absenteeism from prior absenteeism, attitudinal factors and non-attitudinal factors', *Journal of Applied Psychology*, Vol. 68, No. 3, pp. 536-40

63 Industrial Society (1985). See Chapter 5, reference 64.

64 CBI (1987). See Chapter 4, reference 2.

Chapter 8

1 See:

Mann, F. (1964), 'Studying and creating change' in Bennis, W., Benne, K. and Chin, R. (eds), *The Planning of Change*, Holt, Rinehart and Winston, New York, pp. 605-15

Golembiewski, R. and Hillies, R. (1979) *Towards the Responsive Organization: The Theory and Practice of Survey Feedback*, Brighton Publishing, Salt Lake City

Nadler, D. (1977), *Feedback and Organizational Development: Using Data Based Methods*, Addison Wesley, Reading

Chapter 9

1 Glasgow Chamber of Commerce (1979), *The Strike That Never Stops: A Report on Absenteeism in West of Scotland Industry*, Glasgow

2 Latham, G. P. and Napier, N. K. (1984), 'Practical ways to increase employee attendance' in Goodman, P. S. and Atkin, R. S. (eds), *Absenteeism: New*

Approaches to Understanding, Measuring and Managing Employee Absence, Jossey Bass, San Francisco

3 McCurdy, J. and Bowey, A. M. (1982), *Absenteeism*, Working Paper No. 8202, University of Strathclyde Business School, Glasgow

4 Taylor, P. J. (1982), *Absenteeism: Cause and Control*, The Industrial Society, London

5 Matthewman, J. (1985), *Controlling Absence*, Institute of Personnel Management, London

6 Advisory, Conciliation and Arbitration Service (1983), *Absence: Advisory Booklet No. 5*, London

7 Industrial Society (1987), *Study of Absence Rates and Control Policies*, New Series, No. 8, Industrial Society Press, London

8 Scott, K. D. and Markham, S. E. (1982) 'Absenteeism control methods: a survey of practices and results', *Personnel Administration*, June, pp. 73–84

9 Almond, J. M. (1975), 'The Management of Absenteeism', *The Production Engineer*, December, pp. 649–54

10 Steers, R. M. and Rhodes, S. R. (1984), 'Knowledge and speculation about absenteeism' in Goodman, P. S. and Atkin, R. S. (eds), *Absenteeism: New Approaches to Understanding, Measuring and Managing Employee Absence*, Jossey Bass, San Francisco

11 Johns, G. (1980), 'Did you go to work today?', *Montreal Business Report*, Fourth Quarter, pp. 96–106

12 Ford, R. (1973), 'Job enrichment lessons from A. T. and T.', *Harvard Business Review*, Vol. 51, pp. 96–106

13 Kim, J. S. and Campagna, A. F. (1981), 'Effects of flexitime on employee attendance and performance: a field experiment', *Academy of Management Journal*, Vol. 24, pp. 729–41

14 Latham, G. P. and Kinne, S. B. (1974), 'Improving job performance through training in goal setting', *Journal of Applied Psychology*, Vol. 59, pp. 187–91

15 See:

Huczynski, A. A. (1985), 'Designing high-commitment high-performance organizations', *Technovation*, Vol. 3, pp. 111–8

Walton, R. E. (1985), 'From control to commitment in the workplace', *Harvard Business Review*, March–April, pp. 77–85

16 Buchanan, D. (1987), 'Job enrichment is dead: long live high performance work design', *Personnel Management*, May, pp. 40–3

Chapter 10

1 The Industrial Society (1982), *Absenteeism: Causes and Control*, London

2 McCurdy and Bowey (1982). See Chapter 9, reference 3.

3 Matthewman (1985). See Chapter 9, reference 5.

4 Katz, D. and Kahn, R. L. (1966), *The Social Psychology of Work*, Wiley, New York

5 Baum, J. F. and Youngblood, S. A. (1975), 'Impact of an organizational control policy on absenteeism, performance and satisfaction', *Journal of Applied Psychology*, Vol. 60, No. 6, pp. 688–94

6   Rosenthal, R. (1979), 'Arbitral Standards for Absence Discharge', *Labour Law Review*, pp. 732–40

7   Behrend, H. (1974), 'A new approach in the analysis of absences from work', *Industrial Relations Journal*, Vol. 5, No. 4, pp. 4–21

8   McCurdy and Bowey (1982). See Chapter 9, reference 3.

9   Nicholson, N. (1976), 'Management sanctions and absence control', *Human Relations*, Vol. 29, No. 2, pp. 139–51

10   Latham, G. P. and Napier, N. K. (1984), 'Practical ways to increase employee attendance' in Goodman, P. S. and Atkin, R. S. (eds), *Absenteeism: New Approaches to Understanding, Measuring and Managing Employee Absence*, Jossey Bass, San Francisco

11   Long, L. and Hill, M. (1988), *Special Leave*, Institute of Personnel Management, London

12   Scott and Markham (1982). See Chapter 9, reference 8.

13   Industrial Society (1987). See Chapter 9, reference 7.

14   Kuzmits, F. E. (1981), 'No fault: a new strategy for absenteeism control', *Personnel Journal*, May, pp. 387–90

15   Kuzmits, F. E. (1984), Is your organization ready for no fault absenteeism?, *Personnel Administrator*, December, pp. 119–27

16   Rosenthal (1979). See reference 6.

17   Cecchi, L. F. and Plax, T. G. (1984), 'Absence control through sensitive employee monitoring', *Manage*, Vol. 36, No. 3, pp. 8–10

18   Brindle, D. (1987), 'Why absenteeism is a declining fashion', *Financial Times*, October 26

19   Ford, J. E. (1981), 'A simple punishment procedure for controlling employee absenteeism', *Journal of Organizational Behaviour Management*, Vol. 3, No. 2, pp. 71–9

20   Abrose, J. R. (1982), 'Sandvik cuts absenteeism by measuring it accurately', *International Management*, May, pp. 57–8

21   Katz and Kahn (1966). See reference 4.

22   Orpen, C. (1978), 'Effects of bonuses for attendance on the absenteeism of industrial workers', *Journal of Organizational Behaviour Management*, Vol. 1, pp. 118–24

23   Pedalino, E. and Gamboa, V. U. (1974), 'Behaviour modification and absenteeism: intervention in one industrial setting', *Journal of Applied Psychology*, Vol. 59, pp. 694–8

24   The Industrial Society (1985), *Survey of Absence Rates and Attendance Bonuses*, New Series No. 3, Industrial Society Press, London

25   Industrial Society (1987). See Chapter 9, reference 7.

26   Underwood, L. (1987), 'Absent in body and spirit', *The Director*, Vol. 40, No. 11, June, pp. 61–2.

27   Schmitz, L. M. and Heneman, H. G. (1980), 'Do positive reinforcement programmes reduce employee absenteeism?, *Personnel Administrator*, Vol. 25, No. 9, pp. 87–93

28   Schneller, G. O. and Kopelman, R. E. (1983), 'Using incentives to increase absenteeism: a plan that backfired', *Compensation Review*, Vol. 15, No. 2, pp. 40–5

29   'Vauxhall carrot to tempt absentees', *Personnel Today*, October 1987

30   Scott, K. D., Markham, S. E. and Robers, R. W. (1985), 'Rewarding good

attendance: a comparative study of positive ways to reduce absence', *Personnel Administrator*, Vol. 30, August, pp. 72–83

31   Schmitz and Heneman (1980). See reference 27.

32   Incomes Data Survey (1984), *Controlling Absence*, Study 321, London

33   Scheflen, K., Lawler, E. E. and Hackman, J. R. (1971), 'Long-term impact of employee participation in the development of pay incentive plans: a field experiment revisited', *Journal of Applied Psychology*, Vol. 55, pp. 182–6

34   Kempen, R. W. and Hall, R. V. (1977), 'Reduction of industrial absenteeism: results of a behavioural approach', *Journal of Organizational Behaviour Management*, Vol. 1, pp. 1–21

35   Kopelman, R. E. and Schneller, G. O. (1981), 'A mixed consequence system for reducing overtime and unscheduled absences', *Journal of Organizational Behaviour Management*, Vol. 3, pp. 17–28

Chapter 11

1   Steers, R. M. and Rhodes, S. R. (1978), 'Major influences on employee attendance: a process model', *Journal of Applied Psychology*, Vol. 63, No. 4, pp. 391–407

2   Chadwick-Jones, J. K., Nicholson, N. and Brown, C. (1982), *Social Psychology of Absenteeism*, Praeger, New York

3   Industrial Society (1987). See Chapter 9, reference 7.

4   Latham and Napier (1984). See Chapter 10, reference 10.

5   Katz and Kahn (1966). See Chapter 10, reference 4.

6   Hackman, J. R., Oldham, G. R., Janson, R. and Purdy, K. (1975), 'A new strategy for job enrichment', *California Management Journal*, Vol. 17, pp. 57–71

7   Otway, H. J. and Misenta, R. (1980), 'The determinants of operator preparedness for emergency situations in nuclear power plants', Paper presented at the Workshop on Procedural and Organizational Measures for Accident Management, Nuclear Reactors International Institute for Applied Systems Analysis, Laxenburg, Austria, 28–31 January

8   Kelly, M. and Cooper, C. L. (1981) 'Stress among blue collar workers', *Employee Relations*, Vol. 3, pp. 6–9

9   Bula, R. J. (1984), 'Absenteeism control', *Personnel Journal*, Vol. 63, No. 6, pp. 56–60

10   Latham and Napier (1984). See Chapter 10, reference 10.

11   See for example:

Dugoni, B. L. and Ilgen, D. R. (1981), 'Realistic job previews and the adjustment of new employees', *Academy of Management Journal*, Vol. 24, pp. 579–91

Reilly, R. J., Tenopyr, M. L. and Sperling, S. M. (1979), 'Effects of job previews on job acceptance and survival of telephone operator candidates', *Journal of Applied Psychology*, Vol. 64, pp. 218–20

Zaharia, E. S. and Baumesiter, A. A. (1981), 'Job preview effects during the critical initial employment period', *Journal of Applied Psychology*, Vol. 66, pp. 19–22

Makin, P. J. and Robertson, I. T. (1983), 'Self-assessment, realistic job previews and occupational decisions', *Personnel Review*, Vol. 12, No. 3, pp. 21–5

Reilly, R. R., Blood, M. R., Brown, B. M. and Maletsa, C. A. (1981), 'The effects of realistic job previews: a study and a discussion of the literature', *Personnel Psychology*, Vol. 34, pp. 823–34

12   Rosen, R. H. (1984), 'Picture of health in the workplace', *Training and Development Journal*, August, pp. 24–30

13   Cooper, C. L. (1987) 'Stress in the workplace: recent research evidence', Presidential Address to Inaugural Conference, British Academy of Management, Warwick University, 13–15 September

14   Stewart, V. and Chadwick, V. (1987), *Changing Trains*, David and Charles

15   Colligan, M. J. and Murphy, L. R. (1979), 'Mass psychogenic illness in organizations', *Journal of Occupational Psychology*, Vol. 1, pp. 512–32

16   Marshall, J. and Cooper, C. L. (1981) *Coping with Stress at Work*, Gower, Aldershot

17   Peters, R. K. and Benson, H. (1979) 'Time out from tension', *Harvard Business Review*, January–February, pp. 120–4

18   Hinrichs, J. R. (1980), *Controlling Absence and Turnover*, Work in America Institute, Scarsdale, NY

19   Scott and Markham (1982). See Chapter 9, reference 8.

20   Industrial Society (1987). See Chapter 9, reference 7.

21   Abrose (1982). See Chapter 10, reference 20.

22   Lawler, E. E. (1971), *Pay and Organizational Effectiveness*, McGraw-Hill, New York

23   Taylor, P. J. (1982), *Absenteeism: Cause and Control*, Industrial Society, London

24   Dilts, D. A., Deitsch, C. R. and Elsea, S. W. (1987), 'Casual absenteeism cut: the experiences of two manufacturing firms', *Business and Public Affairs*, Vol. 13, pp. 6–8

25   Industrial Society (1987). See Chapter 9, reference 7.

26   Chadwick-Jones, Nicholson and Brown (1982). See reference 2.

27   Krausz, M. and Freibach, N. (1983), 'Effects of flexible working-time for employed women upon satisfaction, strains and absenteeism', *Journal of Occupational Psychology*, Vol. 56, pp. 155–9

Chapter 12

1   ACAS (1983). See Chapter 9, reference 6.

2   The Industrial Society (1982). See Chapter 10, reference 1.

3   Weir, M. and Hughes, J. (1983), 'Lessons in experience', *International Journal of Manpower*, Vol. 6, No. 1–2, pp. 80–102

4   Jones, H. G. (1983), 'Re-grouped success at Volvo', *Management Today*, February

5   Bloggat, T. B. (1983), 'Cadbury Schweppes: more than chocolate and tonic', *Harvard Business Review*, January–February, pp. 134–44

6   Walton, R. (1979), 'From control to commitment in the workplace', *Harvard Business Review*, March–April, pp. 77–84

7   Peters, T. J. and Waterman, R. H. (1982), *In Search of Excellence*, Harper and Row, New York

Chapter 13

1 Cecchi and Plax (1984). See Chapter 10, reference 17.

Chapter 14

1 Peters, T. (1988), *Thriving on Chaos*, Macmillan, London
2 *General Household Survey* (1984), HMSO, London
3 Carlzon, J. (1987), *Moments of Truth*, Harper and Row, New York
4 Scott, K. D. and Markham, S. E. (1982), 'Absenteeism control methods: a survey of practice and results', *Personnel Administration*, June, pp. 73–84
5 Kanter, R. M. (1985), *The Change Masters*, Counterpoint, London
6 Dunphy, D. C. and Dick, R. (1981), *Organizational Change by Choice*, McGraw-Hill, Sydney
7 Bedeian, A. G. (1980), *Organizations: Theory and Analysis*, The Dryden Press, Homewood, Illinois
8 Kotter, J. P. and Schlesinger, L. A. (1979), 'Choosing strategies for change', *Harvard Business Review*, Vol. 57, No. 2, pp. 106–14
9 Boddy, D. and Buchanan, D. A. (1987), *Technical Change Audit*, Manpower Services Commission, Sheffield

Index

Ability to attend, 32, 37, 77–80
  Absence Cause Analysis Checklist, 170
  absence control techniques, 123, 136–8
  Arlanda Electronics case study, 223–4, 228, 229
Absence Cause Analysis Checklist, 169–70, 174, 220, 221
Absence control techniques, 89–152
  ALIEDIM, 155–95
    Arlanda Electronics case study, 155, 156, 196–256
  deciding on, 97–9
  measuring effectiveness of, 93–5
  organizational techniques, 97, 98–9, 139–48
  people techniques, 97, 98, 100–22
  work techniques, 97, 98, 123–38
Absence data analysis, 166–7
ACAS (Arbitration and Conciliation Advisory Service), 8, 92, 140, 199,
Accidents, 77, 79, 126
Active jobs, 43
Age of employees
  and absence due to illness, 77
  and absence rates, 33, 55, 56–8, 59, 62, 68
  and shift workers, 254
Alcoholism, 77, 78–9, 130
ALIEDIM absence control strategy, 155–95
  Arlanda Electronics case study, 155, 156, 196–256
Assessing the absence problem, 156, 157–66
  Arlanda Electronics case study, 209–14
Attendance
  deciding on clear expectations of, 103–4
Attendance behaviour
  pressure to attend, 65–77
  process model of, 4, 34–7, 65, 76–7, 83, 124, 167
Attendance bonuses, 113–16, 119, 122
Attendance lists, 139
Attitudes of employees
  and absence rates, 52–4
  and absence-proneness, 61–2
  to absenteeism, 110–11
  ALIEDIM method of absence control, 186–91, 191, 194
  Arlanda Electronics case study, 206–8, 218–19, 243–4, 248, 249, 250
  Diamond Manufacturing case study, 142–7
  personal work ethics, 75–6

surveys, 129, 168, 194, 218–19
Authority
  and absence control programmes, 102
AV (Added Value)
  in absence cost analysis, 163, 165

Barlow, D.H., 8
Belgium, absence rates in, 5
Benchmarking, 23–5
  Arlanda Electronics case study, 210–11
  external, 23–4, 158–60, 210
  internal, 23, 24–5, 161–3, 210–11
Bendell, E.R.D., 51
Blue-collar workers see Hourly-paid workers; Manual workers
Boddy, David, 188–9
Bonus schemes, 113–16, 119
Boring jobs
  and absence rates, 39–40, 60
  attitudes to, 46
  and stress, 42
Bowey, A.M., 92
Britain
  absence rates, 5, 6–9
    regional differences in, 66–8
Brooke, P.B., 43
Buchanan, David, 188–9
Bula, R.J., 128

Canada, 19
Career development
  and stress, 44
Causes of absence, 29–88
  Arlanda Electronics case study, 203–5, 224–9, 236–7
  attendance factors, 65–82
  classifying, 31–7
  identifying and prioritizing, 156, 167–74
    Arlanda Electronics case study, 218–29
  job situation factors, 38–51
  personal factors, 52–64
CBI (Confederation of British Industry)
  1987 survey, 5, 6, 10–11, 31, 40, 50, 67, 80
Cecchi, L.F., 107, 149, 150
Change, organizational
  checklist of successful programmes, 185–6
Change Masters, The (Kanter), 180
Changes in absence control procedures
  Arlanda Electronics case study, 250

implementing, 188–91
resistance to, 186–8
Diamond Manufacturing case study, 143–4
Communication
Arlanda Electronics case study, 227–8, 248
Diamond Manufacturing case study, 145–6
improved systems of, 127
with supervisors, 133
Companies
attitudes to absence, 9
benchmarking, 23–5
inter-company comparisons of absence rates, 20–1
loyalty to
and absence rates, 75–6
size of, and absence rate, 50–1
see also Managers/Management
Comparison analysis
of absence causes, 173–4
Arlanda Electronics case study, 224–9
see also Benchmarking; International comparisons
Conditions of work
and absence rates, 41–50
changes in, 98, 126–7
Contracts of employment, 103
Control plans (absence), 54
Cooper, Cary, 41–2, 44, 47, 130
Costs of absence, 4, 8, 91
Arlanda Electronics case study, 201–2, 211–14, 252
assessing/measuring, 15–27
calculating, 163–6
international comparisons, 5
Counselling of employees, 133, 136
Arlanda Electronics case study, 202, 253
Crèche facilities, 137
CSO (Central Statistical Office)
Annual Abstract of Statistics, 6
Customers
Diamond Manufacturing case study, 145–6
Czechoslovakia, absence rates in, 5

Danger, physical
and absence due to stress, 41–2
Day of week
and absence rates, 80–1
Delivery deadlines
and absenteeism, 15, 17–18
Designing absence control programmes, 156, 179–84
Arlanda Electronics case study, 234–46
Diamond Measurements Ltd
case study of organizational techniques, 141–7
Doctor's certificates, 72, 109–10
Dunphy, D.C., 185

Economic conditions
and absence rates, 65–8
Employees, see Attitudes; Expectations; Individuals; Values
Employment Protection Act (Consolidated) 1980, 202
Environmental factors
and absence rates, 41–2, 48–50, 62–3
change in, 98, 126–7
Evaluating current absence control methods, 156, 175–9

Arlanda Electronics case study, 230–4
Expectations of employees
and absence control techniques, 123, 127–8
and absence rates, 52–4
Arlanda Electronics case study, 222
Extroversion
and absenteeism, 62

Family responsibilities
and absence rates, 60, 61, 80
and organizational loyalty, 76
Females, see Women
Financial benefits
absence control through, 113–19
Finniston, M., 8
Flexibility
and overtime, 68
as reason for absence, 54
Flexible manning
Arlanda Electronics case study, 242–3
Diamond Manufacturing case study, 144–5
Flexible time working (flexitime), 137–8
Arlanda Electronics case study, 237
Diamond Manufacturing case study, 145
Ford, J.E., 110
4–40 hours approach, 137
France, absence rates in, 5
Freibach, N., 137
Frequency of absence
Arlanda Electronics case study, 215, 217–18, 235
identifying, 167
Fringe benefits
and absence control, 101
sick leave as, 128
GAS (General Adaptation Syndrome), 41
General Household Survey (1984), 5, 6, 7–8, 11, 57, 58, 159, 160, 214
Gibson, R.O., 61
Gifts, for perfect attendance, 120, 121
Groups (work)
and absence control, 117
cohesion of, 44–6, 50–1
hourly-paid workers, 188
Industrial Society booklet on, 140
norms, 73–4
encouragement of desirable, 134–6
size of, 50–1, 73–4
see also Industry groups

Health and fitness programmes, 129–30
Health status
and absenteeism, 77–8
Hedges, J.N., 60
Herzberg, Frederick, 50
High strain jobs, 43, 44
Hill, M., 104
Holland, absence rates in, 5
Horgan, J.F., 56
Hourly-paid workers
Arlanda Electronics case study, 197, 200–1
group identity, 188
sick-pay committees. 190–1
Hours of work
and absence rates, 47
Diamond Manufacturing case study, 145
flexitime, 137–8, 145, 237

Illness, absence due to, 77–9
Implementing absence control programmes, 156, 184–91
  Arlanda Electronics case study, 246–50
In Search of Excellence (Peters and Waterman), 148
Individuals
  and absence control techniques, 123, 128–31
  and absenteeism, 31, 32, 71
  absent-prone, 61–2
  good attenders
    attitudes to absenteeism, 18–19
    rewards for, 119, 252
  Industrial Society booklet on, 140–1
  past absence patterns, 81–2
  personal work ethics, 75–6
  responsibility for absence, 248
Industrial citizenship programmes, 248
Industrial Society, 19
  1985 survey, 6, 7, 50, 59, 66, 67, 82, 113, 114
  1987 survey, 7, 10–11, 21, 22, 50, 59, 66, 67, 81, 92, 105, 114, 122, 124
  absence control programmes, 101
  booklet on absenteeism, 140–1
  and causes of absence, 33, 34
Industry groups
  absence rates by, 159–60
International comparisons
  of absence rates, 5–6, 20
Introversion
  and absenteeism, 62
Italy, absence rates in, 5
Ivancevich, J.M., 82

Japan, absence rates in, 5
Job enrichment, 46, 98
  and absence control, 125–6, 127
  Diamond Manufacturing case study, 146–7
Job involvement
  and organizational loyalty, 76–7
Job moves, frequency of
  and absence rates, 44–6
  Arlanda Electronics case study, 202, 219
Job rotation, 46
  and absence control, 125, 127, 254
Job satisfaction
  and absence rates, 33, 62–4
  Arlanda Electronics case study, 225–6, 228
  Industrial Society booklet on, 140
  and organizational loyalty, 76
Job scope, level, design and type
  and absence rates, 38–40
Job situation
  Absence Cause Analysis Checklist, 169
  and absence control techniques, 123, 124–7
  Arlanda Electronics case study, 219, 222
  and attendance behaviour, 35, 36, 37
  as cause of absence, 38–51
Job strain
  and absence rates, 33
  model, 43–4
Journal articles on absence, 12, 91

Kanter, R.M., 180
Karasek, Richard
  job strain model, 43–4
Klein, B., 5

Kopelman, R.E., 115
Krausz, M., 137

Latham, G.P., 92, 103
Lawler, Edward, 24
Leadership style
  and absence rates, 47–8
Legislative changes, 8–9, 104
Length of service
  and absence rates, 55–6, 68
Locating the absence problem, 156, 166–7
  Arlanda Electronics case study, 214–18
Long, L., 104
Lorsch, Jay, 255–6
Lost time *see* Time lost rates
Lotteries, 118, 121
Low strain jobs, 43

Management review questions
  on absence control methods, 96, 150–2
  on causes of absence, 85–8
Managers/Management
  absence control programmes
    accountability for, 185
  and absence costs, 17
  absence rates, 7
  Arlanda Electronics case study, 196, 203–5, 208, 225, 233, 255
  attendance records, 124
  attitudes to employees, 128
  attitudes to positive reinforcement, 121–2
  Diamond Manufacturing case study, 142–7
  leadership style
    and absence rates, 47–8
  organizational techniques, 140
  personal theories of absence, 11–12, 13–14, 34, 62–3, 83, 92–3
    and absence control programmes, 186, 196, 203–5, 225, 255
  responsibility for absence, 157
  stress in, 41
  technical training for, 146
  will to control absences, 107–9
Mann, Floyd, 47
Manual workers (Blue-collar workers)
  absence rates, 7, 10, 11, 124
  attendance bonuses, 114
  and family responsibilities, 80
  financial benefits to, 116–17
  and group size, 74
  patterns of absence, 81
  and self-certification, 82
  and special leave, 104
  United States, 50
Manufacturing companies
  attendance bonuses, 113
Market conditions
  and absence rates, 65–8
Markham, S.E. *see* Scott K.D., and Markham, S.E.
Marriage leave, 104
Married women, 60, 137
Mason, Andrew, 40
Maternity leave, 103, 104
Matthewman, J., 8, 92
MBWA (Management By Walking About), 255
McCurdy, J., 92
Men, absence rates of, 57, 58–61

Miles, Raymond, 13
Mixed consequence system
  of absence control, 98, 122, 139, 179, 182
  Arlanda Electronics case study, 237, 240
Moments of Truth (Carlzon), 161
Monday payday plans, 118
Monitoring absence control programmes, 156,
    191—5
  Arlanda Electronics case study, 250—5
Motivation
  for absences, 54
  to attend, 32
  Herzberg's theory of, 50
  increasing, 135
  pressure to attend, 65—77
  valency theory of, 24

Napier, N.K., 92, 103
National Economic Development Council, 7
Negative (punishment) incentive
  for controlling absence, 54, 98, 100—12, 122,
    131, 139, 179, 182
No-fault Absenteeism approach, 106, 237
  Arlanda Electronics case study, 205—9, 236,
    240, 241, 248, 250, 252
Noise levels, 126, 127
Non-manual workers
  absence rates, 7, 10, 11
  and special leave, 104
  see also Salaried employees; Staff employees
North-south divide
  and absence rates, 66—8

Office workers
  survey on office environment, 49—50
Organizational climate/structure
  and stress, 44
Organizational commitment, 75—6
Organizational permissiveness, 48
Organizational techniques
  of absence control, 97, 98—9, 139—48, 149,
    151—2, 180, 181, 182
  Arlanda Electronics case study, 238—9
Overmanning
  and absence costs, 15, 16—17
Overtime
  and absence costs, 15, 16
  and absence rates, 68, 69—71
  Arlanda Electronics case study, 202, 220,
    242—3, 254—5
Overwork, and stress, 42

Paringer, L., 60
Parkinson's Law of Sick Leave Abuse, 71—2
Part-time employees
  absence rates, 7, 59
Passive jobs, 43
Past absenteeism, 81—2
Pay-for-performance systems, 249
Pay rises
  absence control through, 116
  see also Wage levels
Pay structures, reviewing, 241—2
People techniques
  Arlanda Electronics case study, 237, 240—1
  for controlling absence, 97, 98, 100—22, 149,
    151—2, 179, 181, 182

Performance, monitoring of
  ALIEDIM approach to, 191—5, 252—5
Personal characteristics
  Absence Cause Analysis Checklist, 169
  Arlanda Electronics case study, 222
  and attendance behaviour, 35, 36, 37, 76, 77
  as cause of absence, 52—64
Personality
  and absence rates, 61—2
Personnel departments/managers
  and absence control, 96, 105, 132, 133, 136
Peters, Tom, 158
Physical environment, *see* Environmental factors
Plax, T.G., 107
Pocock, S.J., 55
Poker plans, 118

Poland, absence rates in, 5
Positive incentives approach
  to absence control, 54, 98, 113—22, 131, 133,
    179, 182
  Arlanda Electronics case study, 237, 240
Positive outcomes of absence, 54
Pressure to attend, 35, 36, 228, 229
  Absence Cause Analysis Checklist, 170
  Arlanda Electronics case study, 219, 223, 228,
    229
  and attendance behaviour, 36, 37
Problem groups
  identifying, 166, 168—70, 218—21
Problem-solving tips, 91—3
Procedure for absences, 109—11
Process model of employee attendance, 33, 34—7
Product quality
  and absenteeism, 17, 212—13
Productivity
  increasing, 127
  opportunities
    and absence levels, 25
    Arlanda Electronics case study, 209—11,
      213—14
    for improvement, 21—3
Profit-sharing, 118, 252—3
Project leaders, 249
Protestant ethic, individual adherence to, 75
Psychological disorders, 77—8
Punctuality plans, 118
Punishment *see* Negative (punishment) incentive

Ranking analysis of absence causes, 172—3
Realistic job previews, 129
Reasons for absence *see* Causes of absence
Recognition programmes, 120
Records of absences, 19, 25, 142
  and absence control, 131, 132—3
  keeping, 104—6
Redundancies
  and absence rates, 65, 67
Regional differences
  in absence rates, 66—8
Relationships at work, 44; *see also* Groups
Replacement employees
  costs of, 18, 212
Research literature on absence, 10—14, 33
Retirement bonuses, 118
Reward strategies, *see* Positive incentives
    approach

Rhodes, S. *see* Steers, R., and Rhodes, S.
Role ambiguity/conflict, 42–3, 129
Role conflict, 129
Rosenthal, R., 102, 107
Rules, absence, 111–12

Salaried employees
    Arlanda Electronics case study, 200–1, 218
    see also Non-manual workers; Staff employees
Sargent, Andrew, 25, 105
Schneller, G.O., 115
Scott, K.D., and Markham, S.E., 93–5, 105
    list of absence control methods, 93–5, 105, 109,
        131, 151, 175, 176–8
Self-certification, 3, 72, 105
    Arlanda Electronics case study, 203, 220, 225, 253
    introduction of, 8, 9, 82
    and supervisors, 132
Selye, Hans, 41
Sex differences
    absence rates, 58–61
Shephard, R.A., 14
Shift workers, 33
    and absence rates, 33, 47, 56
    Arlanda Electronics case study, 215, 219–20,
        240, 241, 254
    and stress, 42
Short-term absences
    control of, 106, 107
Sick-leave banks, 118
Sick-leave bonuses, 118
Sick-pay schemes, 33
    and absence control, 116–17, 119, 120
    and absence rates, 68, 71–3
    Arlanda Electronics case study, 226
    committees, 190–1
    costs of, 15, 16
    employees' attitudes to, 128
    punishing absence through, 100, 110, 112
Sickness absence, 3, 105
    Arlanda Electronics case study, 199–200, 201
    behavioural factors in, 32
    factors affecting, 34
    international comparisons, 5–6
    reduction of, 109
    surveys on, 10–11
    in women, 59
Situational constraints, 35, 77
Size of organization
    and absence rates, 50, 73–4
Social psychological disorders, 77–9
Socioeconomic group
    absence rates by, 7
Solutions, 'quick-fix', 12–13, 181
Sparling, John, 47
Special leave, 103–4
Staff employees
    absence rates, 124
    attendance bonuses, 114
    see also Non-manual workers; Salaried
        employees
Staff turnover, 3, 4
State benefits
    and absence rates, 71–3
Steers, R., and Rhodes, S
    process model of absence, 4, 34–7, 65, 76–7,
        83, 124, 167

Stress
    and absence control, 128–31
    and absence rates, 38, 40–4, 77, 128
    management, 128–9, 130–1, 253
    reducing, 238
    and working conditions, 126
Supervisors
    and absence control, 102, 108, 110–11, 131–3
    and absence costs, 17
    Arlanda Electronics case study, 233, 243,
        246–7, 249
    attendance records maintained by, 96
    employee relationships
        and absence rates, 47–8
    and record-keeping, 105
    training, 243, 249
Surveys of absence, 5–9, 10–14; *see also*
        Attitudes of employees: surveys
Sweden, absence rates in, 5

Taylor, P.J., 5, 8, 15, 19–20, 49, 71, 72, 79, 92,
        135
Team-briefing systems, 248, 250
Temporary workers, 208–9, 219, 226
Thorpe, Richard, 22
Time lost rates, 20–1
    Arlanda Electronics case study, 199, 215, 236
    identifying, 167
Time off for good attendance, 119
Trade unions
    and absence control, 135–6
    Diamond Manufacturing case study, 142, 144
    and financial benefits, 118
    and job rotation, 127
    and record-keeping, 105
    and sick-pay committees, 191
    and special leave, 104
Trading stamps/coupons plans, 118
Training
    Diamond Manufacturing case study, 146
    employees, 254
    supervisors, 243, 249
Transportation/travelling problems, 33, 79

Unacceptable absence
    formal definitions of, 111
Unemployment
    and absence rates, 65–8
United Kingdom *see* Britain
United States
    absence control schemes
        negative incentive, 100, 101
    adolescents, attitudes of, 56
    age, and absence rates, 58
    Bureau of Business Practice survey, 48, 49
    company sick-pay schemes, 72
    crèche facilities, 137
    Current Population Survey (CPS), 5
    health care programmes, 129–30
    occupational stress, 40, 126
    sex differences in absence rates, 59, 60
    size of companies
        and absence rates, 50
    supervisory training programmes, 133

Valency theory of motivation, 24

Values of employees
  Absence Cause Analysis Checklist, 169
  and absence control techniques, 123, 127–8
  and absence rates, 52–4
  Arlanda Electronics case study, 222
  and attendance behaviour, 35, 36, 37
  and overtime, 71
  personal work ethics, 75–6

Wage equity, 68
Wage levels
  and absence rates, 68–71
  see also Pay structures
Weir, Mary, 148
Well pay plans, 118
West Germany, 5, 71, 137
Wild, Ray, 22
Winker, D.R., 48
Women
  absence rates, 6, 11, 31, 57, 58–61

Arlanda Electronics case study, 197, 216, 217,
    218–19, 224–6, 236–9
attitudes to job, 53–4
career development, and stress, 44
crèche facilities for, 137
and family responsibilities, 80
and flexitime, 137
managers' attitudes to absence of, 13
positive reinforcement programmes, 121
Work redesign programmes, 249–50
Work techniques
  of absence control, 97, 98, 123–38, 149, 151–2,
    180, 181, 182
  Arlanda Electronics case study, 238, 241–3
Working parties, joint, 249

Year, time of
  and absence rates, 80–1
Young people
  absence rates, 31, 56–8, 59, 60
  work-related accidents, 77